# Productivity Growth and U.S. Competitiveness

*Edited by*

WILLIAM J. BAUMOL and
KENNETH McLENNAN

*A Supplementary Paper
of the Committee for Economic Development*

*New York      Oxford*
OXFORD UNIVERSITY PRESS
1985

Copyright © 1985 by the Committee for Economic Development

All rights reserved. No part of this book may be reproduced in any form without permission in writing from the Committee for Economic Development, 477 Madison Avenue, New York, New York 10022. Manufactured in the United States of America.

Productivity growth and U.S. competitiveness.
"A Supplementary paper of the Committee for Economic Development."
  Bibliography: p.
    1. Industrial productivity—United States—Addresses, essays, lectures.
    2. Industrial productivity—Japan—Addresses, essays, lectures.   I. Baumol, William J.
II. McLennan, Kenneth.   II. Committee for Economic Development.
IV. Title: Productivity growth and United States competitiveness.
HC110.I52P756 1985   338'.06'0973   84-29577
ISBN 0-19-503526-7

Printing (last digit): 9 8 7 6 5 4 3 2 1

Printed in the United States of America

# Preface

This book describes the nature of the productivity problem facing the United States. It summarizes the results of many pieces of empirical research examining the causes of the slowdown in productivity growth that struck the United States in the middle of the 1960s and other leading industrialized countries several years later. It also provides analyses of the poor performance of productivity growth in the United States relative to that of Japan.

Some of the most remarkable material in this volume is to be found in comparisons between Japan and the U.S. Norsworthy and Malmquist provide evidence that Japan's growth in total-factor productivity (TFP) was not significantly more rapid than that of the United States, whereas Japan's manufacturing labor productivity persistently grew almost three times as quickly as America's. The obvious explanation is that most of Japan's remarkable achievement is ascribable to its superior performance in terms of saving and, even more important, investment. Indeed, the estimate provided in the study is that about three-quarters of Japan's relevant achievement in productivity growth during the 1970s is attributable to that source alone.

It is noteworthy that a great deal of historical evidence suggests that similar patterns have occurred elsewhere, that labor productivity and living standards have depended primarily on the level of investment rather than on the rate of rise of TFP. Thus, the remarkable fact that during the first five decades of the Industrial Revolution, per capita income in the United Kingdom apparently grew at the insignificant rate of 0.33 percent a year (see Harley, 1982, p. 286), despite the succession of technological improvement, has been explained by Britain's heavy military expenditures during this period and their crowding-out effect, which kept savings and investment to extraordinarily low levels (see Williamson, 1983). Thus, in this period, growth in TFP has been estimated to account for about 90 percent of the miserable rate of growth in output per worker (see Feinstein, 1978, p. 86). In contrast, during the 1970s, per capita income in the Third World grew at about 10 times the rate achieved by the United Kingdom in the period just after the Industrial Revolution and growth in TFP accounted for only about 10 percent of that growth achievement (Maddison, 1970, p. 53). Similarly, only about 27 percent of the rapid growth in U.S. per capita before the Civil War is explained by the behavior of TFP (see Abramovitz and David, 1973, p. 430).*

One is driven to the conclusion that to an even greater degree than had previously been imagined, the investment rate is the prime long-run contributor to a nation's increase in per capita income and its standard of living. As such, investment may well deserve the highest priority of attention of policy makers concerned with productivity growth.

The other central conclusion of the book is that productivity growth is in every sense a long-run issue. There is probably nothing more important for changes in a nation's economic welfare in terms of developments spanning periods as long as a half century and more. Moreover, the significance and implications of chronically poor productivity growth are virtually invisible in the short run. Once the consequences are widely recognized, it is almost too late—the country will already be bearing the burden of loss of competitiveness, primarily in the form of a reduced relative standard of living and increased difficulty in financing the investments needed for the achievement of widely accepted social goals and improvements in the quality of life.

We must emphasize here, as we do in Chapter 8, that the current productivity problems of the United States cannot be dealt with effectively without some sacrifices. Management will have to accept disturbance of some of its traditional practices in relation both to the labor force and to the exercise of entrepreneurship within the firm, even if such changes make existence less comfortable for those who run the enterprise. Public policies that focus primarily on the short run will have to be reoriented, even if that increases the reelection risks to which politicians are subject. The general public will somehow have to be induced to devote more of its income to saving and more of its savings to productive capital rather than to consumer durables, even if this requires initial sacrifices in living standards.

---

* This and all the other references in this paragraph are taken from Williamson, 1983.

Perhaps some or all of us may not be prepared to make these sacrifices. But if that is the case, we should at least recognize the nature of the burden we thereby impose on future generations.

The idea for this volume originated during preparations for a Committee for Economic Development (CED) policy statement, *Productivity Policy: Key to the Nation's Economic Future* (New York, 1983). CED is a group that brings together leaders of business and representatives of the pertinent disciplines in academia to seek to produce responsible analyses and recommendations on current issues vitally affecting the nation's welfare. CED trustees felt strongly that productivity constitutes just such an issue. The editors of this volume were, accordingly, assigned the task of drafting the report for the trustees' consideration. As is usual in the CED process, background papers were commissioned for the education of both the authors of the draft report and the trustees. Four of the chapters in this volume—those by Martin Bronfenbrenner, Robert McKersie and Janice Klein, Frank Gollop, and E. N. Wolff—were, in earlier drafts, background papers of this type.

We felt that the papers were of high quality and that it would constitute a loss to economists and others concerned with productivity and competitiveness issues if they were not made more widely available. For the deliberations on the earlier drafts of the report, CED also enlisted the advice of a number of persons knowledgeable on the subject. J. R. Norsworthy was among them, and we became acquainted with some of his unpublished research. Two of the articles in this book, one written with David Malmquist and the other with Craig Zabala, are drawn from this valuable material.

Our own two summary chapters were written especially for this volume after Chapters 2 to 7 had been prepared. They are intended to serve as a bridge between the CED report and the other papers included in the book. They also provide some background on the productivity issue generally that we hope will clarify the role of the more specialized materials in the other papers.

We would now like to say a few words about our many obligations. As authors are wont, we shall attempt to pay our debts using no more than the debased currency of mere words.

Above all, we are deeply grateful to the many individuals who have contributed advice and, indeed, wisdom that have helped our efforts. We remember particularly the advice of Albert Rees, George Kuper, and John Stewart and contributions by CED trustees Roy L. Ash, Robert C. Holland, Franklin A. Lindsay, and William F. May. Undoubtedly, there have been others whose names should not have been omitted. We must thank all the trustees of CED and the subcommittee they appointed to guide our earlier work for their patience in bearing with us in the slow and sometimes charged process through which our ideas and theirs evolved.

We also want to express our deep gratitude to the Alfred P. Sloan Foundation for its generous grant to CED that permitted the work underlying this volume to be carried out.

In the preparation of any manuscript containing empirical data, it is necessary to select information from the constant flow of new reports and present the data in a way that makes them relevant to the main thesis of the book. We were assisted most ably in this task by Lorraine Brooker. We must also offer our profound thanks to Hector Guenther and Patricia Murray, who served as victorious defenders of the English language against the many assaults on grammar, comprehensibility, and aesthetics that were predictably launched by the authors of this volume. If this book is readable, the primary credit is surely theirs.

*New York*                                                                          W. J. B.
*December 1984*                                                                    K. McL.


# REFERENCES

M. Abramovitz and P. David, "Reinterpreting Economic Growth: Parables and Realities" *American Economic Review* 63, (May 1973): 428–439.

C. H. Feinstein, "Capital Formation in Great Britain," in *The Cambridge Economic History of Europe* VII, ed. M. P. Mathias and M. M. Postan (Cambridge: Cambridge University Press, 1978).

C. K. Harley, "British Industrialization Before 1841: Evidence of Slower Growth During the Industrial Revolution," *Journal of Economic History* XLII (June 1982): 267–289.

A. Maddison, *Economic Progress and Policy in Developing Countries* (London: Allen and Irwin, 1970).

J. C. Williamson, "Why Was British Growth so Slow During the Industrial Revolution?" (Cambridge: Harvard Institute of Economic Research, forthcoming).

# Contents

**1** U.S. Productivity Performance and Its Implications
WILLIAM J. BAUMOL and KENNETH McLENNAN     **3**

**2** The Magnitude and Causes of the Recent Productivity
Slowdown in the United States: A Survey of Recent Studies
EDWARD N. WOLFF     **29**

**3** Recent Productivity Growth in Japanese and U.S.
Manufacturing
J. R. NORSWORTHY and DAVID H. MALMQUIST     **58**

**4** Japanese Productivity Experience
MARTIN BRONFENBRENNER     **70**

**5** Responding to the Productivity Crisis: A Plant-Level
Approach to Labor Policy
J. R. NORSWORTHY and C. A. ZABALA     **103**

**6** Productivity: The Industrial Relations Connection
ROBERT B. McKERSIE and JANICE A. KLEIN     **119**

**7** Analysis of the Productivity Slowdown: Evidence for a
Sector-Biased or Sector-Neutral Industrial Strategy
FRANK M. GOLLOP     **160**

**8** Toward an Effective Productivity Program
WILLIAM J. BAUMOL and KENNETH McLENNAN     **187**

Contributors     **225**

# PRODUCTIVITY GROWTH AND U.S. COMPETITIVENESS

# U.S. Productivity Performance and Its Implications

WILLIAM J. BAUMOL and KENNETH McLENNAN

This country's productivity growth performance in recent years is extremely disquieting. But the troubling trend is only symptomatic of much more serious productivity problems. For more than one and a half decades before 1983, there was a pervasive and very substantial decline in productivity growth rates throughout most sectors of the U.S. economy. Moreover, for at least the same length of time, productivity grew far less rapidly in the United States than it did in the countries that are our main economic rivals.

The recovery years 1983 and 1984 have brought an upturn in U.S. productivity growth, as is typical at this stage of the business cycle. Unfortunately, this improvement is no better than in previous recoveries, and it provides no evidence that out disappointing longer-term trend in productivity performance has been reversed.

## WHAT IS PRODUCTIVITY?

Productivity measures the relationship between outputs (the amounts of goods and services produced) and inputs (the quantities of labor, capital, and material resources used to produce the outputs). When given amounts of inputs produce larger quantities of outputs, productivity has increased.

The most common measure of the relationship between outputs and inputs is the value of output per worker or per hour worked, which is called *labor productivity*. This is probably the most significant determinant of the nation's standard of living. On the other hand, *total-factor productivity* (TFP) is a measure that attempts to take into account the contributions of all inputs—the services of plant and equipment, energy, and other materials, as well as that of managers and their employees. Total-factor productivity is more difficult to estimate but is especially useful in determining what is causing changes in labor productivity.

In practice, changes in productivity are not simple to measure. For example, the proportion of outputs may change over time or vary among producers, making it difficult to define the behavior of overall output. Public-service output is particularly difficult to quantify because it does not consist of a stream of products or services that have a market value. Few industries or plants produce only one product. Sometimes a single process yields more than one product. Combining these products into a single output figure requires that they be weighted by some measure of relative importance.

Total input is equally difficult to measure properly. Many inputs must be combined to produce an output, but productivity ratios often relate output to a single input, such as labor. When there is a change in a productivity ratio calculated for a single input, it is important not to attribute the change to that one input. In an interrelated economic system, the change may be influenced by any or all of a multitude of variables, such as production techniques, capital equipment, the skill of the work force, managerial performance, the rate of capacity utilization, the scale of operations, materials flow, product mix, the state of labor-management relations, and the quality of the work environment. The relative importance of these influences varies from sector to sector and from organization to organization, as well as over time.

In the short run, productivity growth fluctuates; output falls as the economy slows down during a recession and rises during the subsequent economic recovery. The sources of these productivity changes include variations in the utilization of existing plant and equipment along with time lags in the hiring and laying off of workers over the business cycle.

Short-run cyclical fluctuations in productivity differ among industries. For example, in the first year after the 1981–1982 recession, productivity growth in U.S. manufacturing was larger than the growth rates in the comparable periods following most previous recessions. On the other hand, productivity growth in the entire private business sector was weaker after this recession than in any previous recession since World War II.

It is obviously desirable for the economy to experience a strong upsurge in productivity, but if this improvement quickly dissipates during subsequent phases in the business cycle, the nation will not obtain any significant benefits. The critical issue for economic performance is whether the productivity improvement can be sustained and a high growth rate continued. Changes in capital per worker, the rate of innovation and its adoption throughout industry, and changes in the skill composition of the labor force are the kinds of variables that determine the future productivity growth path of an economy and whether or not it represents a permanent improvement.

What is the significance of lagging productivity growth, and is it a legitimate cause for concern? We review some of the evidence on the magnitude of the deterioration of America's productivity performance and the lag in its performance vis-à-vis that in other countries. The probable major causes of the productivity problem are recapitulated. Finally, we describe some common misunderstandings about the implications of the unimpressive U.S. productivity performance and suggest its implications for the nation's future.

## THE SIGNIFICANCE OF PRODUCTIVITY GROWTH

Productivity growth is important because it is the key determinant of a nation's future standard of living. The inhabitants of a country whose productivity is growing rapidly can expect to be far better clothed and fed, to have available more of the things that are said to contribute to the quality of life, and to be able to enjoy more leisure than they do today. That is, undoubtedly, the consequence of productivity growth that is of most concern for public policy.

Yet, productivity performance has other important implications. The most obvious is that an economy that performs well in this arena will find it easier to provide the means to protect and improve its environment, to educate and offer medical care to its populace, to support cultural activities, and to deal effectively with problems such as poverty and care of the aged. In other words, productivity does more than contribute to the incomes of working individuals and facilitate direct consumption; it also makes it easier to provide for the well-being of others and to release the resources necessary for expansion of general activities and facilities that contribute to the well-being of society as a whole. In sum, the failure of a nation's productivity to grow condemns its work force to a stationary income level and forces the society to forgo improvements in its quality of life.

As we have already suggested, the United States faces a second productivity problem quite different from decline in the growth rate: the low growth rate of U.S. productivity relative to that of most other industrial countries. This comparative lag had already made its appearance before the decline in U.S. productivity growth had begun; and although productivity growth has recently slowed elsewhere, that in the United States has continued to be significantly lower than in other countries.

The comparative productivity performance of the United States has important implications for policy. An economy that falls steadily and substantially behind others loses out in terms of military strength and ability to exercise leadership in the community of nations. There is good reason to believe that America's important international role in the twentieth century, both in peace and in wartime, is attributable in good part to its great industrial strength. In such matters, it is indeed crucial to be second to none. A country is poorly defended if its defensive resources are second-best to those of a potential aggressor, and a country that suffers from relative poverty is apt to be a weak voice in international councils.

Failure of U.S. productivity to keep abreast of that of other countries also has direct economic consequences. In the short run, such a productivity lag may impair U.S. competitiveness in the international marketplace, making it more difficult to find purchasers for U.S. exports and thereby contributing to unemployment and other domestic economic problems.

Although this will not be true in the long run and need not even hold in the short run, lagging U.S. productivity will cause changes in the *pattern* of exports and imports. Products that were once exported without difficulty but in which the relative productivity lag is most severe will find foreign markets closed to them. Instead, the United States will be driven toward the production and export of other goods in which its relative productivity performance has not been quite so weak. Such a changeover can exact heavy transition costs, involving obsolescence of the skills of the labor force, unemployment caused by the need to retrain and relocate workers, abandonment of capital in declining industries, and the need to sink additional savings into the industries that replace those whose markets are shrinking.

In short, the poor relative performance of U.S. productivity imposes significant costs on society over and above those attributable to the decline in the productivity growth rate. Each productivity problem is a legitimate cause for concern, and each will have its own unfortunate consequences for the economy unless automatic forces, fortuitous developments, or well-designed policies succeed in improving matters substantially.

## The U.S. Productivity Growth Record

Because there is no single valid measure of productivity growth, and because a variety of data are available for its measurement, it is not possible to provide one set of figures that constitutes *the* record of U.S. productivity performance. The degree of agreement of the available reports is, consequently, very helpful and perhaps not a little surprising.

Between the end of World War II and 1965, the productivity of labor grew at an annual rate of 3.2 to 3.5 percent. Then the decline began. Before the first oil price shock (i.e., in the period from 1965 to 1972), productivity growth fell to between 2.0 and 2.5 percent a year. Thereafter, it slowed to an annual rate of less than 1 percent and came to a virtual halt at the end of the 1970s. Since 1981, it has staged a recovery, but no one is sure how much of the upturn can be considered temporary, a manifestation of the business cycle. The data on total-factor productivity behaved in a manner perfectly parallel to the labor productivity figures.

The decline in productivity growth has not been confined to a few sectors of the economy. On the contrary, it has been pervasive, involving public utilities (where growth fell from 5.5 percent in the period 1948 to 1965, to −2.2 percent during the 1979 to 1981 period), construction, transportation, trade, and manufacturing as a whole. The communications sector has been the only persistent exception, with productivity growth actually *rising* from 3.2 percent a year in 1965–1973 to 4.0 percent in 1979–1981.[1]

Within manufacturing, too, the decline has been pervasive, with petroleum, chemicals, transportation equipment, and lumber among the subsectors in which the falloff has been most substantial. According to Bailey (1982), a breakdown of manufacturing into twenty subsectors showed that total-factor productivity after 1973 fell below its 1958–1973 average in all but three areas (apparel, furniture, and leather).[2] The extensiveness of the productivity decline is supported by the U.S. Bureau of Labor Statistics index of productivity for 116 industries in all sectors of the economy. These data show that the decline occurred in about 80 percent of the industries.[3]

In sum, the deceleration in U.S. productivity has not been brief, minor in magnitude, or confined to isolated areas of the economy. It has gone on for more than fifteen years. The annual growth figure in labor productivity has fallen by more than 70 percent. It has affected almost all of manufacturing and most of the remainder of the economy. It cannot, in good conscience, be disregarded.

## MAJOR CAUSES OF THE PRODUCTIVITY SLOWDOWN

Although the data are quite consistent in their evaluation of the intensity and pervasiveness of the slowdown, the statistical analyses differ widely in their evaluation of the causes. As shown in Chapter 2, a number of very able analysts have examined the issue; but using different data and analytic techniques, they have produced conclusions that differ considerably in quantitative terms. Yet, for our purposes, that is not as serious an obstacle as it may appear; it is not terribly important in this context whether lagging investment accounts for 20 percent of the slowdown or nearly 50 percent. Rather, what is important from the review of the slowdown's causes in Chapter 2 is the general agreement that this influence was significant and substantial.[4]

The presentation of the results of the new Multifactor Productivity Index, prepared by the U.S. Bureau of Labor Statistics (BLS), appears to contradict the conclusion that insufficient capital investment was one of the causes of the productivity decline. According to this interpretation, a slowdown in capital formation accounted for about 14 percent of the post-1973 productivity slowdown in the private business sector as a whole. In the nonfarm business sector, inadequate capital formation accounted for 11 percent of the slowdown but insufficient capital investment played no role in explaining the decline in the manufacturing slowdown.[5]

Most of the discrepancy between the BLS interpretation of their new multifactor productivity data and the results of the research reported in Chapter 2 is due to differences in the time periods selected for measuring the slowdown. The BLS compares the slowdowns between 1948–1973 and 1973–1981, and it does not believe it is appropriate to separate the trend in productivity in the mid-1960s since this was not a peak in the business cycle. Technically, BLS is correct since comparisons of productivity growth should be based on periods starting and finishing at the peak of a business cycle. Many researchers feel, however, that while the mid-1960s was not an official peak in the business cycle, the economy experienced some major changes, including a rapid rise in prices and an increase in the labor force participation of some demographic groups, and that this justifies selecting either 1965 or 1966 as a break in the 1948–1973 period.

The selection of 1981 as the end point for comparing the productivity decline is even more questionable since most economic indicators confirm that during 1981, the economy was well into the severest post-World War II recession. If the comparison is to rely consistently on the peak-to-peak criterion, the appropriate period for comparing the productivity slowdown is 1973–1979, and perhaps even 1973–1978. Indeed, on the basis of the BLS data, if the comparison periods for the slowdown are 1965–1973 and 1973–1979, insufficient capital explains about 40 percent (0.7 percentage points out of a decline of 1.6 points) of the slowdown in the private business sector's productivity after 1973. Insufficient investment explains a smaller proportion of the slowdown of productivity growth in the manufacturing sector of the economy.

Estimates of the effect of changes in the rate and level of investment in plant and equipment on the productivity slowdown vary substantially according to the time periods being compared. There is general agreement that insufficient investment in plant and equipment played a smaller role in explaining the productivity slowdown in manufacturing than in other sectors of the economy as a whole. But on the basis of the reviews of recent empirical studies and the data provided by the new multifactor index, we conclude that for the private business sector as a whole, lack of capital investment accounts for over 20 percent of the decline during the 1970s. The evidence that insufficient investment is one of the major causes of the U.S. productivity slowdown is particularly significant because government policies are enormously important in determining the rate of investment in new plant and equipment.

Among the other major sources of the slowdown, according to the econometric studies, are low outlays for research and development, the rise in the direct and indirect costs of regulation, and the increase in energy prices during the 1970s. About 10 to 15 percent of the problem has been ascribed to each of these candidate causes. In addition, although it has been a source of considerable controversy, a number of analysts have attributed a substantial role to changes in the composition of U.S. output and, particularly, to the shift of the labor force from manufacturing to the services, whose productivity growth has historically been relatively slow. Estimates of the effect of this influence range from 10 to 40 percent, and several more extreme figures have also been proposed.

While low saving and investment rates have contributed substantially to the slowdown in U.S. productivity growth, as we have seen, recent studies indicate that they have played an even greater role in our poor performance relative to other countries.

Low investment rates handicapped productivity in two ways: (1) They have obviously meant that in a period when the labor force grew rapidly, American workers had less equipment at their disposal and could therefore be expected to turn out fewer products in a given time. As is shown in Figure 1-1, investment in equipment began to accelerate in the late 1970s and early 1980s. If this trend is maintained, it will raise the stock of nonresidential equipment—especially manufacturing equipment, which is so important for international competitiveness. (2) A slowdown in investment also reduces the opportunity for modernization of the productive techniques embodied in plant and equipment and therefore condemns the output processes to increasing obsolescence. The investment figures on new structures indicate that this was a problem for the nonresidential sector as a whole and was especially serious in manufacturing.

The history of the outlays for research and development is also not quite straightforward. Between 1964 and 1977, the share of the gross national product (GNP) devoted to research and development declined by more than 20 percent; however, all of that decrease is attributable to reductions in outlays for defense and space exploration. Research and development

| Type of capital | AVERAGE ANNUAL RATE OF INCREASE | | | | | |
| | 1960 – 1973 | | | 1973 – 1981 | | |
| | Structures | Equipment | Total | Structures | Equipment | Total |
|---|---|---|---|---|---|---|
| Manufacturing | 1.9 | 4.5 | 3.3 | 1.2 | 6.8 | 4.7 |
| Nonresidential | 4.1 | 5.2 | 4.6 | 2.1 | 4.8 | 3.4 |
| Residential | | | 3.5 | | | 2.2 |

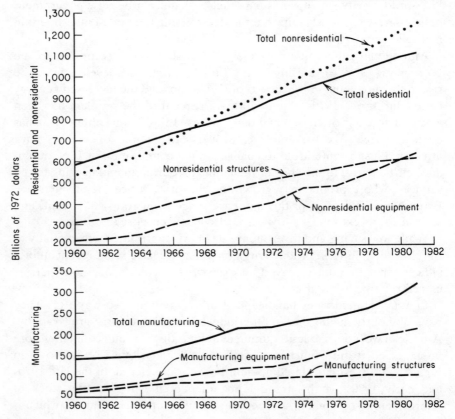

Figure 1-1. Net stocks of residential, nonresidential business, and manufacturing capital, in constant dollars. (*Source*: *Survey of Current Business*, February 1981 and October 1982.)

expenditures in other areas have actually increased as a share of GNP. The issue, then, is how much of an influence on general productivity growth can be ascribed to the relative cutbacks in financing of research and development in the military and space arenas.

Another issue may be pertinent here. There are areas of economic activity whose technological character impels their costs to rise at a faster rate than those in other sectors of the economy. Because they are relatively impervious to productivity improvements, and because technological change seems to increase the complexity of their equipment requirements, outlays in these areas must rise cumulatively faster than the general price level if their outputs are not to lag. For example, this seems to be true of health care, and at least some crude evidence suggests it is true of research and development as well. If so (i.e., if research and development is an investment in which it is necessary to keep running ahead financially in order to be a leader in innovation), the absence of a decline in nonmilitary (and space) R&D outlays may have been insufficient to prevent a slowdown in the flow of new ideas. In any event, the statistical analyses, as we have already indicated, ascribe a significant role, but one of relatively moderate proportions, to this influence.

There is reason to suspect that the influence of the rise in energy prices has been undervalued by the statistics. The data themselves indicate that energy constitutes a fairly small proportion of total expenditures on inputs in the U.S. economy. Hence, sheer statistical inference leads to the conclusion that the rise in energy costs during the 1970s, while significant in its effects on productivity growth, could not have been of overwhelming importance. Yet, many observers feel that the single phenomenon that made a marked difference for U.S. economic performance was the *suddenness* of the rises in energy prices, which occurred largely in several great jumps following military and political upheavals in the Middle East. The abruptness of the change in prices of such an important input caused severe disruptions in the economy, stimulating inflation, rendering obsolete all sorts of plant, equipment, and consumer durables that were not efficient in their use of energy, and leading to adjustment costs that could have been avoided if a price rise of similar total magnitude had occurred very gradually.

The initial 1973 energy shock may also be related to the role of capital in the 1973–1979 slowdown. The resulting obsolescence of capital was probably much more rapid than is indicated by the depreciation rates used to estimate the growth in the net stock of capital. Consequently, even though statistics show that investment in capital did increase in the 1970s, the effect of that increase on the productive potential of the economy was probably overestimated. The energy shock required an upward shift in capital investment if a decline in productivity growth was to be avoided.

The most controversial of the causes suggested by statistical investigations is the change in the composition of output and the allocation of the labor force among the sectors of the U.S. economy. There has been a shift in the labor force away from agriculture and, to some degree, out of manufacturing into the services. The reduction in the share of farm labor is judged to have raised productivity, but there is some dispute about the magnitude and even the direction of the consequences of the move toward the services. It is generally agreed that productivity in the services as a whole tends to rise more slowly than in manufacturing, but the difference between the two is not very large. However, there is considerable variability in this respect from service to service, and part of the question is whether the labor force has moved toward those services that are more stagnant or those that are less stagnant. There is an a priori reason to expect a tendency of inputs to shift toward outputs whose productivity grows slowly: Those sectors whose productivity growth record is outstanding are, by virtue of that very fact, least likely to find themselves needing additional quantities of inputs. However, this tendency can be offset if the demand for such items grows comparatively rapidly. In any event, there is little agreement on which data are pertinent or on which methods should be used to examine the issue, so it is hardly surprising that the available estimates vary widely.

### Additional Contributing Causes

The statistics suggest some other influences that may have played a role in the productivity slowdown, including the stage of the business cycle and trends in unionization and union behavior. But none of these appears, on the basis of the data, to have been of major significance.

Several candidate causes have not proved amenable to statistical testing but have been cited by a number of observers as important. The most notable are the magnitude of the inflation during the 1970s and the alleged decline in the quality of entrepreneurship and in the intensity with which it is exercised.

There is no doubt that much of the period of the slowdown in productivity growth was accompanied by an inflation unparalleled in intensity and duration in recent U.S. history. Such a disturbing influence can certainly impede productivity. Inflation has upset the capital markets and made the acquisition of funds riskier and sometimes more expensive, even in real terms. It has used up managerial resources by forcing firms and individuals to devote time and effort to preventing the erosion of the purchasing power of their assets. It has increased the risk involved in entering into long-term contracts. It has even contributed to political uncertainties. Obviously, inflation is no aid to productivity.

Those who believe that both management and entrepreneurship in the United States have declined in quality and vigor may not be clear on what may have led to such a development. However, many commentators ascribe part of the problem to a rising tide of protectionism, in many cases in response to the wishes of members of the business community. Firms threatened by bankruptcy have sought protection from the effects of their bad fortune or management through various forms of government assistance; industries whose markets were threatened by foreign rivals have demanded the adoption of a variety of impediments to imports. There is no doubt that U.S. businesses have faced competition from foreign producers who receive subsidies from their governments, sometimes in violation of international trading agreements. But the solution is not adoption of domestic-content rules, orderly market agreements, or other barriers to trade. Innovation and productivity growth have rarely flourished in a protected economy. Quite the contrary, impediments to trade will reduce the incentives for management and labor to innovate.

Enterprises whose markets are endangered by the success of domestic competitors have often turned to the antitrust authorities and the regulatory agencies for protection. Where that has been judged insufficient, private lawsuits have been employed, and vast resources have been expended. In the 1950–1954 period, the Department of Justice and the Federal Trade Commission initiated the vast majority of antitrust suits; only 184 private suits were filed. But during the 1970–1974 period, 1,260 suits were initiated by private parties.[6] In the later period, relative to government suits, the number of private suits had increased dramatically.

When outstanding success is certain to bring a business firm before the courts accused of the crime of competing vigorously and effectively, when poor performance by an enterprise is grounds for public assistance, when legal costs become a substantial portion of a company's outlays and an increasing share of management is made up of lawyers rather than engineers, the impediments to entrepreneurship and effective management are fairly obvious. Whether there has, in fact, been a decline in the quality of management and entrepreneurship, and whether pressures for protectionism have been an important cause of such a decline, can only be conjectured. However, it is hard to believe that productivity growth has not been impeded by the extent of business involvement in related legal activities and the undermining of market forces that is an inevitable result of protectionism.

## COMPARATIVE PRODUCTIVITY GROWTH

As we have already indicated, U.S. productivity growth has lagged substantially behind that of many other industrialized countries. It should also be pointed out that the slowdown in productivity growth has not been confined to the United States; almost every industrial country has suffered a similar difficulty. But the United States was behind many of the others before the decline began, and the general decline has left the American economy in its lagging position. Thus, in the 1960–1973 period, labor productivity grew at an average annual rate of 3.1 percent in the United States, 3.8 percent in the United Kingdom, 4.2 percent in Canada, 5.8

percent in Sweden and West Germany, 5.9 percent in France, 7.8 percent in Italy, and 9.9 percent in Japan.

Between 1973 and 1979, all these figures fell. Growth was only 1.1 percent in the United States and 1.0 percent in Canada; but the rates were 1.6 percent in Italy, 1.9 pecent in the United Kingdom, 2.5 percent in Sweden, 3.8 percent in Japan, 4.2 percent in France, and 4.3 percent in Germany.[7] Thus, most leading industrial countries were gaining rapidly on the United States in the earlier period and continued to do so in the later one. Indeed, the leading industrial nations have achieved growth rates in productivity two to three times as large as ours (see Figure 1-2). Between

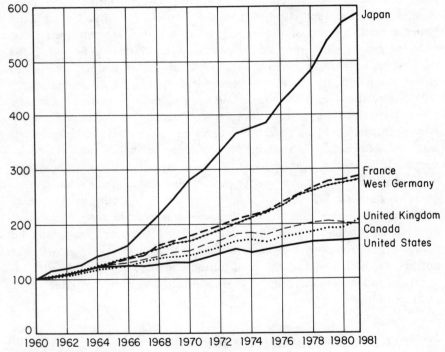

For each country, 1960 = 100

In order to compare productivity growth rates, each country's growth rate for 1960 is assigned a value of 100. If this figure were to compare *levels of productivity* (instead of growth rates), it would show each country starting at a different level. While the United States began at a higher level than did the other countries shown, by the end of the 1970s the more rapid growth rates in other countries resulted in a convergence of productivity levels in much of the manufacturing sector.

Figure 1-2. Trends of productivity growth rates: indexed labor productivity—growth rates for manufacturing industries, 1960–1981. (*Source*: Prepared from unpublished data provided by the U.S. Department of Labor.)

1960 and 1980, Japan's labor productivity in manufacturing industry increase approximately sixfold and that in Germany multiplied some two and a half times, whereas America's rose by only about 75 percent.

Inevitably, such trends mean that productivity *levels* in at least some other countries are converging on that of the United States. Figure 1-3

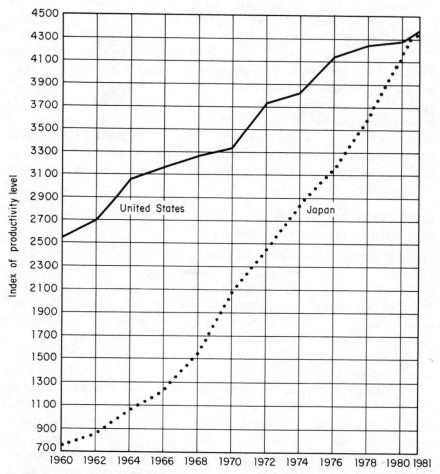

The benchmark year for the comparative levels is 1977. The relative productivity levels for 1977 are based on the Japan Productivity Center's industry comparison of most manufacturing industries in each country for the 1970s. These results, including productivity growth rates, were similar to available data from the U.S. Bureau of Labor Statistics. To determine the estimates for the period 1960-1981, the U.S. government's growth rate statistics were applied to the Japan Productivity Center's 1977 productivity level estimates.

Figure 1-3. Convergence of U.S. and Japanese manufacturing productivity levels.

compares the convergence of U.S. and Japanese productivity levels in manufacturing. These estimates clearly show that, on the average, Japanese manufacturing is just about as productive as U.S. manufacturing. In some industries, U.S. productivity may still be the leader; but in others, the United States may have been outstripped by its chief competitors. In a number of industries—notably steel and automobiles—this already seems to have happened; in others, such a position is well on its way to realization. In the steel industry, for example, Japanese output per person-hour was some 5 to 20 percent behind U.S. output in 1972 but now exceeds ours by 20 to 50 percent.[8]

The convergence of productivity levels would not be cause for serious concern if the United States could somehow quickly double or triple its productivity growth rate to match those of its leading competitors and maintain this improvement over at least the next decade. But such a miraculous improvement cannot possibly occur without significant changes in government policies and in management and labor practices. Growth in U.S. productivity is now far behind that in a number of leading industrial countries, and the international competitiveness of many U.S. industries will continue to be threatened.

## EXPLANATIONS OF THE DIFFERENCES IN PRODUCTIVITY PERFORMANCE

A comment that is frequently offered in response to such data as those just presented is that a country that comes from behind always has an important advantage over the leading economy. Previously laggard countries can advance through imitation. By copying the leader's methods and equipment, a country can achieve very rapid productivity growth with little outlay on research and development. Indeed, the country that is catching up thereby acquires an advantage over the leader because newly acquired equipment can be more up to date and in better condition than the older plant and equipment employed by the leader. But according to those who espouse this view, such an imitation process is self-terminating. As the gap between the countries' performances grows smaller, the nation that is coming from behind will find it increasingly difficult to move faster through imitation. In the end, the older leader may well find itself with its position intact.

There is unquestionably some truth to this analysis, but there is more to the story. No doubt there has been a good deal of learning from American business methods and American techniques, but now, in many areas, matters have begun to reverse themselves. American business executives are attending seminars on Japanese approaches to labor relations. Japan's use of robots is setting targets for U.S. industry, and in many lines of endeavor it is the United States that now must catch up. Yet, there is little evidence that Japanese productivity growth rates in those areas have slowed relative to ours.

What else accounts for the differences in performance? Once again, the answers are not unambiguous, but some broad conclusions can be drawn from the evidence. There is strong evidence, as we have already noted, that a primary source of the disparity lies in the inferior U.S. performance in terms of saving and investment. One study reported that in 1980, 21.0 percent of total disposable income was saved in Japan, 15.5 percent in France, 15.0 percent in the United Kingdom, 13.2 percent in Germany, 10.3 percent in Canada, but only 5.6 percent in the United States.[9] That is, four of the five countries had saving rates more than twice as high as the U.S. rate.

Differences in industrial investment, although not quite so large as those in saving, were also substantial. According to the Bureau of Labor Statistics, between 1970 and 1977, investment in manufacturing as a proportion of the value of manufacturing output was 28.8 percent in Japan, 15.9 percent in West Germany, 14.7 percent in Canada, but only 9.6 percent in the United States (see Table 1-1).[10] For many years, in fact, U.S. investment rates trailed those of all major industrial nations. Recently, however, Japan's industrial investment rate dropped while the U.S. rate rose, and today they are about the same.

The U.S. rate of investment in new plant and equipment is significantly lower than the rate in Japan but is quite similar to the rates in other industrial nations. In addition to the lower rate of *manufacturing* capital investment, the United States has had a long-term comparative deficiency in its rate of investment in new structures.

When such differences persist and are compounded year after year, they must soon impose a substantial handicap on the lagging economy in terms of plant and equipment per worker. The statistical analysis of the sources of the differences in manufacturing productivity growth rates in the U.S. and Japan presented in Chapter 4 indicates that much of Japan's substantial advantage in productivity growth is attributable to its superior investment performance. During the 1960s and early 1970s, Japan's average annual rate of investment in new manufacturing plant and equipment was four times greater than the U.S. rate. It may be, as some say, that Japanese workers have a stronger commitment to the work ethic than the current members of the U.S. labor force, but most of the difference in manufacturing productivity growth is explainable by the fact that Japanese workers use more modern plant and equipment than their American counterparts.

**Table 1-1. Fixed Capital Investment, Excluding Residential Construction as Percentage of Gross Domestic Product, for Selected Countries (constant $)[1]**

| Country | 1965–1972 | | | 1973–1979 | | | 1980–1981 | | |
|---|---|---|---|---|---|---|---|---|---|
| | Total | Non-residential Structures | Machinery & Equipment | Total | Non-residential Structures | Machinery & Equipment | Total | Non-residential Structures | Machinery & Equipment |
| U.S. | 14.3 | 7.3 | 7.1 | 13.5 | 5.4 | 8.1 | 13.9 | 5.1 | 8.8 |
| Canada | 17.6 | 10.1 | 7.4 | 17.4 | 9.0 | 8.4 | 18.8 | 9.7 | 9.1 |
| Japan | 24.3 | 14.3[a] | 12.9[a] | 25.5 | 13.6 | 11.9 | 25.8 | NA | NA |
| Denmark | 16.2[b] | 8.9[c] | 7.4[c] | 15.5 | 7.5 | 7.9 | 12.5 | 5.5 | 7.0 |
| France | 16.4 | 6.9[a] | 10.0[a] | 15.9 | 5.8 | 10.1 | 15.2 | 5.0 | 10.1 |
| Germany | 16.4 | 8.1 | 8.3 | 15.0 | 6.8 | 8.2 | 15.2 | 6.5 | 8.8 |
| Italy | 14.3 | 6.5[a] | 8.2[a] | 13.3 | 5.4 | 7.9 | 13.5 | 4.9 | 8.6 |
| Sweden | 17.0 | 9.3 | 7.7 | 16.5 | 7.8 | 8.2 | 15.3 | 6.9 | 7.8 |
| U.K. | 15.7 | 7.8 | 8.3 | 15.3 | 6.7 | 8.6 | 15.0 | 5.6 | 9.4 |

NA Not Available.

[a] Period 1970–1972.

[1] These figures are based on *gross* current expenditures on new durable goods (less sales of secondhand goods) by industries, producers of government services, and nonprofit services. Such expenditures do not adjust for changes in the *net* stock of durable goods since no account is taken of the depreciation of existing capital goods. Military capital goods are excluded but capital expenditures by industry to produce military hardware are included. The table was compiled from unpublished data provided by the Bureau of Labor Statistics, U.S. Department of Labor.

[c] Period 1966–1972.

Why do the inhabitants of other countries save and invest more than Americans do? No one can be sure of the answer, which is undoubtedly a combination of cultural and historical differences as well as differences in institutional arrangements and legislative rules. However, there is considerable evidence for the view that in the United States there are a variety of influences biasing the use of disposable income toward consumption rather than saving. The federal tax code has long worked in that direction. For example, by permitting the deduction of interest income, it has favored borrowing and induced purchases on credit. In various ways, the tax rules have favored investment in housing rather than in industry. Moreover, U.S. tax procedures are harsher in their treatment of capital gains than the tax codes in a number of other countries are.

The problem of the treatment of capital gains has been exacerbated by inflation because the tax rules have assessed tax liability on the basis of what economists call *nominal* (as opposed to *real*) capital gains. Between 1972 and 1982, inflation cut the purchasing power of the dollar roughly in half. A person who invested $1,000 in stocks in 1972 and sold them ten years later for $1,500 would therefore have suffered a loss in purchasing power amounting to 25 percent of the investment. Yet, a full capital gains tax would have been imposed on the $500 increase in the number of dollars involved, as though it had really constituted a profit. Add to the biases toward consumption in the tax code the fact that U.S. consumers have available more highly developed credit arrangements than other countries provide, and the differences in saving rates become considerably less surprising.

It has also been said that U.S. productivity growth has been impeded by government policies that have intervened in the market system through an array of ad hoc federal expenditure, loan, and tax subsidy programs as well as economic and social regulatory policies. This explanation of the productivity problem and the declining international competitiveness of many U.S. industries has led to several proposals for a more explicit U.S. industrial policy to raise U.S. productivity growth rates and respond to the industrial policies of its competitors in international markets.

The empirical research reported in Chapter 2 supports the view that the growth of government intervention in markets has played an important role in retarding productivity growth. Certainly, fiscal, economic development, and regulatory policies have distorted the allocation of resources among industries in a way that has unnecessarily impeded productivity growth.[11]

A more explicit and systematic approach to industrial policies could rationalize current government policies to increase productivity by facilitating the reallocation of resources among industries as the economy adjusts to change. However, most advocates of an industrial policy believe this requires more government intervention to facilitate the movement of capital and labor to those sectors of the economy that are potential winners and the adoption of adjustment policies or temporary measures of protection from imports as resources gradually move out of declining industries.

These proposals all attempt to manage the rate of structural economic change, to introduce specific adjustment programs, and to modify in varying degrees the existing institutional policy-making processes through some form of economic planning system. The role of planning agencies in Japan and some European countries, such as France, is usually cited as an illustration of how the particular components of an industrial policy can be determined and executed.[12]

Whether a more explicit industrial policy accompanied by a government planning process can reverse the adverse productivity trend only with the aid of increased government intervention is by no means clear. It is noteworthy that even in Japan and France, government plans designating which industries and regions will be assisted in the future are not binding on policy makers. Even when firms do follow the plan, they have often proved unsuccessful in achieving the goals adopted for the course of the planning exercise. In contrast, some of the most notable corporate success stories in Japan have involved firms which did not follow the government's plan.

In designing a program for dealing with this country's productivity problems, the basic issue is whether a more explicit industrial policy should be based on increased reliance on competitive markets for the allocation of resources among industries or whether the government can somehow achieve the optimal allocation through more targeted policy intervention in the market system. Chapter 7 presents some empirical estimates indicating how in the past the market system reallocated resources and contributed to U.S. productivity performance. From this analysis, it is possible to judge more rationally whether an industrial policy intended to improve U.S. productivity performance should rely more on the market system or whether the government should intervene directly to reallocate resources.

No doubt other explanations for the poor comparative record of U.S. productivity growth can be found. For example, relations between labor and management are often judged to be far less felicitous than those in Japan. A few words should therefore be said about the much publicized Japanese institutional arrangements for worker participation in management. A great deal of attention has been elicited by such devices as quality circles, in which voluntary groups of workers meet periodically to discuss productivity in their area of the firm; labor-management participation teams, which are assigned the task of solving particular operational and production problems; and job tenure, which is intended to secure the loyalty of the worker and reduce resistance to labor-saving technological changes. There is, however, some question whether such innovations in labor-management arrangements have contributed substantially to the Japanese productivity achievement; and, more to the point, there is considerable dispute about the transferability of such arrangements to the American scene.

Some observers attribute a good deal of the Japanese success to cultural differences and differences in tradition and interpret special worker-management institutions more as a manifestation of these differences than as an independent source of productivity growth. On the other hand, in a few cases in which Japanese managements have taken over plants in the United States and the United Kingdom using mostly local personnel, the effects on productivity are reported to have been extremely favorable. It is not possible to derive a set of categorical conclusions on the basis of the available evidence. One can only venture the judgment that there *is* something to be learned from successful Japanese experience in labor relations, that its moral does not consist of the advisability of adoption of a few widely publicized devices that, unless carefully thought out, may prove little more than gimmicks. The main lesson is the opportunity for achievement offered by full and genuine commitment to worker consultation and participation in the pertinent portions of managerial activities. (For fuller discussion of these issues, see Chapter 4, which examines the worker participation approach in the context of the Japanese cultural and social environment; Chapter 5, which focuses on worker-management relations at the plant level; and Chapter 6, which reviews some of the innovations in labor and management practices in the United States.)

## MISUNDERSTANDINGS ABOUT PRODUCTIVITY ISSUES

Much of what we have said so far amounts to a recitation of facts and commonsense observations. However, there are a number of issues in which the pertinent relationships are less obvious and about which the results of careful analysis may differ substantially from those derived from hasty judgment. Among the topics that fall into this category are the effects of productivity growth on unemployment, its consequences for inflation, and the implications of the relative U.S. productivity lag for the nation's balance of payments and the overall competitiveness of the U.S. economy in international marketplaces.

### Productivity Growth and Unemployment

It is widely believed that increased productivity is one sure way to exacerbate the nation's unemployment problem. With unemployment rates at double-digit levels in the early 1980s and projected to remain high throughout the decade, the adoption of measures to encourage productivity growth may be resisted because of fear of unemployment.

There is some truth to this conjecture in the short run and for particular firms and industries. If a productivity improvement permits an industry to match its previous output using a labor force 20 percent smaller than before, the market mechanism may force the enterprise to reduce its costs by decreasing the number of workers it employs. True, any resulting reduction in price will elicit some offsetting rise in demand, but the net result may nevertheless be some reduction in jobs.

However, unqualified extension of this reasoning to the economy as a whole commits the fallacy of composition. Labor-saving innovations automatically also provide some new jobs in other industries, most immediately in the production of the labor-saving equipment itself. Moreover, even if, say, there is a decrease in total spending on X when productivity cuts its price, consumers of X will be left with more purchasing power which they can devote to products Y and Z, thereby providing new jobs in those industries. In this process, some workers are almost always displaced permanently from their current jobs, and unemployment will grow temporarily because it takes time to shift workers from industry X to industries Y and Z and to retrain them for their new jobs.

Even in the short run, only a small proportion of the unemployed are laid off because of changes in demand brought about by measures taken to improve productivity. Most workers who are unemployed through involuntary layoffs have lost their jobs temporarily because of cyclical changes in demand. Even during the relatively severe recession of 1975, about 80 percent of laid-off workers eventually returned to their previous employers.[13]

The introduction of new technology as a means to increase productivity is a gradual process. It usually takes many years before the results of successful research and development are incorporated into the production process.[14] The rate at which more productive plant and equipment are introduced depends on many factors, including the rate of saving and the cost of financing the capital investment relative to the expected rate of return on the investment. During this diffusion process, there is substantial labor mobility within occupational and geographic labor markets; much of the potential displacement of workers from their jobs never occurs because of gradual attrition of the workers as some retire or move to other jobs before the more productive innovation is actually introduced.

In any labor market, workers will be permanently displaced only if the employment declines brought about by the productivity-enhancing measures are both absolutely large and *relatively* large compared with the attrition rate in the local labor market. In the short run, this may occur in some local labor markets if the work force is heavily concentrated in a narrow range of industries that have become uncompetitive. Unless these industries regain their competitive position, some of the work force will be displaced permanently and may experience permanent income losses through long-term unemployment and the need eventually to accept lower paying jobs. Government policies can assist workers during that difficult transition, but the greatest threat to employment and income security in firms that have lost their competitive position comes from failure to maintain a high rate of productivity growth.

In the long run, there simply is no reason for enhanced productivity to reduce employment in the economy as a whole. History confirms this conclusion. We estimate that the almost uninterrupted sequence of productivity improvements that U.S. manufacturing has enjoyed since the beginning of the Industrial Revolution increased the productivity of labor by as much as twenty times. Naive reasoning suggests that if 100 percent of the manufacturing labor force was employed in 1800, only about 5 percent of our workers would have jobs today because our 1800 per capita output can be produced today with one-twentieth of the labor hours that were required then. Of course, that is not what has happened. Instead, our standard of living and our demands for goods and services have risen so dramatically that the average unemployment rate in the postwar period was no higher than it was at the onset of the Industrial Revolution.

In sum, productivity improvement may not be an unmixed blessing for some workers, and it may add to unemployment in particular industries and in the economy as a whole for limited periods, but there is little reason to fear that productivity growth will contribute to long-run unemployment problems.

## Productivity Growth as a Cure for Inflation

Perhaps as a balance to those who are overly pessimistic about enhanced productivity as a threat to employment, there are those who are overly optimistic in considering it as a relatively costless cure for inflation. Once again, there is some truth to the basic proposition. For example, enhanced productivity growth permits firms to raise wages without increasing product prices commensurately and thus may reduce the inflationary consequences emerging from the collective bargaining process and from compensation decisions made by management. More generally, all other things remaining equal, a 1-percentage-point rise in productivity growth may reduce the rate of inflation by about the same amount. But a sustained rise in productivity growth from 1 percent to 2 percent a year in the very near future would be no minor achievement; indeed, it would constitute an astonishing improvement in our productivity if maintained over many years. Reliance on this sort of development rather than on monetary and fiscal policy as the main means to bring inflation to an end is a commitment to a Herculean task. It involves productivity goals that would be difficult enough to approximate in a decade; it also involves the unrealistic assumption that, on the average, none of the benefits of increased productivity will be used to increase wages and income from capital.

### Reduced Taxation, Decreased Inflation, and Deregulation as a Productivity Problem

There are those who have attributed much of the decline in U.S. productivity growth to government interference in the market mechanism and to its failure, at least until recently, to make much headway against inflation. From this observation, it is implied that all that is needed to "get America going again" is to decrease business taxes sharply, reduce the severity of regulatory restraints, and bring the rate of inflation back down to what it was before the Vietnam War.

No doubt each of these proposals would serve as a stimulus to productivity. The question is not about the direction in which they would work, but whether such a painless path out of the country's productivity problem actually exists. There is no evidence supporting the proposition that such a simple set of programs will prove sufficient for the task; there are, in fact, reasons for doubting it. Here history is at least suggestive. Economic historians indicate that the period during which Great Britain began to lose its economic preeminence extended roughly from 1870 to 1914. During that period, Britain's productivity growth declined sharply and it was overtaken in productivity growth by the United States and Germany. In this respect, then, there is a direct parallel to the current American performance record. Yet, during the entire period of British decline, prices were not rising, taxes on business were negligible by any standards, and there was certainly no regulatory interference of any substance in the conduct of business. Despite the fact that all three conditions were ideal, the British economy was unable to muster sufficient energy to divert it from the path that today has left it with a per capita income level perhaps half of that in most prosperous European countries.

We conclude that although containment of inflation, reduction of the burden of regulation, and elimination of the most onerous business taxes may be steps in the right direction, it is self-delusion to believe that these alone can be relied on to bring the United States up to the productivity growth rates of its leading industrial competitors.

## Productivity and International Competitiveness

It is widely believed that lagging productivity growth must raise the cost and the price of American products, which will, in turn, drive those products, one after another, out of the foreign markets that previously imported them, and that at the same time all U.S. markets will become increasingly vulnerable to foreign imports. The consequences envisaged are growing unemployment in the United States, collapse of most of its industries, increased trade deficits, and takeover of vast segments of American markets by foreign competitors.

The future that economic analysis leads us to expect in the event that U.S. productivity growth continues to lag is very different. Some U.S. industries will certainly decline or even disappear, but others will inevitably take their place. In the short run, unemployment may well be increased, but there is no reason for it to persist in the long run. Some foreign products will replace ours in the purchases of American consumers, but along with this, the use of some U.S. products will rise. Above all, there is very little likelihood that the United States will be driven from all foreign markets or that it will be saddled with persistent trade deficits from which it cannot extricate itself.

A number of influences virtually guarantee such a scenario in the long run. One—the exchange rate mechanism—is able to achieve all these results by itself. Its role is easily described. Suppose that poor productivity performance raises the cost of American products relative to their foreign counterparts and causes a sharp shrinkage in the markets for U.S. goods. This would indeed imply that we will spend more on foreign goods than foreigners will spend on ours, and a deficit in our balance of payments can be expected to follow. But in the long run, the value of the dollar will fall relative to the mark, franc, yen, and other foreign currencies because the currency markets, like other markets, are regulated by demand and supply.[15] When foreigners do not want U.S. goods, they will not demand the dollars they would otherwise need to carry out these imports, and the value of the dollar will fall. Such a decline in the dollar, however, makes it cheaper for residents of other countries to buy American goods. A 50 percent drop in the mark price of the dollar means that the purchase of an American car becomes half as expensive for a German as it was before; at the same time, it doubles the cost of a pair of German binoculars to an American customer.

In that way, a decrease in the price of the dollar can offset any relative lag in U.S. productivity growth. Moreover, the decline in the dollar's value in such circumstances is not a fortuitous matter, which may or may not occur. It is an inevitable consequence of any very protracted balance-of-payments deficit stemming from the productivity lag.

This may seem to be a very optimistic view of the situation. The productivity lag will produce no permanent deficit in the U.S. balance of payments because the resulting reduction in the value of the dollar will bring it to an end. That same decline in the dollar's value will discourage foreign exports to the U.S. and will preserve world markets for American goods despite our relative productive inefficiency. But, in fact, this scenario is not optimistic at all. The mechanism just described can preserve the competitiveness of American products, but only at a terrible cost to the economy. It has at least two most unfortunate consequences: (1) It would reduce the standard of living; indeed, in the final analysis, it would make low U.S. wages the means by which U.S. products as a group retain their place in world markets. (2) Although it would not destroy the economy, it would undermine some industries that were previously the mainstays of U.S. prosperity and, in the process, would impose some very high and painful adjustment costs.

A reduction in the value of the dollar has immediate and unfortunate consequences for American income levels because such a decline amounts to a huge markdown sale in which U.S. products are offered to the world at bargain prices while the prices of foreign products offered to Americans are increased commensurately. If we, in effect, sell our computers, our wheat, and our other export products at large discounts, and if we pay a great deal in return for our imports, we automatically impoverish ourselves. If the yen price of the dollar doubles, it will take twice as many hours as before for a U.S. worker to earn enough to buy a Japanese television set. Thus, reductions in the value of the dollar automatically serve to impoverish the U.S. labor force and enable this country to retain its place on the world's markets through the export of the products of cheap U.S. labor.

Such a process must also change the composition of U.S. exports. Instead of exporting the sophisticated outputs of a skilled, productive, and well-paid labor force, we will be driven to specialize in goods best suited to the abilities of a badly paid labor force. Industries like steel, automobiles, and others in which the U.S. formerly excelled will become vulnerable to competition from abroad, and the costs in obsolescent skills of workers and redundant equipment will be enormous. This is hardly an attractive picture, but it is just part of the price of failure to adopt an effective productivity program.

## NOTES

1. These figures demonstrate the dangers of generalization about productivity in the services taken as a whole. The services are, technologically, extremely heterogeneous and include activities ranging from nearly pure handicrafts such

as teaching and live orchestral performance to the highly sophisticated field of telecommunications. This fact that all of these yield intangible products is about their only common attribute. It is hardly surprising, as a consequence, that (if we make no adjustment for quality changes) productivity growth in teaching and live musical performance has been virtually zero while that in telecommunications has achieved perhaps the most outstanding record of any sector of the economy. Of course, such differences do not necessarily imply that one group is inefficient and unimaginative and the other the epitome of virtue and progressivity. Rather, much of the difference can be ascribed to differences in the technological characteristics of service subsectors. It is also noteworthy that services as a whole, whose historical record involves growth rates of productivity somewhat lower than those in manufacturing, have actually performed relatively well during the period of productivity slowdown. The source of the data is the American Productivity Center, *Productivity Perspectives*, rev. ed. (Houston: APC, 1982).

2. Martin Neil Bailey, "The Productivity Slowdown by Industry" (Washington, D.C.: The Brookings Institution, photocopy, 1982).
3. See "Productivity Measures for Selected Industries, 1954–1981," *Bulletin 2155* (Washington, D.C.: U.S. Department of Labor, Bureau of Labor Statistics, 1982).
4. Chapter 2 shows that most studies of the effects of lagging capital investment attribute between 20 percent and 50 percent of the slowdown to this factor. The only exception is a study by Edward F. Denison, which attributes no significant role to capital investment.
5. "Trends in Multifactor Productivity, 1948–1981," *Bulletin 2178* (Washington, D.C.: U.S. Department of Labor, Bureau of Labor Statistics, 1983), p. 20.
6. Based on table in Robert D. Tallison, ed., *The Political Economy of Antitrust* (Lexington, Mass: Lexington Books, 1980), p. 2.
7. These figures are taken from New York Stock Exchange, *U.S. Economic Performance in a Global Perspective* (New York: NYSE, 1981), p. 9.
8. U.S. Department Labor of Labor, Bureau of Labor Statistics, unpublished data.
9. Chase Econometrics.
10. Unpublished data provided by U.S. Department of Labor, Bureau of Labor Statistics.
11. The word *unnecessarily* is *not* meant to argue implicitly for a weakening of all regulatory programs (e.g., for a reduction in objectives for the purity of air and water). Rather, we are referring to evidence that alternative approaches are capable of meeting those targets fully while considerably reducing the degree to which they hold back growth in productivity.
12. For a review of alternate approaches in industrial policy, see *Strategy for U.S. Industrial Competitiveness* (New York: Committee for Economic Development, 1984).
13. Harry J. Gilman, "The Economic Costs of Worker Dislocation: An Overview" (Paper presented to the National Commission on Employment Policy, Washington, D.C., 1979).
14. Robert Ayers and Steve Miller, *The Impact of Industrial Robots* (Pittsburgh, Pa.: The Robotics Institute, Carnegie-Mellon University 1982). Also, see S. A. Levitan and C. M. Johnson, "The Future of Work: Does It Belong to Us or the Robots?" *Monthly Labor Review* 105, no. 9 (September 1982): 10. Genetic engineering (based on research conducted in the 1930s) will also require at least a decade before other industries are affected significantly. See testimony of David A. Jackson, "Impact on Developments in Biotechnology on Productivity," Senate Subcommittee on Employment and Productivity, 96th Cong., 2d session.

15. In the short run, of course, other influences may offset this influence of low
    U.S. productivity. As this book goes to press, the dollar's value is considered
    high in relation to other currencies because high U.S. interest rates are
    attracting foreign investors who must buy dollars to acquire bonds, stocks, and
    other assets in this country. The high interest rates are, in turn, attributed
    primarily to the prospect of large federal deficits and the resulting borrowing by
    the government, as well as the accompanying fear of renewed inflation. If the
    strength of the dollar attributable to very large budget deficits extends over a
    period of several years, the resulting rise in the exchange rate for the U.S.
    dollar relative to other currencies can have a detrimental effect on future
    productivity growth. Since the United States has a relatively low saving rate,
    large-scale government borrowing to finance expenditures on programs that
    provide income for current consumption can raise the cost of private borrowing
    for investment in plant and equipment.

    The disparity among real interest rates in the United States and other
    countries cannot persist, since the capital flows it elicits will eventually bring
    the rates more closely into line. The dollar's exchange value will then have to
    fall and the trade adjustments described in this chapter will begin to occur.

# 2

# The Magnitude and Causes of the Recent Productivity Slowdown in the United States: A Survey of Recent Studies

EDWARD N. WOLFF

The slowdown in the rate of productivity growth (the *productivity slowdown*) that has occurred in the United States over the past fifteen years or so has been a major focus of policy debate. Because of its enormous implications for the improvement of per capita well-being, the productivity slowdown has engendered a rapid increase in scholarly literature on the subject. A whole host of possible causes has been diagnosed, and a corresponding menu of remedies has been proposed.

This chapter surveys the literature dealing with the recent productivity slowdown and concentrates on the major studies and the major factors cited as causes; no new work is attempted here. It should be mentioned at the outset that there are wide differences of opinion both on the identity of the relevant factors and on their likely quantitative importance. Because much of this is highly technical in nature, this survey avoids a detailed discussion of modeling and measurement problems. Instead, it provides a summary of the pertinent arguments and positions on the central issue.

The first section, "What Is Productivity?," presents a brief discussion of how productivity is measured both at the sectoral level and overall. The second section, "Magnitude of the Productivity Slowdown," examines the evidence both by industrial sector and for the economy as a whole. The third section, "Causes of the Slowdown," surveys much of the available literature. The fourth section, "An Evaluation," takes a brief look at the relative merits of the arguments on the causes of the productivity slowdown.[1]

## WHAT IS PRODUCTIVITY?

Before discussing the causes of the productivity slowdown, it is necessary to show that such a slowdown has, in fact, occurred; and before doing that, it is necessary to define the concept of productivity. There is perhaps as much divergence of opinion about the proper measure of productivity as there is about the causes of its growth over time (see National Research Council, 1979, for an extended discussion of measurement). Generally speaking, productivity is defined as a ratio of some measure of output to some measure of input. The disagreements are about what to include in (or exclude from) the numerator and denominator of the fraction. This is true for the measures of both overall or aggregate productivity and sectoral or industry productivity.

For *aggregate productivity*, the numerator is some measure of the total output of the economy, such as gross national product (GNP) or net national product (NNP). However, there has been extensive discussion about the desirability of excluding certain components of traditional net output indexes such as police services and including certain nonmarket activities such as homemaker services in the NNP (see, for example, Rees, 1979). There is disagreement about how to define the output of the government sector, which is currently valued on the basis of its inputs.[2] Of particular relevance for the current debate over the productivity slowdown is the desirability of including such items as worker safety, environmental improvements, and other measures of *externalities* as part of the output measure. Another major issue is whether to use the GNP, as Kendrick (1980a) and Thurow (1979) do, or the NNP, as Denison (1979a) does. The difference between the two is the amount of depreciation of fixed capital. Many observers, particularly growth theorists, believe it is more proper to exclude the depreciation of fixed capital because this is an intermediate cost that, like the consumption of raw materials and semifinished goods, is excluded from the measure of final output. However, others, particularly those looking at the issue from the standpoint of production theory, prefer the GNP measure because for them depreciation is part of the measure of the services of the primary factor—capital.

In calculating the denominator of the productivity measure, two measures are commonly used. The first is the total labor input, and the resulting ratio is referred to as *labor productivity*; the second is a weighted sum of factor inputs, including labor and capital stock and sometimes land and other natural resources, and the ratio is referred to as *total-factor productivity (TFP)*. Labor productivity is usually considered the better measure of welfare because it bears a rough correspondence to per capita income; TFP is considered the better measure of an economy's efficiency and its rate of technical change because it measures the ratio of output to the sum of all basic inputs. Moreover, whereas the labor productivity measure can, in essence, be used with any model or theoretical framework, the use of TFP involves some fairly restrictive assumptions. The reason is that the denominator is normally construed as a weighted average of the various inputs, where the weights are value shares (i.e., shares received by the factor in total income). For this to be legitimate analytically, the production functions that characterize each sector of the economy must fall within a certain class (i.e., those with constant elasticities of substitution), and labor and capital must receive in payment the value of their marginal products. In addition, it must be assumed that the economy is operating efficiently (or, in more technical terms, that the economy is on the production-possibility frontier). (See Hulten, 1978.)

There are also questions about the appropriate way to define the inputs used in the two kinds of measures. In the case of labor, the simplest measure is the total number of hours worked per year or the number of full-time-equivalent workers. These are referred to as *unweighted* measures of labor input. However, some researchers use *weighted* measures of labor input. The case for a weighted figure is that more skilled labor represents a larger number of input units per unit of time worked, and thus makes for a better measure of factor input in a production function. There is, however, disagreement about whether to use schooling, training, or some combined measure of human capital or relative wages as the appropriate weight.[3] It should be noted that most standard labor input measures, such as those issued by the Bureau of Labor Statistics, are effectively weighted.

In the case of the principal input—capital stock—three major issues arise. (1) What is the appropriate measure of the *net capital stock?* Gross investment in a given year can be measured adequately in standard national accounts. However, in any given year, part of the existing capital stock wears out physically, and part of it becomes obsolete technologically or economically. The net increase in capital stock is equal to gross investment less this depreciation. The difficulties concern the measurement of *true* economic depreciation, which is necessary to estimate the net capital stock. (2) How should the *capital stock of the business sector and its components* be measured? The gross investment figure in the national accounts lumps together business investment in various sectors (as well as residential investment). Alignment of investment in plant and equipment with the sector making the investment is often a major measurement task. (3) What is the measure of the *utilization rates of capital stock?* This is particularly important in the use of TFP because TFP is designed to measure the ratio of output to a weighted sum of actual labor services and capital services. Capital services, in turn, depend on the amount of the existing capital stock actually utilized in production. A failure to measure such utilization rates properly may therefore bias the TFP measure.

Additional complications beset measurement of productivity by sector. Almost all researchers use value added originating by sector divided by employment as the measure of sectoral productivity. Two problems affect the use of the sectoral value-added measure: (1) It is sometimes difficult to interpret what is meant by "value added in constant prices," a concept that is essential to the analysis of productivity change over time. The physical gross output of a sector—such as wheat—has a price whose movement over time can be ascertained. But the components of value added—such as wages, profits, rent, net interest, and depreciation—all change at different rates over time. Normally, therefore, researchers use a technique called *double deflation*, in which the prices of the gross output and the material inputs are deflated by their respective price changes. The difference between the two is used as the measure of value added in constant prices. (2) More important, perhaps, the actual output produced by a sector and its value added may move in different directions over time. The agricultural sector provides the clearest example. A bumper crop causes the price of the output to fall, perhaps yielding lower profits and a reduction in value added, depending on the elasticity of demand in response to prices. For these two reasons, consequently, value added may not be the optimal measure of sectoral output. In summary, it is probably fair to say that different concepts of productivity are useful for different purposes and different ways of measuring productivity are advantageous for some uses but not for all.


## MAGNITUDE OF THE PRODUCTIVITY SLOWDOWN

There is almost universal agreement among researchers that the rate of productivity growth in the United States began to decline from its postwar rate in the mid- to late 1960s. Moreover, most researchers believe that there were two distinct phases in the decline, one lasting from about 1965 to 1973 and the other from about 1973 to 1978. Table 2-1 presents various estimates of the change in aggregate productivity growth between 1948 and the late 1970s. Even though different definitions of productivity are used, the results are quite uniform. For the 1948–1965(1966) period, the estimated annual rate of productivity growth ranges from 3.3 to 3.5 percent; for the 1965(1966)–1972(1973) period, the range is 2.1 to 2.3 percent; and for the 1972(1973)–1977(1978) period, the range is 1.1 to 1.2 percent. Kendrick (1980a), Norsworthy, Harper, and Kunze (1979), and Thurow (1979) all find that there was about a 1-percentage-point drop in

**Table 2-1. Selected Estimates of Change in Aggregate Rate of Productivity Growth over Postwar Period**

| Source | Concept | Period | Annual Rate of Productivity Growth (percent) |
|---|---|---|---|
| Denison (1979a) | National income per person employed in nonresidential business | 1948–1973<br>1973–1976 | 2.43<br>−0.54 |
| Kendrick (1980a) | Real product per unit of labor in the business economy | 1948–1966<br>1966–1973<br>1973–1978 | 3.50<br>2.10<br>1.10 |
| Kendrick (1980a) | TFP in the business economy | 1948–1966<br>1966–1973<br>1973–1978 | 2.70<br>1.60<br>0.80 |
| Norsworthy, Harper, and Kunze (1979) | Gross domestic product per hour of labor input | 1948–1965<br>1965–1973<br>1973–1978 | 3.32<br>2.32<br>1.20 |
| Thurow (1979) | GNP per labor-hour in private sector | 1948–1965<br>1965–1972<br>1972–1977 | 3.30<br>2.30<br>1.20 |

the labor productivity growth rate between the first two periods and another drop of about 1 percentage point between the second and third periods. Denison (1979a) compares the rate of growth of labor productivity in the 1947–1973 and 1973–1976 periods and finds a more precipitous drop of 3 percentage points.

Kendrick (1980a) presents a separate set of estimates for the rate of growth of TFP. These are uniformly lower than his estimates of labor productivity growth because the effect of a rising capital-labor ratio on labor productivity is factored out. Even so, Kendrick finds a 1-percentage-point drop in the rate of growth of TFP between the first and second periods and the second and third periods.

Table 2-2 presents various estimates of the decline in the rate of productivity growth in particular industries. In contrast with the aggregate estimates, there is much greater variation in the actual point estimates for particular sectors, although the assessments of the *direction* of change are fairly uniform.[4] All seven researchers find that the rate of productivity growth for the mining sector had declined and also that this was the sector that had experienced the largest decline. There was also general agreement that productivity growth had declined in both durable and nondurable manufacturing (Bennett found no change), in construction (Kendrick found an increase), in agriculture (Wolff found no change), and in transportation, utilities, wholesale and retail trade, and general services. There were mixed reports for finance, insurance, and real estate, with four papers reporting increases and two papers finding declines, and for the government sector, with two reporting modest declines and one a modest increase. By all accounts, the decline in productivity growth before 1970 and after 1970 characterized almost all sectors. However, the actual magnitude of the decline varied considerably among sectors, from a high in mining to a low in government services and to an actual increase in productivity in communications.[5]

## CAUSES OF THE SLOWDOWN

A full explanation of the productivity slowdown would have to account not only for the aggregate slowdown but also for the relative productivity movements of the various sectors. Moreover, it would have to account for the two-phase nature of the slowdown and for the fact that the patterns in productivity growth in the two phases varied considerably by sector.

Needless to say, no one has yet come up with a full explanation. Indeed, most research has been geared to explaining the change in aggregate productivity growth. Most of the aggregate analysis comes out of what is usually called *growth accounting*, in which the economy is treated as a

**Table 2-2. Selected Estimates of Change in Overall and Sectoral Productivity Growth Rates (percent)**

| Source / Productivity concept | Denison (1979a) GNP/hours worked[a] | Thurow (1979) Value added per employee-hour[b] | Kendrick (1980a) TFP[c] | Nadiri (1980) Value added per worker | Bennett (1979) Output per employee-hour[d] | Norsworthy, Harper, and Kunze (1979) Gross domestic product per employee-hour[e] | Wolff (1981) Total labor productivity[f] |
|---|---|---|---|---|---|---|---|
| Periods | 1948–1973, 1973–1976 | 1948–1965, 1972–1977 | 1948–1973, 1973–1976 | 1948–1974, 1974–1978 | 1948–1967, 1967–1978 | 1948–1965, 1973–1978 | 1947–1967, 1967–1976 |
| Overall | -2.97 | -2.1 | -1.8 | -0.93[g] | -0.7 | -2.1 | -2.7 |
| Sector: | | | | | | | |
| Agriculture, forestry, fisheries | -3.4 | -3.6 | -2.2 | -1.17 | — | -2.6 | +0.1 |
| Mining | -10.2 | -9.4 | -7.0 | -6.79 | -5.2 | -8.2 | -4.0 |
| Construction | -0.7 | -4.2 | +0.9 | -1.06 | -5.1 | -4.7 | -3.2 |
| Nondurable manufacturing | -1.3 | -0.7 | -2.2 | -0.94 | 0.0 | -1.0 | -3.7 |
| Durable manufacturing | -1.5 | -1.5 | -0.6[h] | -1.07 | -0.2 | -1.6 | -2.9 |
| Transportation | -2.9 | -1.0 | +0.1 | -2.45 | +0.5 | -2.4 | -0.9 |
| Communications | +3.2 | +1.1 | | +2.52 | | +1.6 | |
| Utilities | -4.0 | -5.3 | -6.7 | -2.66 | -3.7 | -6.1 | |
| Wholesale trade | -4.6 | -3.3 | | | -0.3 | -2.9 | -1.5 |
| Retail trade | -1.3 | -1.6 | -2.4 | -1.86 | -0.6 | -1.6 | |
| Finance and insurance | — | — | | | | | |
| Real estate | — | -0.6 | +0.3 | +1.59 | -1.1 | +0.4 | +0.1 |
| Services | -1.2 | -1.0 | — | -1.37 | -0.2 | -1.0 | -3.1 |
| Government | — | — | — | -0.33 | — | +0.1[i] | -0.3 |

[a] The overall productivity figure is the national income per person employed in nonresidential business.

[b] The overall figure is GNP per employee-hour in the private sector.

[c] The overall figure is for the business economy.

[d] The growth rates are adjusted for business cycles, and the overall figure is for the nonfarm private economy.

[e] The overall figure is for the private business economy.

[f] Total labor productivity is defined as the sum of the direct plus indirect labor time (employee-years) required per unit of gross output. The overall figure is the NNP per employee-year for the whole economy.

[g] This figure is for the total economy; for the business economy, the overall figure is -0.78.

[h] Excludes railroads.

[i] This figure is for government enterprises only. Government enterprises are businesses owned and operated by various government agencies that sell their output directly to the public. Examples are local utilities and transit systems and the U.S. Postal Service.

single aggregate production function, with total output related to a set of input factors. Each factor is assigned a weight in the determination of total output, usually based on its factor share (i.e., the proportion of total income received by the factor), and the total growth of output can be related to the growth of these inputs over time. It is then possible to estimate the contribution of each of these factors to output growth. The remaining part or residual is then attributed to technological change.

It is also possible to use this framework to determine the sources of labor productivity growth. Many growth accounting analyses (e.g., Kendrick's) use a fairly simple production function, called a *Cobb-Douglas function*.[6] It is also possible to use a more complex production function to relate aggregate output to the various input quantities, such as the translog function used by Norsworthy, Harper, and Kunze.

It is perhaps most convenient to use a production function to investigate the factors cited as causes of the slowdown. Seven causes have been suggested. The first three relate to inputs: the rate of capital formation, the composition of the labor force, and energy prices. The fourth relates to the residual in the production function: research and development (R&D) and technological progress. The fifth concerns the shares of the economy's different products: the composition of output. The remaining two are government regulation and the business cycle. It should be mentioned at the outset that these seven causes are not really mutually exclusive. For example, much of the discussion concerning the effect of the energy price rise on productivity growth involves its impact on capital formation. This division is made more for heuristic purposes than for analytical reasons.

## Rate of Capital Formation

Many believe that the decline in capital formation was a major culprit in the overall productivity slowdown. On the surface, the evidence seems to belie this belief because the ratio of gross private domestic investment to gross domestic product actually *rose* from 12.3 percent in 1948–1965 to 13.5 percent in 1965–1973 and then fell to 12.8 percent in 1973–1978, a figure that was still above the level prior to the slowdown.[7] However, this is not the whole story; employment also increased more rapidly during the slowdown periods. The same source indicates that total hours of labor input increased at annual rates of 0.38 percent in 1948–1965, 1.44 percent in 1965–1973, and 1.42 percent in 1973–1978. From the viewpoint of labor productivity, the important issue is what happened to the *capital-labor ratio* during this period because labor productivity increases as the capital-labor ratio rises. Despite the seeming simplicity of the issue involved, there are wide disparities in the results obtained in different studies depending on which definition and which data source were used.

Eckstein (1980) maintains that the stagnation in the capital-labor ratio was perhaps the largest element in the productivity slowdown. Kendrick (1980a), using a growth accounting framework, finds that of the 2.4-percentage-point decline in the rate of growth of real product per unit of labor between the 1948–1966 and 1973–1978 periods, 0.5 was accounted for by the deceleration in the substitution of capital for labor. Kopcke (1980), using an aggregate Cobb-Douglas production function, ascribes half of the productivity slowdown between 1950–1965 and 1965–1978 in the nonfarm, nonresidential economy to slower growth in plant and equipment. In the case of manufacturing, he attributes the entire drop to slower growth in investment. Nadiri (1980), using a three-input Cobb-Douglas production function and sectoral data, estimates that the change in the capital-labor ratio accounted for 38 percent of the productivity slowdown between 1948–1974 and 1974–1978 for the economy as a whole and 33 percent in the private economy. Tatom (1979) estimates that the slowdown in capital formation accounted for 0.7 percentage points of a 1.8-percentage-point decline in the productivity growth rate between 1950–1972 and 1972–1979. Moreover, P. Clark (1977) estimates that 0.26 points of the 0.75-point decline in the 1965–1973 trend rate in productivity growth came from the slow growth in the capital-labor ratio.

Another view of the effect of capital formation on the productivity slowdown is offered by Norsworthy and Harper (1979), who examine the effect of the rate of capital formation on labor productivity growth after 1965 in the nonfarm business sector. They find that the rate of capital formation had little to do with the slowdown during the 1965–1973 period but played a significant role during 1973–1977. Divisia aggregates of capital stock were used in conjunction with a translog production function.[8]

A problem affecting the capital stock measures used in many studies is their misalignment with the output and labor input measures. The equipment and structures of nonprofit institutions are normally included but, for consistency, should be left out; the stock of tenant-owned housing is normally excluded but should be included. The misalignment is found to have significant effects on conclusions about the comparative rate of growth of capital stock and the capital-labor ratio. Norsworthy and Harper find that when this problem is corrected for, there was about a 20 percent increase in the figure for the rate of growth of net stocks of equipment and structures in the nonfarm business sector in the 1965–1973 period. They conclude, on the basis of an examination of both corrected and uncorrected rates, that there was no slowdown in the capital-labor ratio during the 1965–1973 period regardless of the aggregation method. However, they find a slowdown in the capital-labor ratio of 1 percentage point a year since 1973. Moreover, they conclude that the effect of capital accumulation on labor productivity growth was actually *greater* in 1965–1973 than in earlier periods. In the 1973–1977 period, on the other hand, they estimate that the contribution of capital stock growth to productivity growth fell by one-half. Of the 0.87-percentage-point decline in productivity growth between 1965–1973 and 1973–1977, the slowdown in capital formation explained 0.43 percentage points.

In a follow-up study, Norsworthy, Harper, and Kunze (1979) look at productivity growth over the 1965–1973 and 1973–1978 periods for the entire business sector (including the farm sector). Using regression analysis, they reach conclusions similar to those of the previous study: Capital formation contributed to productivity growth in the private business sector over the 1965–1973 period. During the 1973–1978 period, capital effects accounted for 0.79 percentage points of the 1.12-percentage-point decline in productivity growth.

Denison (1979a) presents the opposing view that capital formation was not a major contributory factor in the productivity slowdown. His estimates show that there was a very small decline in the rate of growth of the capital-labor ratio in the nonresidential business economy between the 1948–1973 and 1973–1976 spans and that this factor explains *only 1 percent* (*not percentage point*) of the slowdown. Denison (1980) extends his analysis through 1978. He finds that for the nonresidential business economy, the growth rate of fixed capital to hours worked was only slightly lower in 1965–1978 than in 1950–1965 (0.1 percent for gross stocks and 0.5 percent for net stocks of capital). In manufacturing, in fact, the growth rate of gross stocks per hour worked *rose* 0.61 points in the second period, and the rate for net stocks *rose* 1.12 points. Denison's findings probably differ from those of the other studies because he excludes the residential sector and because he uses NNP instead of GNP, which results in a lower estimate of capital's contribution to output. Finally, Wolff (1981), using sectoral capital stock data provided by the Bureau of Labor Statistics (1979), also finds a very small retardation in the annual rate of increase in the overall capital-labor ratio from 2.49 percent in 1947–1967 to 2.41 percent in 1967–1976. However, because the unemployment rate was high in 1976 and low in 1967, the peak-to-peak decline might have been somewhat greater.

Besides holding back the rate of increase of the capital-labor ratio, a slowdown in capital formation will have secondary effects on the rate of growth of labor productivity (see Griliches, 1980). Because new technology is normally embodied in new capital stock, a decline in capital formation will slow down the rate of introduction of new technology and therefore the rate of technical change. There is also an effect usually referred to as the *vintage effect* because the more rapidly new vintages of capital stock are introduced, the more rapidly new technology is diffused. In this way,

Kendrick (1980a) uses the average age of capital goods as an indicator of the rate of diffusion of new technology. He finds that between 1948 and 1966, the average age declined by three years, contributing 0.25 percentage points to the overall productivity growth rate. Between 1966 and 1973 the decline in average age slowed to one year; and between 1973 and 1978 there was no decline in the average age of capital stock. P. Clark (1979), using a Cobb-Douglas aggregate production function and assuming that new capital stock is 1 percent more productive than last year's capital stock, finds a somewhat smaller vintage effect than Kendrick does. He estimates that of the 0.66-point decline in the labor productivity growth rate between 1948–1965 and 1965–1973, the vintage effect explains 0.09 points; of the 1.17-point decline between 1965–1973 and 1973–1978, the vintage effect accounts for 0.10 points.

One additional argument that has been offered in connection with capital formation is that much of the new capital investment since the mid-1960s has been made in order to comply with safety regulations and pollution rules and therefore does not add to productivity. Rama (1980) estimates that if one subtracts this unproductive portion from the total capital stock, the capital-labor ratio *actually fell* from an index of $258 in 1967 to $220 in 1973. Denison (1979a) estimates that the amount of capital installed to comply with pollution and safety regulations grew from zero percent of net stocks in 1967 to 2.6 percent in 1975. Such compliance explains 0.30 points of the 3.07-point decline in the productivity growth rate from 1948–1973 to 1973–1976.

## Composition of the Labor Force

Another candidate cause of the productivity slowdown is the changing composition of the labor force, particularly the increase after 1966 in the relative number of young workers and women. Eckstein (1980) and Perloff and Wachter (1980) argue that the productivity of these groups is generally lower than that of the labor force as a whole because they have fewer skills and less experience; therefore, a shift in labor force composition toward these groups will lower overall productivity. Perry (1977) estimates the labor-force participation rates of various demographic groups. For persons of both sexes aged 16 to 24 and women aged 25 to 44, a statistically significant speedup in participation rates was found after 1966. For teenagers and women aged 25 to 44, this acceleration was 3 to 4 percent a year. Men aged 25 to 64 and women 45 years of age and older showed a statistically significant slowing in participation rates. Perry also argues that these changes in labor force participation by women are the result of fairly permanent sociological changes, such as the deferral of marriage or childbearing, rather than short-run influences, such as inflation and declining real earnings.

Kendrick (1980a), using a growth accounting framework, estimates that the changing proportion of women and youths in the labor force reduced annual productivity growth by 0.1 percentage points in 1948–1966, 0.4 points in 1966–1973, and 0.2 points in 1973–1978. Filer (1980), using a correlation analysis from a regression model, estimates that a significant part of the productivity slowdown was caused by the accelerated influx of women into the labor force since 1966. Norsworthy, Harper, and Kunze (1979) estimate that the changing age composition of the work force played some role in the productivity slowdown between 1948–1965 and 1965–1973 but not between 1965–1973 and 1973–1978, whereas they find that the changing sex composition was a factor in the second slowdown but not in the first. Denison (1979a) attributes only 0.08 points of the 2.97-percentage-point productivity slowdown to the change in age-sex composition between the 1948–1973 and 1973–1976 periods. Clark (1977) estimates that the shifts in age and sex explained almost one-third of the 1965–1973 slowdown.

A counteracting influence during this period was the increase in the education and training of the work force. Kendrick (1980) estimates that it accounted for 0.7 points in the overall productivity growth rate between 1973 and 1978, compared with 0.6 points between 1948 and 1966. Norsworthy, Harper, and Kunze (1979) also find that the contribution of this factor increased steadily, from 0.46 points in 1948–1965 to 0.95 points in 1965–1973 and 1.05 points in 1973–1978, although these figures are not corrected for interactive effects with the change in the occupational mix. Denison's (1979a) figures indicate a rise in the contribution of this factor from 0.52 points in 1948–1973 to 0.88 points in 1973–1976, but because 1976 was a year of high unemployment, the average education of the labor force is probably overstated.[9]

## Energy Prices

Another event that many observers believe is connected with the productivity slowdown is the dramatic rise in energy prices that began in the early 1970s. A study by Rasche and Tatom (1977) estimates that 4 to 5 percentage points of the decrease in national income in 1974 was due to the quadrupling of oil prices by the Organization of Petroleum Exporting Countries (OPEC). They conclude that this loss of national income was permanent, as was the associated reduction in potential GNP. The Council of Economic Advisers (1977) also cites evidence supporting the view that the drop in productivity of labor and capital resources since 1973–1974 was permanent and was caused by the higher costs of energy resources. Rasche and Tatom estimate a Cobb-Douglas production function using annual data for the period from 1949 to 1975. The results indicate that capacity in the manufacturing sector fell 5 percent in 1974 as a result of the 45.3 percent increase in the nominal price of energy over the 1973–1974 span. There is also evidence that these results are representative for the entire private business sector.

An analysis by Hudson and Jorgenson (1978) also examines the effect of the 1973–1974 oil price increase using a dynamic general equilibrium model of the U.S. economy to simulate two economic growth paths over the 1972–1976 period. The first simulation uses actual values for the exogenous variables, including world oil prices. This gives an estimate of the actual development of the economy over that period. A second simulation keeps energy prices constant at their 1972 level for the entire period. A comparison of the two simulations indicates that the increase in the price of energy over that period reduced real GNP in 1976 by 3.2 percent. This is attributed to the behavior of producers who tried to substitute other inputs for energy in the production process. This tended to decrease productivity because the substitution is imperfect and the substitute inputs must be taken away from other uses. The decline in energy use is found to redirect the patterns of net input away from energy. The greatest relative reductions in energy use are estimated to have occurred in services and manufacturing.

At the same time, higher energy prices led to increased use of labor per unit of output as producers substituted labor for energy. The largest increases in the demand for labor occurred in services and manufacturing; significant increases were also found in agriculture and construction. However, because real GNP fell by 3.2 percent between 1972 and 1976, the demand for labor also fell by 3.2 percent. The net effect of the increase in the price of energy was found to be a decrease in labor demand of only 0.6 percent. As a result, there was a decrease in the average output per worker. The economic restructuring represented by the differences in the two simulations involves a 2.57 percent decline in the growth rate of average labor productivity over four years, or 0.6 percent a year. Hudson and Jorgenson note that these are once-and-for-all effects; they will persist even in the absence of further price increases.

Denison (1979a) disputes this analysis. He argues that the value of energy used in the nonresidential business sector is less than 4 percent of the total value of the factor inputs in the entire economy. Hudson and Jorgenson (1978) estimate that the use of energy per unit of factor input was reduced 7.7 percent between 1973 and 1976. According to Denison, "The usual procedure would then yield a reduction in output per unit of labor, capital, and land of only 0.3 percentage points (7.7 × 0.04)";[10] this is about one-seventh of the Hudson-Jorgenson estimate of 2.57 percentage points. Denison thus estimates that the 1973–1974 energy price increase reduced the productivity growth rate by 0.1 percentage points a year, not 0.6 percentage points a year. However, it should be noted that Denison's analysis implicitly assumes a Cobb-Douglas production function for the economy, an assumption that might not be entirely supportable.

Norsworthy, Harper, and Kunze (1979) use a dynamic model of the manufacturing sector to simulate the effect of energy price movements on productivity. In their analysis, the energy price effect on the productivity slowdown is subsumed in its effect on capital formation. The results show a strong complementarity between labor and capital over both the short and the long terms. The simulation assumes that the price of energy increased at the same rate as the implicit price deflator for manufacturing (rather than the 22.3 percent that occurred). On this basis, the model suggests that the capital-labor ratio would have risen at an annual rate of 2.3 percent instead of the actual 1.7 percent, implying that the annual labor productivity growth rate would have increased 0.18 points if the change in the relative price of energy had not occurred.

Finally, Berndt (1980) argues that the direct effect of the energy price increase on the productivity slowdown in U.S. manufacturing during the 1973–1977 period was not significant. He identifies two reasons for the small direct effect: (1) Energy costs were a very small proportion of total costs, and therefore, energy price variations did not weigh heavily in productivity calculations. (2) Observed variations in energy-output ratios were very small between 1973 and 1977, despite the substantial energy price increases. Berndt grants that energy price increases could have had an indirect effect on labor productivity through price-induced substitutions of labor for energy, which would have led to reductions in the ratios of capital to labor and energy to labor. This requires energy-capital complementarity and energy-labor substitutability. But he points out that the evidence on this is not strong. There was only a very slight slowdown in the rate of growth of the capital-labor ratio, from 2.88 percent in 1965–1973 to 2.52 percent in 1973–1977, and in the rate of growth of the energy-labor ratio, from 2.79 percent in 1965–1973 to 2.54 percent in 1973–1977.

## Research and Development and Technological Progress

The decline in R&D expenditures since 1965 has been cited by several authors as a contributor to the slowdown over the 1965–1978 period. The ratio of R&D expenditures to GNP peaked in 1964 at 2.97 percent and then fell to 2.27 percent over the 1976–1977 period (Denison, 1979a). The decline was ascribable primarily to the drop in federal expenditures on defense and space programs. Expenditures financed by other sources actually increased from 0.99 percent of GNP in 1963–1964 to 1.15 percent in 1969–1970. There was a decline in private R&D to GNP ratio to 1.07 percent in 1972–1973, but it recovered to 1.12 percent in the 1974–1977 period.

Research and development affects productivity through advances that reduce the unit cost of final outputs already available or through the introduction of new products. However, not all R&D expenditures contribute to productivity growth. Much is spent on defense and space exploration, health, environment, and goods and services, and the qualitative improvements brought about by such spending are not captured in the national income accounts. Because much of the relative decrease in R&D outlays occurred in these areas, the slowdown in productivity-augmenting research and development may be considerably smaller than these figures indicate.

Griliches (1980) estimates that there was a decline in R&D capital spending of approximately 3 to 6 percentage points during the period of the slowdown. Assuming an elasticity of aggregate output with respect to R&D capital of 0.06 points, Griliches estimates that the reduction in the R&D capital growth rate contributed only 0.14 percentage points to the productivity decline in manufacturing during the recent slowdown.[11] Denison (1979a) estimates that the slowdown in R&D expenditures contributed only about 0.1 points to the decline in overall productivity growth rate. Thurow (1980) also argues that the retardation in R&D spending could not have contributed much to the productivity slowdown because whereas this lessened expenditure did not really begin until the early 1970s, the slowdown began in the mid-1960s, and there must be a substantial time lag between R&D expenditures and measured productivity growth.

On the other side of the ledger, Kendrick (1980) claims to find that 13 percent of the decline in TFP (0.25 percentage points out of an overall decline of 1.9 percentage points) can be attributed to the decline in research and development. However, as Denison points out, Kendrick does not adjust his R&D series for that portion financed by the federal government for space and defense work. Moreover, Nadiri (1980), using a Cobb-Douglas production function with three inputs (labor, capital, and R&D stock), estimates that 17 percent of the productivity decline in the economy as a whole and 37 percent of the decline in the private sector can be attributed to diminished research and development. Nadiri's estimates may, however, be biased upward because he omitted such variables as the average age of capital and total number of labor-hours. The total number of labor-hours, in particular, reflects the short-run productivity movements during the business cycle (see the later section "Cyclical Factors"). In a later work, Nadiri and Shankerman (1980) specify cost and demand functions for total durables and nondurables manufacturing. Cost, price, and income elasticities are estimated and used to examine the slowing of TFP growth over the 1958–1965, 1965–1973, and 1973–1978 periods. Nadiri and Shankerman use an average variable cost function that is shifted by disembodied technological change and the change in the stock of research and development, as well as an output demand function and pricing rule that equates output price to average variable costs and quasirents accruing to capital. They find that the decline in the growth of R&D stock contributed only 5 to 10 percent of the slowdown in TFP for total manufacturing from 1958–1965 to 1965–1973, with a similar figure applying to nondurables from 1965–1973 to 1973–1978. For total manufacturing and durables, the R&D slowdown accounted for about one-quarter of the TFP slowdown between the 1965–1973 and 1973–1978 periods.[12]

In seeking to determine whether there was a slowdown in the rate of technical change, most studies measure this variable by treating it as the residual in the analysis. That is, any change not attributable to any other source is simply ascribed to technical change. Fraumeni and Jorgenson (1980) report that after 1966, the rate of technical change measured in this way almost disappeared as a source of economic growth. Indeed, they calculate that in the 1973–1976 period, the rate of technical change was actually *negative*. But it is hard to evaluate these findings because there is no independent measure of technical change. Since R&D investment continued during these periods, their results would seem to imply that R&D activity yielded no innovative techniques.[13]

## Composition of Output

The relation between the composition of output and the productivity slowdown is also a topic on which there is some disagreement. It should be noted that this treatment of the productivity problem is distinct from the others discussed so far in that it deals with a new set of issues: namely, how the composition of the product has changed over time. However, this treatment is not entirely separable from the others; a change in the composition of output has direct implications concerning the growth of inputs, particularly the capital stock, and the composition of the labor force. Thus, effects on productivity growth estimated from the change in output composition may have been partly picked up in other analyses from changes in input or labor force composition. These results are not therefore strictly additive with other results.

The difference in findings concerning the effect of output composition on productivity growth is ascribable to differences in research methods. Two basically different procedures are employed in this context.

The first calculates the aggregate productivity *level* as a weighted average of the productivity *levels* of the individual sectors. A shift in employment or output between sectors will therefore change the level of overall productivity, assuming that the values of all other variables remain unchanged. It is then possible to isolate the effect of shifts in the composition of output or employment on the change in overall productivity. This *decomposition* technique is used by Nordhaus (1972), Kutscher, Mark, and Norsworthy (1977), Denison (1973, 1979a), and Thurow (1979).

The second approach calculates the overall rate of productivity growth as a weighted average of individual sectoral rates of productivity growth.[14] The theory underlying this approach was provided by Baumol (1967) in his model of unbalanced growth and was later extended by Grossman and Fuchs (1973) and Baumol, Blackman, and Wolff (forthcoming). Using this technique, one can break down the change in overall productivity growth into two effects: the first ascribable to changes in sectoral rates of productivity growth and the second to the composition of output or employment. This technique was used by Wolff (1981).

In the earliest of these studies, Nordhaus (1972) estimates productivity levels for twelve sectors and then projects what the overall rate of productivity growth would have been if the sectoral productivity levels had remained constant over the period while the employment weights shifted as they did over that time. He finds that of the 1.17-percentage-point decline in aggregate productivity growth that occurred between 1948–1965 and 1965–1971 (from 3.20 to 2.03), 0.90 points were attributable to the change in the composition of output.

Kutscher, Mark, and Norsworthy (1977), using Bureau of Labor Statistics sectoral gross output and employment data, estimate that between 1947 and 1966, the shift in the labor force out of agriculture contributed 0.4 points a year to the overall productivity growth rate; whereas from 1966 to 1973, it contributed only 0.1 points annually. Moreover, the shift of employment toward services decreased the overall productivity growth rate by only 0.1 percentage points a year, and this effect was fairly steady over the entire 1947–1973 period. Taken together, the shift in hours of work was responsible for 0.3 to 0.4 points of the 1.5-point decline in overall productivity (from 3.2 to 1.7 points) between 1947–1966 and 1967–1973.

Denison (1973) finds that the shift to services had very little bearing on the productivity slowdown. Although the share of total employment in service industries rose from 54 percent in 1948 to 64 percent in 1969, service employment as a share of total employment in the nonfarm, nonresidential business sector remained almost constant. Moreover, service output as a percent of total nonfarm, nonresidential business output also remained constant. As a result, Denison estimates that the change in composition between commodities and services had less than a

0.05-percentage-point impact on the annual productivity growth rate. Norsworthy, Harper, and Kunze (1979) use a sixty-two-sector breakdown of employment by industry. They estimate that despite the 1.00-percentage-point decline in annual labor productivity growth between 1948–1965 and 1965–1973, the interindustry effect from employment shifts actually boosted productivity growth by 0.05 points. Between 1965–1973 and 1973–1978, the interindustry effect accounted for 0.27 of the 1.12-point decline in the productivity growth rate. However, these results may be understated because the farm-to-nonfarm shift was actually captured by the change in occupational composition.

In contrast, Thurow (1979) finds somewhat stronger compositional effects on productivity growth. Using a twelve-sector breakdown and defining sectoral productivity as value added per worker, Thurow also found that between 1948–1965 and 1965–1972, changes in the industrial composition of employment had no effect on productivity. However, Thurow estimates that from 1965–1972 to 1972–1977, 45 to 50 percent of the observed decline in productivity growth was ascribable to the shifts in the mix of output toward low-productivity sectors. However, this effect may result in part because the shift occurred to sectors with lower capital-to-labor ratios. Finally, Wolff uses U.S. input-output data for 1947, 1967, and 1976 and separates the overall rate of productivity change into two effects: (1) that produced by the sectoral composition of final output and (2) that stemming from individual sectoral rates of technical change. He estimates that the sectoral composition of final output, mainly because of its constancy, accounted for 20 to 25 percent of the decline in the overall productivity growth rate.

**Government Regulation**

Increased government regulation during the 1965–1978 period has also been cited as contributing to the decline in productivity growth. Denison (1979a) argues that there has been a diversion of inputs in the process of complying with government regulations. Government regulations also impose extra paperwork, which uses resources. The federal government estimated that in 1976, this cost was between 2.4 and 3.1 percent of national income of the business sector; when state and local government regulations are included, the cost was approximately 3.0 to 4.6 percent. Regulation and taxes also divert executive attention. The profitability of business is affected by the way in which it responds to rapid changes in government regulations that discriminate among types of income and business costs. Denison concludes that this is a psychological deterrent to performance. On balance, he thinks the effect of such regulations on productivity growth accounted for perhaps 13 percent of the decline.

Government regulation also extends the maturation and fruition period of new investment projects and this delay, too, retards productivity growth. In addition, regulation may cause a misallocation of resources to those items in whose favor it is biased. The largest misallocation effect results from the induced uncertainty about the future. Future benefits of a project become more difficult to assess if there is uncertainty about future regulations. In this way, growing government regulation may serve to reduce growth. Kendrick's results suggest that 16 percent of the weakening in productivity growth between the 1948–1966 and 1973–1978 periods was attributable to government regulations and related policies. Fellner (1979) also concludes that 1 *percentage point* of the worsening in productivity growth is difficult to explain without including the effects of federal government policy changes.

Denison (1979b) estimates the effect of pollution controls on measured output per unit of input. He concludes that by 1975, the change in environmental controls introduced since 1967 had diverted nearly 1 percent of labor, capital, and land used in the nonresidential business sector from production of measured output to pollution abatement, which does *not* result in measured output. By 1978, this had risen to 1.2 percent. He concludes that output per unit of input in 1978 was 98.8 percent as large as it would have been if environmental regulations had stayed as they were in 1967.

Crandall (1980) suggests that there are two ways in which government regulation may reduce productivity growth: (1) Government regulation restricts competition and protects regulated firms from new technology and new competitors. (2) Health, safety, and environmental regulations divert large quantities of resources to the control of various hazards, thereby reducing normally measured output-to-input ratios. Between 1969 and 1972, for example, the Occupational Safety and Health Administration, Environmental Protection Agency, National Highway Traffic Safety Administration, Consumer Product Safety Commission, and the National Environmental Policy Act all came into existence. However, the only hard evidence Crandall presents is for the mining sector, where the annual productivity growth rate declined from 4.2 percent in 1948–1965 to 2.0 in 1965–1973 and −4.0 in 1973–1978.[15]

## Cyclical Factors

Another view attributes much of the productivity problem to the business cycle and thus considers the problem temporary. Productivity growth is known to decrease during the tail end of an economic expansion and during recessions. But during periods of economic recovery, productivity growth usually increases.

An economic recovery begins with the resurgence of sales and decreases in inventory accumulation. Output is initially increased by more intensive use of the existing labor force and capital stock. This increases average weekly working hours and leads to a sharp rise in output per labor-hour. As output increases, so do employment and productivity. In later stages, the increase in labor input continues to grow at a rapid rate for one or two quarters after the rate of growth slows down, thus decreasing the growth of output per labor-hour.

Cyclical productivity movements are explained by the hoarding of labor by firms. During recessions, firms are reluctant to lay off workers because they want to avoid rehiring costs when the expansion occurs. For this reason, hours of employment per worker also display a cyclical pattern. Therefore, hours worked vary more than employment. An alternative explanation of the observed cyclical behavior of productivity is that the use of capital relative to labor is procyclical. Firms use relatively more capital-intensive methods as the economy expands and reduce capital usage relative to labor during economic contractions.

Gordon (1979) examines the short-run behavior of aggregate productivity from 1954 to 1977. Specifically, he investigates the short-run increasing returns to labor and the tendency for productivity to decline during the last stages of the business expansion. Cyclical fluctuations in labor productivity are described in his model as a partial adjustment of the ratio of actual labor hours to potential hours (i.e., the full employment level of labor hours) in response to the fluctuation in the ratio of actual to potential GNP. He includes a dummy variable in the regression to capture the effect of overhiring in the last two quarters of the business expansion. Estimates show that the dummy variable is highly significant. Of the total end-of-expansion effect of 1.8 percentage points, employment accounts for 1.26 points, and hours per employee for 0.54 points. This implies that the end-of-expansion effect primarily involves the retention of too many workers relative to output. Gordon has two explanations for this phenomenon: (1) Labor and capital are interdependent factors of production. When capital investment is relatively high, additional employees are required for installation and training. This implies that experienced labor must work overtime to train new employees. When investment is low, installations of this type are decreased. (2) Firms may maintain slack in their labor force when the quit rate is high to guard against being caught shorthanded.[16]

Kendrick (1980a) notes that there was full employment in 1948 and 1966 and that, as a result, the ratio of actual to potential GNP in 1973 was 1.5 percent below that of 1966 and 2.7 percent lower in 1978 than in 1966. This subtracted 0.1 points from annual growth rates in 1966–1973 and 0.3 points in 1973–1978. A related phenomenon is that the deceleration in the growth of total real GNP means a lessening of the contribution of economies of scale to productivity growth. Kendrick estimates that this explains 0.2 points of the decline in TFP growth between 1948–1966 and 1973–1978.

A basic difficulty with the cyclical explanations of the productivity decline is the evidence that this decline has now been going on for fifteen years and does not seem to have been affected by changing business conditions. All in all, it is not easy to believe that the business cycle has been one of the prime culprits.

## AN EVALUATION

It is rather difficult to form a summary judgment or discern a consensus on either the quantitative or the qualitative importance of the various factors cited by the studies discussed here as possible causes of the productivity slowdown. Results differ among economists because of differences in data sources, time periods, concepts, sector of the economy studied, research methods, measurement errors in the raw data, and the underlying assumptions and models used (e.g., the specification of the production function). The range of estimates is summarized in Table 2–3. Perhaps it is best, therefore, to offer some rather general and guarded statements about the importance of the various factors.

### Capital Formation

Except for Denison, most observers seem to agree that the slowdown in the growth of the capital-labor ratio was an important cause of the productivity slowdown. In addition, there seems to be a marked difference in its importance between the first slowdown period (1965–1973) and the second (from 1973 onward). The evidence seems to suggest, although not with unanimity, that this factor was not very important in explaining the first slowdown. However, the slowing in the growth of capital employed per worker does seem to explain between one-third and two-thirds of the second slowdown. It should be emphasized, though, that the underlying cause is not a decline in the gross investment-to-GNP ratio but, rather, the rapid growth in the labor force after 1965.

Moreover, when other effects associated with capital formation are added in, its importance becomes even greater. The vintage effect stemming from a slowdown in capital formation may explain about another 10 percent of the decline in both the first and the second periods. The fact that a part of the new capital equipment went to meet new pollution and safety standards instead of increasing productivity means the growth of the

**Table 2-3. Estimates of the Importance of Selected Factors in the Productivity Slowdown (percent)**

| Factor and Source | Period | Percent of Slowdown |
|---|---|---|
| **Capital Formation** | | |
| Capital-labor ratio growth | | |
| Denison (1979a) | 1948–1973, 1973–1976 | 4 |
| Kendrick (1980) | 1948–1966, 1973–1978 | 21 |
| Clark (1979) | 1948–1965, 1965–1973 | 35 |
| Nadiri (1980)[b] | 1948–1974, 1974–1978 | 38 |
| Tatom (1979) | 1950–1972, 1972–1979 | 39 |
| Norsworthy and Harper | 1948–1965, 1965–1973 | — |
| (1979) | 1965–1973, 1973–1977 | 49 |
| Norsworthy, Harper, and | 1948–1965, 1965–1973 | — |
| Kunze (1979) | 1965–1973, 1973–1978 | 71 |
| | | |
| Vintage effect | | |
| Kendrick (1980a) | 1948–1966, 1973–1978 | 10 |
| Clark (1979) | 1948–1965, 1965–1973 | 14 |
| | 1965–1973, 1973–1978 | 9 |
| | | |
| Pollution and regulation | | |
| Denison (1979a) | 1948–1973, 1973–1976 | 13 |
| Kendrick (1980a) | 1948–1966, 1973–1978 | 16 |
| | | |
| Energy price effect | | |
| Denison (1979a) | 1948–1972, 1972–1976 | 3 |
| Norsworthy, Harper, and | 1965–1973, 1973–1978 | 16 |
| Kunze (1979) | | |
| Hudson and Jorgenson | 1948–1972, 1972–1976 | 20[a] |
| (1978) | | |
| | | |
| **Research and Development** | | |
| Denison (1979a) | 1948–1972, 1972–1976 | 3 |
| Griliches (1980) | 1965–1973, 1973–1977 | 10 |
| Kendrick (1980) | 1948–1966, 1973–1978 | 13 |
| Nadiri (1980)[b] | 1948–1974, 1974–1978 | 17 |
| Nadiri (1980)[c] | 1948–1974, 1974–1978 | 37 |
| | | |
| **Output Composition** | | |
| Denison (1979a) | 1948–1972, 1972–1976 | 13 |
| Kutcher, Mark, and | 1947–1966, 1966–1973 | 23 |
| Norsworthy (1977) | | |
| Norsworthy, Harper, and | 1948–1965, 1965–1973 | — |
| Kunze (1979) | 1965–1973, 1973–1978 | 24 |
| Thurow (1979) | 1948–1965, 1965–1972 | — |
| | 1965–1972, 1972–1977 | 45–50 |
| Wolff (1981) | 1947–1967, 1967–1976 | 48 |
| Nordhaus (1972) | 1948–1955, 1965–1971 | 79 |
| | | |
| **Government Regulation** | | |
| Denison (1979a) | 1948–1972, 1972–1976 | 13 |
| Kendrick (1980a) | 1948–1966, 1973–1978 | 16 |

[a] Approximate; percentage contribution based on Denison's estimate of 2.97-percentage-point decline in overall productivity growth.
[b] Percentage for economy as a whole.
[c] Percentage for private economy.

*effective* capital stock is overvalued by the investment data. This diversion of capital stock to meet new government regulations may have explained 10 percent of the slowdown in the second period, at least. And the rapid increase in energy prices after 1972 also may have slowed the rate of new capital formation. Moreover, because higher energy prices made part of the existing capital stock uneconomical and therefore obsolete, the rate of growth of the *net* capital stock may have been even further depressed. This factor may explain another 10 percent of the productivity slowdown of the second period. Altogether, capital formation effects may well account for over half of the productivity slowdown in the second period and perhaps a quarter of that of the first period.

## Composition of the Labor Force

Changes in the labor force involved two counteracting tendencies during the slowdown period: (1) the increased rate of labor force participation of women and the relative rise in the number of young workers and (2) the increased educational level of new entrants into the labor force. On this, there is a strong consensus that the net contribution to the productivity slowdown was very small (and, as a result, these estimates are not shown in Table 2-3).

## Research and Development and Technical Change

The consensus seems to be that the rate of disembodied technical change did decline after 1965 (although perhaps not as much as Fraumeni and Jorgenson found). But because the ratio of privately financed research and development to GNP did not decline (and, in any event, was largely confined to manufacturing), research and development was probably not a major contributory factor. There seems to be general agreement that about 10 percent of the productivity slowdown of the second period was caused by a decline in R&D investment.

## Composition of Output

Most observers seem to concur that output shifts were responsible for part of the productivity slowdown, but their estimates differ quite widely. For the first period, the estimates vary from zero to three-quarters; for the second period, they vary from zero to one-quarter. These differences largely reflect methodological differences. Conservatively, one might guess that about one-fourth of the slowdown in both periods was attributable to composition effects.

**Other Factors**

Of the remaining possible causes (government regulation and cyclical factors), only increased government regulation may have played any significant role in the productivity problem, perhaps as much as 15 percent in the second period. On the surface, it is hard to believe that the increased stringency of safety, health, and environmental regulations did *not* divert some resources away from *measured output*. However, in this context in particular, measurement issues play an especially vital role; and if the benefits generated by those regulations had been reflected in the measures of output utilized, the reported productivity slowdown probably would have been somewhat smaller.

In conclusion, this look at the consensus accounts for nearly all the productivity slowdown in the second period and perhaps one-third of the decline in the first period. Of course, this chapter has not attempted to discuss all the proposed causes of the productivity slowdown. One major omission is contributing institutional factors, particularly those related to the structure of employer-employee relations. The reason for this omission is that although many studies have investigated the effect of various institutional arrangements on the productivity of individual companies, there are almost no estimates of the quantitative significance for the economy as a whole. A second major omission involves industry-specific factors, such as the effect of the depletion of natural resources on the productivity performance of the mining sector. Here, too, the reason is the lack of a sufficient number of industry-specific studies to permit estimation of their effects on the economy as a whole.

**NOTES**

1. A corresponding literature presenting policy recommendations for the improvement of America's productivity performance will not be examined here. See also Committee for Economic Development, *Productivity Policy: Key to the Nation's Economic Future* (New York: Committee for Economic Development, 1983).
2. In education, for example, the labor input of teachers and other personnel, rather than the number of graduates or the improvement in test scores, is currently used to measure its output.
3. The justification for the use of relative wages is that in a competitive labor market, wage differences should reflect differences in marginal productivity. However, there is considerable reason to believe that discrimination, unions, and other factors make the assumption of perfectly competitive labor markets questionable.
4. The differences in the estimates reflect the actual periods chosen, the productivity concepts used, and the sources of data.
5. The productivity growth declines by sector were not uniform between the 1948–1965 and 1965–1973 periods in comparison with the 1965–1973 and 1973–1978 periods. The Norsworthy, Harper, and Kunze (1979) data indicate

that productivity growth in both argiculture and transportation slowed very little between 1965 and 1973 but substantially between 1973 and 1978. Productivity growth in communications fell slightly between the first two periods, increased in the second period, and fell precipitously in the third. In construction, there was a tremendous drop in the second period and a slight rise in the third. In finance, insurance, and real estate, a large decline in the second period was followed by a sharp rise in the third.

6. The Cobb-Douglas production function is an algebraic function that relates the output of an industry to its inputs. In its simplest representation, the function takes the following form:

$$X = CL^a K^b$$

where
$X$ = output
$L$ = labor input
$K$ = capital input
$a$, $b$, and $c$ = parameters of the production function, which are usually estimated for various industries

7. See Norsworthy, Harper, and Kunze (1979), p. 390.

8. A divisia aggregate is an index formed by weighting each component (in this case, of capital stock) according to its current value share. A translog production function is a fairly complex representation of the technology of an industry. It relates the output of the sector to the various inputs used in production. See, for example, Gallop and Jorgenson (1980), pp. 25–28, for a discussion of the translog production function.

9. A related factor cited by Kendrick (1980a) is the reduction in the ratio of hours worked to hours paid as a result of increased vacations, holidays, coffee breaks, and the like since 1966. Norsworthy, Harper, and Kunze (1979) estimate that this may have made a minor contribution to the first slowdown but actually had a slightly positive effect between the 1965–1973 and 1973–1975 periods.

10. The "usual procedure" that Denison refers to is the use of the Cobb-Douglas production function, with energy included as a separate input. In such a framework, the factor share of each input is assumed to be fixed. Therefore, a certain percentage increase in the price of energy requires a corresponding percentage decrease in the input of energy in order to maintain a constant factor share. One can then compute the effect on output per unit of labor, capital, and land that results from the decreased input of energy.

11. Griliches (1980) also points out that almost all research and development is carried out by manufacturing, agriculture, communications, transportation, and public utilities and that with the exception of public utilities, the productivity slowdown has not been at all notable in these areas. However, his estimates of the R&D effect do not capture any spillover effects of research and development within and among industries.

12. Another argument has been proposed by Baumol and Wolff (1983): that R&D activity itself may be subject to significantly lower rates of productivity growth than the sectors whose productivity it increases. Thus, the price of research and development may be increasing relative to the general price level. As a result, any series of constant R&D expenditures using a GNP or investment goods deflator will overvalue the true level of R&D activity increasingly over time. Therefore, the true quantity of research and development may be decreasing over time much more rapidly than previously thought, and its effect on the productivity slowdown may be considerably greater than is currently believed. No test of this has yet been carried out.

13. Some independent evidence is provided by Rama (1980), who reports, for example, that private industry in the United States actually employed 5 percent *fewer* scientists and engineers in 1975 than in 1970. In 1979, U.S. manufacturers expected R&D budgets to equal less than 50 percent of capital investment budgets, compared with 80 percent in mid-1960s.

14. It is easy to see how the two approaches can yield very different conclusions. Suppose that current productivity in the services and in manufacturing is about the same but that the rate of growth of productivity is much greater in manufacturing. Suppose also that there is a shift in output from manufacturing to services. If the economy's overall productivity is taken to be a weighted average of productivity in the two sectors, there will clearly be no effect on the economy's productivity calculated in this way. But if, instead, the economy's productivity *growth* rate is taken to be the average of the growth rates in the two sectors weighted by their shares in total output, the assumed shift toward the services will reduce the growth rate of productivity in the economy as a whole, according to this method of calculation.

It is important to note that absolute productivity in the two sectors will always have a tendency to *appear* on the basis of the statistics to be about the same. That is, paradoxically, even though productivity in manufacturing has grown more rapidly than that in the services, certainly throughout this century, the measured absolute productivities as indicated by the statistics would have been about the same in 1900, and they are also about the same today. This is, of course, only a consequence of the method of measurement. It occurs because it is not possible to compare directly the physical productivity of a service, such as education, with that of a manufactured good, such as alarm clocks. (If an average teacher has classes of 40 students, is that teacher's productivity greater or smaller than that of a clockmaker who produces 500 clocks?) Therefore, we use *value* of output (i.e., price times quantity) as the relevant measure. Suppose, then, that the physical productivity of labor in clockmaking doubles. If, as a result, the price of a clock falls by half, the *value* of the output of a worker (the worker's *value* productivity) will remain unchanged. This is a rather general relationship; whenever there is a rise in the physical productivity of the inputs used to produce an item, the price of the item will tend to fall. Moreover, the competition will tend to equalize the ratio of the value of output to the value of input for all sectors, giving an appearance of equality of productivity of inputs. For this reason, intersectoral comparisons of absolute productivity tend to show that the differences are small and do not change greatly with the passage of time, even though physical productivity in some grows far more rapidly than in others.

15. Of course, this argument might simply suggest that output is improperly measured. If output measures reflected improvements in the quality of work life or in the environment, the measured productivity slowdown might have been somewhat more moderate.

16. This explanation follows from several strains of contract and search theory, which views the quit rate as high during periods of recession or relatively lower wages, when search costs are low. However, this view is inconsistent with the observed behavior of labor, which shows quit rates to be relatively low during recessionary phases. Tatom (1979) presents a related argument. He gives two rationales for cyclical productivity movements: (1) During recessions, firms are reluctant to lay off workers because they want to avoid relatively large rehiring costs in the subsequent expansion. (2) Management is really "overhead employment," and as output changes, there is little change in managerial employment. These explanations work fairly well for the 1967–1973 period but predict very poorly for the 1973–1979 span.

# REFERENCES

Baumol, William J. "Macroeconomics of Unbalanced Growth: The Anatomy of Urban Crisis." *American Economic Review* 57 (June 1967): 415–426.

——, and Edward N. Wolff. 1980. "On the Theory of Productivity and Unbalanced Growth." C. V. Starr Center for Applied Economics, New York University, New York. No. 80–03, January 1980.

——, and Edward N. Wolff. "Feedback from Productivity Growth to R&D." *Scandinavian Journal of Economics* 85, no. 2 (1983): 147–157.

——, Sue Anne Butcy Blackman, and Edward N. Wolff. "Unbalanced Growth Revisited: Asymptotic Stagnancy and New Evidence." *American Economic Review*. Forthcoming.

Bennet, Paul. "American Productivity Growth: Perspective on the Slowdown." *Federal Reserve Bank of New York Quarterly Review* (Autumn 1979): 25–31.

Berndt, Ernst R. 1980. "Energy Price Increases and the Productivity Slowdown in United States Manufacturing." In *The Decline in Productivity Growth* (Boston: Federal Reserve Bank of Boston).

Clark, Peter K. "Capital Formation and the Recent Productivity Slowdown." (Paper presented to the American Economic Association and the American Finance Association, December 30, 1977).

——. "Issues in the Analysis of Capital Formation and Productivity Growth." *Brookings Papers on Economic Activity*, 2 (1979): 423–431.

Crandall, Robert W. 1980. "Regulation and Productivity Growth." In *The Decline in Productivity Growth* (Boston: Federal Reserve Bank of Boston).

Congressional Budget Office. 1981. *The Productivity Problem: Alternatives for Action.* (Washington, D.C.: U.S. Government Printing Office).

Council of Economic Advisers. 1977. *Economic Report of the President, 1977* (Washington, D.C.: U.S. Government Printing Office).

Denison, Edward F. "The Shift to Services and the Rate of Productivity Change." *Survey of Current Business* 53, 10 (October 1973): 20–35.

——. 1979a. "Explanations of Declining Productivity Growth." *Survey of Current Business* 59, no. 8, pt. 2. (August 1979a): 1–24.

——. 1979b. "Pollution Abatement Programs: Estimates of Their Effect Upon Output per Unit of Input, 1975–78." *Survey of Current Business* 59 (August 1979b): 58.

——. 1979c. *Accounting for Slower Economic Growth* (Washington D.C.: Brookings Institution).

——. 1980. "Discussion." In *The Decline in Productivity Growth* (Boston: Federal Reserve Bank of Boston).

Eckstein, Otto. 1980. "Core Inflation, Productivity, Capital Supply, and Demand Management." In *The Economy and the President: 1980 and Beyond*, edited by Walter E. Hoadley (Englewood Cliffs, N.J.: Prentice-Hall).

Fellner, W. 1979. "The Declining Growth of American Productivity: An Introductory Note." In *Contemporary Economic Problems, 1979*, edited by W. Fellner (Washington D.C.: American Enterprise Institute for Public Policy Research).

Filer, Randall K. 1980. "The Downturn in Productivity Growth: A New Look at its Nature and Causes." In *Lagging Productivity Growth*, edited by Shlomo Maital and Noah M. Meltz (Cambridge, Mass: Ballinger Publishing Co.).

Fraumeni, Barbara, and Dale W. Jorgenson. 1980. "Capital Formation and U.S. Productivity Growth, 1948–76." Mimeo.

Gallop, Frank M., and Dale W. Jorgenson. 1980. "U.S. Productivity Growth by Industry." In *New Developments in Productivity Measurement and Analysis*, edited by John W. Kendrick and Beatrice N. Vaccara (Chicago: University of Chicago Press).

Gordon, Robert J. 1979. "The End-of-Expansion Phenomenon in Short-Run Productivity Behavior." *Brookings Papers on Economic Activity*, no. 2 (1979): 447–461.

Griliches, Zvi. "R&D and the Productivity Slowdown." *American Economic Review* 70, no. 2 (May 1980): 343–347.

Grossman, Michael, and Victor R. Fuchs. "Intersectoral Shifts and Aggregate Productivity Change." *Annals of Economic and Social Measurement* 2, no. 3 (1973): 227–243.

Hudson, E. A., and Dale W. Jorgenson. "Energy Prices and the U.S. Economy, 1972–76." *Natural Resources Journal* 18, no. 4 (October): 877–897.

Hulten, Charles. "Growth Accounting with Intermediate Inputs." *Review of Economic Studies* (October 1978): 511–518.

Kendrick, John. 1980a. "Productivity Trends in the United States." In *Lagging Productivity Growth*, edited by Shlomo Maital and Noah M. Meltz (Cambridge, Mass.: Ballinger Publishing Co.).

————. 1980b. "Remedies for the Productivity Slowdown in the United States." In *Lagging Productivity Growth*, edited by Shlomo Maital and Noah M. Meltz (Cambridge, Mass.: Ballinger Publishing Co.).

Kopcke, Richard W. 1980. "Capital Accumulation and Potential Growth." In *The Decline in Productivity Growth* (Boston: Federal Reserve Bank of Boston).

Kutscher, R. E., J. A. Mark, and J. R. Norsworthy. "The Productivity Slowdown and Outlook to 1985." *Monthly Labor Review* 100 (May 1977): 3–8.

Nadiri, M. Ishaq. "Sectoral Productivity Slowdown." *American Economic Review* no. 2 (May 1980): 349–352.

————, and Mark A. Shankerman. 1980. "Technical Change, Returns to Scale and the Productivity Slowdown." (Paper presented at the annual meeting of the American Economic Association.)

National Research Council. 1979. *Measurement and Interpretation of Productivity* (Washington, D.C.: National Academy of Sciences).

Nordhaus, W. D. "The Recent Productivity Slowdown." *Brookings Papers on Economic Activity*, no. 3 (1972): 493–536.

Norsworthy, J. R. and Michael Harper. 1979. *The Role of Capital Formation in the Recent Slowdown in Productivity Growth*. Bureau of Labor Statistics Working Paper no. 87 (Washington, D.C.: U.S. Government Printing Office).

————, M. J. Harper, and K. Kunze. "The Slowdown in Productivity Growth: Analysis of Some Contributing Factors." *Brookings Papers on Economic Activity*, no. 2 (1979): 387–421.

————, and L. J. Fulco. "Productivity and Costs in the Private Economy 1973." *Monthly Labor Review* 97 (June 1974): 3–9.

Perloff, Jeffrey M., and Michael L. Wachter. 1980. "The Productivity Slowdown: A Labor Problem." In *The Decline in Productivity Growth* (Boston: Federal Reserve Bank of Boston).

Perry, G. L. "Potential Output and Productivity." *Brookings Papers on Economic Activity*, no. 1 (1977): 11–47.

Rama, Simon. 1980. "The U.S. Technology Slip: A New Political Issue." In *The Economy and the President: 1980 and Beyond*, edited by Walter E. Hoadley (Englewood Cliffs, N.J.: Prentice-Hall).

Rashe, R. H., and J. A. Tatom, "The Effects of the New Energy Regime on Economic Capacity, Production and Prices." *Federal Reserve Bank of St. Louis Monthly Review* (May 1977): 2–12.

————. "Energy Resources and Potential GNP." *Federal Reserve Bank of St. Louis Monthly Review* (June 1977): 10–24.

Rees, Albert. "Improving the Concepts and Techniques of Productivity Measurement." *Monthly Labor Review* (September 1979): 23–27.

Tatom, John A. "The Productivity Problem." *Federal Reserve Bank of St. Louis Monthly Review* (September 1979): 3–16.
Thurow, Lester. "The U.S. Productivity Problem." *Data Resources Review* (August 1979).
———. 1980. "Comment." In *The Decline in Productivity Growth* (Boston: Federal Reserve Bank of Boston).
Wolff, Edward. 1981. "The Composition of Output and the Productivity Growth Slowdown of 1967–76." New York University, Department of Economics. Mimeo.
U.S. Bureau of Labor Statistics. 1979. *Time-Series Data for Input-Output Industries*. Bulletin 2018.

# 3

# Recent Productivity Growth in Japanese and U.S. Manufacturing

## J. R. NORSWORTHY and DAVID H. MALMQUIST

This chapter presents the major conclusions of a comparative study of productivity growth in manufacturing in Japan and the United States conducted by the authors at the Bureau of Labor Statistics. Japan was chosen for the comparison because the growth of productivity there has been extraordinary despite a less than favorable economic environment and because the U.S. and Japanese productivity growth experiences over the past fifteen years or so lie at opposite ends of the spectrum of Western industrialized countries' productivity performance (see Table 3-1).

It is important at the outset to clarify a few technical points. Our study has examined productivity *growth*, rather than productivity *levels*. It is much harder to compare productivity levels of countries with different currencies, business environments, and technologies. Although U.S. pro-

**Table 3-1. Average Annual Rates of Productivity Growth in Selected Countries, 1960 to 1980 (percent)**

|  | *1960–1973* | *1973–1980* |
|---|---|---|
| United States | 3.4 | 1.3 |
| Canada | 4.7 | 1.5 |
| Japan | 10.5 | 6.4 |
| France | 5.8 | 4.4 |
| West Germany | 5.5 | 4.5 |
| United Kingdom | 4.3 | 1.6 |
| Italy | 7.3 | 3.8 |

*Source*: Division of Foreign Labor and Statistics and Trade, Bureau of Labor Statistics, unpublished data.

ductivity growth in manufacturing has been much lower than Japan's, the levels of productivity in the two countries are probably not very far apart.[1]

An earlier study by Norsworthy, Harper, and Kunze (1979) found that capital formation played a major role in the productivity slowdown in the private business sector in the United States. However, the slowdown in manufacturing was less pronounced. It is not so much the pattern of recent decline in U.S. manufacturing productivity growth that raises concern as the U.S. performance relative to that of manufacturing in other industrialized countries.

The measure commonly called *multifactor* or *total-factor productivity* represents the productivity performance of all factors combined; in the case of manufacturing, these are labor, capital, energy, and materials. Although a consensus has emerged in the economics literature about the general framework for adding the separate inputs to productivity in order to create a multifactor productivity measure, researchers differ on some details of application.[2] Interpretation of U.S.-Japanese productivity trends is not sensitive to alternative practices for measuring capital input within the commonly used neoclassical framework for productivity analysis.

This discussion of U.S. and Japanese productivity growth is based on a different output measurement concept from that underlying the data in Table 3-1 which are based on the gross national product accounts of the several countries. We used the gross output concept in our study because we wanted to examine the roles of energy and materials as well as those of labor and capital. A gross output approach permits us to look at all purchased inputs, whereas GNP accounting methods exclude all inputs other than labor and capital.

The time periods covered in this study are 1965 to 1978 for Japan and 1965 to 1977 for the United States. Earlier data are available for this country, but our study of Japan does not extend back beyond 1965. Some inconsistencies in the historical data prevented our extending farther into the past. Because the U.S. data are only through 1977, those for the 1973–1977 period may not reflect the full recovery from the 1974–1975 recession. This effect probably results in a downward bias in the growth rates of capital and energy productivity for that time period.

## TRENDS IN PRODUCTIVITY GROWTH

Table 3-1 shows the growth in labor productivity in manufacturing for the United States and six other industrialized nations for the periods from 1960 to 1973 and from 1973 to 1983.[3] All countries show a slowdown in productivity growth after 1973, with France and West Germany experiencing the smallest declines. Japan, however, even after a significant slowdown

60 Productivity Growth and U.S. Competitiveness

(the largest among the seven countries) still led in productivity growth after 1973.

The multifactor productivity measure used in this study can be thought of as a supplement to the labor productivity measure (output per hour of labor input) that is commonly used. In fact, as Table 3-2 shows, the growth in the productivity of all factors (multifactor productivity growth) can be thought of as an *average* of the productivity growth rates of the several factors of production (labor, capital, energy, and materials). The labor productivity growth rate was about $2\frac{1}{2}$ percent a year in the United States in 1965–1973, compared with more than 11 percent a year in Japan. This substantial difference was accompanied by declining capital productivity in both countries. The decrease in capital productivity was small in the United States but about 4 percent a year in Japan.

How could Japan afford declining capital productivity? The answer is that even though capital productivity was falling, multifactor productivity was rising thanks to the tremendous gains in labor productivity. Taken together, however, the productivity of all factors rose at nearly 0.8 percent a year from 1965 to 1973, not much more than in the United States.

Energy productivity grew very little in the United States and at only about $1\frac{1}{2}$ percent a year in Japan during the 1965–1973 period. In materials, which account for about 60 percent of the total cost of production in each country, productivity was down slightly in the United States and rose at a 1 percent rate in Japan.

As the rates of productivity growth for the several inputs indicate, each country has directed its greatest efforts toward raising labor productivity. Because it is labor productivity that ultimately determines the standard of living in a country, it is gratifying to see that labor productivity growth is leading in this way. But the probable reason for the more rapid growth of labor productivity is a mundane one: The price of labor services rose more rapidly in each country than the prices of other factors of production. Under these circumstances, it is to be expected that producers would try to raise labor productivity by increasing the input of other factors (capital, energy, and materials) and decreasing labor input. And that appears to be what happened.

In 1973, the energy crisis occurred. Crude petroleum prices escalated rapidly; and, for a while, there were fuel shortages as well. The impact on both the U.S. and the Japanese manufacturing sectors was severe. (The same was true in other industrialized countries.) The result was two kinds of effects on the economies of both countries: price effects associated with the surge in energy prices and output effects from the recession that swept most industrial nations.

Table 3-2. **Average Annual Rates of Growth of Productivity Factors in U.S. and Japanese Manufacturing, Gross Output Basis** (percent)

| | Capital Productivity | | Labor Productivity | | Energy Productivity | | Materials Productivity | | Multifactor Productivity | |
|---|---|---|---|---|---|---|---|---|---|---|
| | United States | Japan | United States | Japan | United States | Japan | United States | Japan | United States | Japan |
| 1965–1973 | -0.11 | -4.09 | 2.50 | 11.08 | 0.05 | 1.50 | -0.14 | 1.03 | 0.59 | 0.91 |
| 1973–1978[a] | -0.87 | -0.78 | 1.83 | 5.42 | -0.73 | 3.27 | 0.00 | 1.15 | 0.38 | 1.64 |

Source: J. R. Norsworthy and David H. Malmquist, "Input Measurement and Productivity Growth in Japanese and U.S. Manufacturing," *American Economic Review* 73 (December 1983), Table 3, p. 954.

[a] Data for the United States are for 1973 to 1977.

The price effects took shape with immediate increases in energy costs where price controls were not imposed (Japan was one such country). Transportation costs, both domestic and international, also rose. Where some nonmarket rationing of energy supplies took place (as in the United States and Canada), fuel and transport costs did not increase as rapidly, but the process whereby the economy as a whole adjusts to price hikes took correspondingly longer. As the effect of higher energy prices worked through the economy, the costs of energy-intensive goods (certain raw materials, aluminum, and steel) were the next to be affected, followed finally by the prices of other goods and services. Feeding back through cost-of-living increases, the general surge in prices acquired its own momentum.

Thus, there were two types of price effects at work in the post-1973 period: sharp hikes in energy prices and a general price inflation. Because of different general economic conditions and tax institutions in the two countries, similar price effects had somewhat different consequences for productivity growth.

One effect of energy price increases was to reduce investment in capital goods. This proposition, which has been explored independently by Jorgenson[4] and by Berndt,[5] is somewhat subtle but important. The normal relationship between factors of production is *substitution*. When two goods are substitutes, the quantities used in production of a fixed level of output tend to move in opposite directions. Capital and labor are normally substitutes; that is, an increase in the price of labor will encourage greater use of capital, and vice versa. In contrast, energy and capital are *complements* in the production process. That is, they are used in close conjunction with each other, like bread and butter: When the capital input rises, so does the associated energy input. Because the sharp rise in energy prices discouraged energy use, it also discouraged the use of the complementary good—capital. The rise in the price of energy encouraged U.S. producers to use less energy *and* less capital. Unfortunately, because studies of the capital-energy relationship have not been done for Japan, we do not know whether the same mechanism was at work there.

The general price inflation also discouraged capital formation. In the United States, this negative influence has had a twofold effect: (1) Inflation has led to higher interest rates and thus has raised the cost of funds for capital investment. (2) Although higher prices for capital goods pushed up the cost of replacing the capital stock, depreciation for tax purposes continued to be based on historical costs (the acquisition cost of the assets). Because economic depreciation exceeded allowable depreciation for tax purposes, part of the cost of replacing existing capital stock at current prices was taxed as profits, leading to a higher effective tax rate and a higher cost of investment. This effect was widely discussed in connection with the tax legislation passed in 1981, and most economists judge that it was eliminated by the depreciation provisions in the Economic Recovery Tax Act.[6] Japanese producers were insulated from this second effect because depreciation costs for tax purposes are indexed to prices of capital goods.

The period after 1973 tells a different productivity growth story. Labor productivity growth slowed down in both countries, but the decline was much larger in Japan. In the United States, multifactor productivity growth also slowed. In Japan, however, the total factor-growth rate increased; that is, overall efficiency in Japan grew more rapidly after 1973 in the prior period—despite the energy shock. In the United States, both energy productivity and capital productivity dropped. These declines may be traceable in part to the fact that the U.S. data end in 1977 and therefore do not fully reflect the recovery from the 1974–1975 recession. In addition, some have argued that environmental regulations may have contributed to the U.S. decline, in that air pollution control equipment is energy-intensive in its operation. Whatever the source of the problem, energy productivity did not improve in U.S. manufacturing in the 1973–1977 period.

In Japan, the rate of energy productivity growth nearly doubled after 1973. This result is not surprising. Whereas U.S. domestic supplies of energy were relatively abundant, Japan relies on imports for most of its energy, and its domestic price was (and is) higher than the U.S. price. We would therefore expect Japan to have had a stronger incentive than the United States had to develop energy-saving technology before 1973.

In both countries, materials productivity growth after 1973 was almost unchanged from the prior period.

The growth rate of labor input in the two countries after 1973 shows two quite different patterns (see Table 3-3). Although labor input in the United States declined somewhat, it fell more rapidly, at about $2\frac{1}{2}$ percent a year, in Japan. In fact, during the 1973–1978 period, the size of the labor force in Japanese manufacturing declined by more than 10 percent, but the productivity of those workers who remained grew by more than 5 percent annually. What is especially significant is the fact that this was accomplished in an economic environment of much slower growth in output than in the 1965–1973 period.

These, then, are some of the elements of the "miracle" of Japanese productivity: very high rates of labor productivity growth accompanied by very rapid growth in output and capital input before 1973 and rapid, although diminished, labor productivity growth after 1973 despite much lower output growth and capital formation.

Table 3-3. Average Annual Rates of Growth of Gross Output and Input Factors in U.S. and Japanese Manufacturing (percent)

| | Capital | | Labor | | Energy | | Materials | | Gross Output | |
|---|---|---|---|---|---|---|---|---|---|---|
| | United States | Japan | United States | Japan | United States | Japan | United States | Japan | United States | Japan |
| 1965–1973 | 3.65 | 16.54 | 1.26 | 1.37 | 3.71 | 10.96 | 3.90 | 11.43 | 3.76 | 12.46 |
| 1973–1978[a] | 1.95 | 2.05 | -0.75 | -2.57 | 1.81 | -0.42 | 1.08 | 1.70 | 1.08 | 2.85 |

*Source:* J. R. Norsworthy and David H. Malmquist, "Input Measurement and Productivity Growth in Japanese and U.S. Manufacturing," Table 4, p. 955.

[a] Data for the United States are for 1973 to 1977.

# SOME SOURCES OF PRODUCTIVITY GROWTH

What is the source of Japan's productivity miracle? The framework provided by multifactor productivity analysis makes it possible for us to quantify some of the factors that have contributed to productivity growth in both countries. This approach permits us to gauge the effects of changes in the intensity of the various inputs relative to labor and of changes in overall efficiency on the growth in labor productivity.[7] Using this relative-intensity approach, we can measure a kind of substitution or supplementation effect in the growth of labor productivity that does not depend on an elaborate econometric model. In a more limited framework, the capital-labor ratio is often used to measure the change in capital intensity relative to labor. Our analysis includes not only the effect of the capital-labor ratio but also those of the energy-labor and materials-labor ratios.

The results are shown in Table 3-4, which indicates the effects on labor productivity of growth in capital, energy, and materials and growth in overall efficiency (multifactor productivity) in both countries. One impression is immediate: Growth in other inputs relative to labor outweighs growth in overall efficiency as a contributor to labor productivity growth in both countries.

Also, the largest source of labor productivity growth in each country is growth of materials. However, this should not be mistaken as meaning that capital (or, indeed, labor) is not critical in a structural sense to enhancing labor's capacity to process an increasing flow of materials. Because materials inputs constitute such a large share of the total cost of production in each country, they play a major role in this type of analysis.[8] It is clear that the more rapid growth in Japan of other inputs (capital, energy, and materials) accounts for most of the difference between U.S. and Japanese rates of labor productivity growth, compared with the rates for multifactor

Table 3-4. Sources of Labor Productivity Growth in U.S. and Japanese Manufacturing Based on Factor Intensities Relative to Labor (percent)

|  | Capital Effect | Energy Effect | Materials Effect | Multifactor Productivity Effect | Labor Productivity Growth |
|---|---|---|---|---|---|
| | | U.S. Manufacturing | | | |
| 1965–1973 | 0.25 | 0.04 | 1.62 | 0.59 | 2.50 |
| 1973–1977 | 0.23 | 0.05 | 1.17 | 0.38 | 1.83 |
| | | Japanese Manufacturing | | | |
| 1965–1973 | 3.72 | 0.27 | 6.19 | 0.91 | 11.08 |
| 1973–1978 | 1.13 | 0.06 | 2.58 | 1.64 | 5.42 |

Source: J. R. Norsworthy and David H. Malmquist, "Input Measurement and Productivity Growth in Japanese and U.S. Manufacturing," Table 6, p. 956.

productivity growth. The difference in multifactor productivity growth contributed about 1 percent a year in the post-1973 period, compared with a difference of 3.6 percent a year in labor productivity. Before 1973, the growth in multifactor productivity was only about 0.25 percent a year, whereas the difference in the rates of labor productivity growth was about $8\frac{1}{2}$ percent.

The results of this method of analysis should do much to dispel the aura of mystery that surrounds some discussions of productivity growth in Japan. In the main, we believe that rapid growth in the capital stock, which can be viewed as raising the workers' capacity to process a greater volume of materials, is a major source of Japanese growth. And although this rapid growth in capital and materials inputs can be thought of as representing substantial technological change, the overall efficiency of Japanese manufacturing as measured by growth in the productivity of all inputs has not shown remarkable progress relative to that of U.S. manufacturing.

What of the widely discussed dedication and motivation of the Japanese worker? The framework of this analysis does not permit us to address that issue directly. However, if the source of the Japanese advantage in productivity improvement derived primarily from the higher quality of the Japanese worker, we might expect to see a greater increase in overall efficiency (i.e., in multifactor productivity). Instead, the pattern seems to rely on more conventional sources of growth: greater investment and greater throughput of materials.[9] Nevertheless, the role of labor relations in Japan should not be underestimated. In general, workers' willingness to accept and accommodate to new technology is an important element in the cost of introducing new capital equipment and new working techniques.[10] And that willingness may, in turn, derive partly from the job tenure system that guarantees lifetime employment to many Japanese workers. So it may be that labor-management relations in Japan have indeed played a major part in smoothing the assimilation of the new technology that has resulted in rapid labor productivity growth.

Another result of our research illustrates the role of greater capital investment in Japan. In the value-added portion of U.S. manufacturing — the portion attributable to capital and labor alone, excluding intermediate goods (energy and materials) — labor's share is about 75 percent, and capital's share is 25 percent. In Japan, capital accounts for about two-thirds of value added, with labor contributing one-third. Roughly speaking, manufacturing wages in Japan are about half those in the United States. Consequently, if wages in Japan were doubled to approximately the U.S. level, value added in Japan would be about evenly divided between labor and capital. In other words, every hour of Japanese labor would be supplemented by an equal expenditure on capital services; whereas in the

United States, every hour of labor is supplemented by capital services worth only one-third as much. Clearly, even with the wage differences accounted for, the Japanese worker has much more capital services to work than his or her U.S. counterpart.

## SUMMARY

In examining recent manufacturing productivity trends in the United States and other industrialized countries, we find that the slowdown in labor productivity growth after 1973 was quite general. Rising energy prices and slower output growth were widespread during this period.

A comparison of the U.S. and Japanese experiences indicates that greater capital investment and greater processing of materials per worker have led to far greater labor productivity growth in Japan. However, growth in the efficiency of all productive inputs combined has not been much greater in Japan than in the United States. The major source of the difference stems from the higher rates of growth in the capital and materials inputs used in conjunction with the Japanese labor force.

## NOTES

*Author's Note:* The views expressed in this chapter are those of the authors alone and do not necessarily reflect those of the Bureau of the Census or the Securities and Exchange Commission or their staffs. Material in this chapter is taken from testimony before the Subcommittee on Employment and Productivity of the U.S. Senate Committee on Human Resources on April 2, 1982. A similar version of this chapter, titled "Input Measurement and Productivity Growth in Japanese and U.S. Manufacturing," appeared in the *American Economic Review* 73 (December 1983): 947–967. Used by permission.

1. Jorgenson and Nishimizu (1978) conclude that in most major manufacturing industry groups in the standard industrial classification (SIC), the levels of Japanese and U.S. total-factor productivity were about the same in the early 1970s.
2. See Nadiri (1970).
3. These statistics are based on the GNP accounts of the countries listed in Table 3-1. The measurement basis is somewhat different from that used in the detailed comparison between the United States and Japan.
4. For example, see E. Hudson and D. W. Jorgenson (1978).
5. See especially Ernst R. Berndt and David O. Wood (1979).
6. The 1982 tax legislation reversed some of the investment incentives provided in the 1981 act. Charles Hulten of the Urban Institute estimates that about two-thirds of the corporate cash flow aided by the 1981 act was rolled back in the 1982 act.
7. This framework is an extension of that in the study of the sources of the productivity slowdown in major sectors of the U.S. economy by Norsworthy, Harper, and Kunze (1979).
8. In particular, the effect of materials on labor productivity is computed as the growth rate in the materials-labor ratio multiplied by 0.6, the materials share in

the cost of production. Thus, a 10 percent growth in the materials-labor ratio multiplied by 0.6 yields a contribution of 6 percent to labor productivity growth. Similarly, the capital-labor and energy-labor ratios contribute. The sum of these factor-intensity contributions and overall efficiency growth exactly equals labor productivity growth. This growth accounting method is elaborated in Berndt (1980).

9. F. R. Lichtenberg of Columbia University has found that worker "quality," as measured by experience in the present job, is more strongly associated with multifactor productivity than with labor productivity alone. See Lichtenberg (1981).

10. C. A. Zabala argues that worker acceptance of new technology is a necessary part of realizing the cost savings that new capital is designed to achieve. Otherwise, worker resistance to new technology may raise costs. See Zabala (1983).

## REFERENCES

Berndt, Ernst R. 1980. "Energy Price Increases and the Productivity Slowdown in U.S. Manufacturing." In *The Decline in Productivity Growth*, 342–354 (Boston: Federal Reserve Bank of Boston).

———, and David O. Wood. "Engineering and Econometric Interpretations of Energy-Capital Complementarity." *American Economic Review* 69 (June 1979): 342–354.

Binswanger, Hans P. "The Measurement of Technical Change Biases with Many Factors of Production." *American Economic Review* 64 (December 1974): 964–976.

Christensen, Laurits R., Dianne Cummings, and Dale W. Jorgenson. 1978. "Productivity Growth, 1947–1973: An International Comparison." In *The Impact of International Trade and Investment on Employment*, 211–233 (Washington, D.C.: U.S. Department of Labor, Bureau of International Labor Affairs).

Hudson, Edward A., and Dale W. Jorgenson. "Energy Prices and the U.S. Economy," *Data Resources Review* (September 1978): 1.24–1.37.

Hulten, Charles R., and Mieko Nishimizu. *The Japanese Productivity Slowdown.* Urban Institute Project Report (Washington, D.C.: The Urban Institute, 1982).

Jorgenson, Dale W., and Barbara M. Fraumeni. 1982. "Relative Prices and Technical Change." In *Modeling and Measuring Resource Substitution*, edited by Ernst R. Berndt and Barry C. Fields, Chapter 2 (Cambridge: MIT Press).

———, and Mieko Nishimizu. "U.S. and Japanese Economic Growth, 1952–1974: An International Comparison." *Economic Journal* 88 (December 1978): 707–726.

———. "Sectoral Differences in Levels of Technology: An International Comparison Between the U.S. and Japan, 1955–1972." Paper presented at the North American Summer Meeting of the Econometric Society, Montreal, June 27–30, 1979.

Lichtenberg, F. R. 1981. "Training, Tenure and Productivity." Ph.D. dissertation, University of Pennsylvania.

Nadiri, M. Ishaq. "Some Approaches to the Theory and Measurement of Productivity: A Survey." *Journal of Economic Literature* 8, no. 4 (December 1970): 1137–1177.

Nishimizu, Mieko, and Charles R. Hulten. "The Sources of Japanese Economic Growth." *Review of Economics and Statistics* 60 (August 1978): 351–361.

Norsworthy, John R., and Michael J. Harper. "The Role of Capital Formation in the Recent Productivity Slowdown." Bureau of Labor Statistics Working Paper no. 87.
————, Michael J. Harper, and Kent Kunze. "The Slowdown in Productivity Growth: Analysis of Some Contributing Factors." *Brookings Papers on Economic Activity* (Fall 1979): 387–421.
————, and David H. Malmquist. "Input Measurement and Productivity Growth in Japanese and U.S. Manufacturing." *American Economic Review* 73, no. 5 (December 1983): 947–967.
Zabala, Craig A. 1983. "Collective Bargaining at UAW Local 645, General Motors Assembly Division, Van Nuys, California, 1976–1981." Ph.D. dissertation, University of California, Los Angeles.

# 4

# Japanese Productivity Experience

## MARTIN BRONFENBRENNER

To confirm or disconfirm the hypotheses of specialists on the American economy about the causes and implications of the decline in American productivity in the wake of the Vietnam War and the oil price actions of the Organization of Petroleum Exporting Countries (OPEC), it is helpful to compare the American record with that of another country for the same period. For this purpose, we have chosen Japan because it is both an important trading partner (and rival) of the United States and a country whose productivity increase rate remains decidedly positive, despite a decline in the 1970s.

One hears with increasing frequency that the Japanese economy has now become more productive than our own. Some definitions of productivity make this statement correct. But according to the more usual definitions— those of common speech—it is false.

The ordinary individual, both in Japan and in the United States, uses *productivity* in its average sense, leaving the complexities of marginalism to the theoretical economist. If productivity is used to mean the real gross output or the gross value added (without deductions for depreciation of fixed capital) per employee or per labor-hour,[1] and if the dollar is evaluated relative to the yen (and vice versa) in terms of a purchasing power index over the gross domestic product (GDP),[2] American productivity in the late 1970s remained well above the Japanese in most major sectors of the two economies, although the American advantage had decreased in most sectors since 1970 (see Table 4-1).

For individual manufacturing sectors, Table 4-2 compares value added per labor-hour in 1970 prices, using an exchange rate of 244 yen to the

**Table 4-1. Labor Productivity Levels, Japan and United States, 1970, 1974, and 1978, by Economic Sector (in yen of 1970 purchasing power per worker-year)**

| | 1970 | | | 1974 | | | 1978 | | |
|---|---|---|---|---|---|---|---|---|---|
| | United States | Japan | Ratio | United States | Japan | Ratio | United States | Japan | Ratio |
| Agriculture | 1,860 | 504 | 3.69 | 1,937 | 747 | 2.59 | 2,111 | 763 | 2.77 |
| Mining and quarrying | 6,417 | 3,105 | 2.07 | 5,946 | 4,807 | 1.24 | 5,255 | 5,060 | 1.04 |
| Manufacturing | 2,958 | 1,913 | 1.55 | 3,312 | 2,407 | 1.38 | 3,759 | 3,271 | 1.15 |
| Electricity, gas, and water | 7,528 | 5,561 | 1.35 | 6,336 | 6,209 | 1.02 | 6,633 | 6,841 | 0.97 |
| Construction | 2,422 | 1,437 | 1.68 | 2,129 | 1,426 | 1.49 | 2,038 | 1,354 | 1.51 |
| Transportation, communication, and storage | 3,238 | 1,550 | 2.09 | 3,640 | 1,934 | 1.88 | 4,189 | 2,004 | 2.09 |
| Commerce and service industries | 3,140 | 1,564 | 2.01 | 3,144 | 1,827 | 1.72 | 3,171 | 2,038 | 1.56 |

*Source:* Japan Productivity Center Report on International Comparison on Labor Productivity (Tokyo: Nihon Seisansei Hombu, March 1981): Table 1.1.4., pp. 12–19.

Table 4-2. Worker-Hour Productivity Levels, Japan and United States, 1970, 1975, and 1979, by Specific Industries (in yen of 1970 purchasing power)

| | 1970 | | | 1975 | | | 1979 | | |
|---|---|---|---|---|---|---|---|---|---|
| | United States | Japan | Ratio | United States | Japan | Ratio | United States | Japan | Ratio |
| Food and related products | 2,296 | 836 | 2.75 | 2,974 | 1,265 | 2.35 | NA | NA | 1.98 |
| Textile mill products | 1,188 | 357 | 2.13 | 1,857 | 989 | 1.88 | NA | NA | 1.60 |
| Apparel and other fabricated textiles | 1,144 | 421 | 2.72 | 1,806 | 548 | 3.30 | NA | NA | 3.05 |
| Lumber and wood products | 1,271 | 594 | 2.14 | 1,471 | 714 | 2.06 | NA | NA | 1.59 |
| Furniture and fixtures | 1,332 | 590 | 2.26 | 1,845 | 494 | 3.74 | NA | NA | NA |
| Paper and allied products | 1,957 | 1,065 | 1.84 | 2,367 | 1,395 | 1.70 | NA | NA | 1.54 |
| Printing and publishing | 1,986 | 1,008 | 1.97 | 1,915 | 872 | 2.20 | NA | NA | NA |
| Chemicals and allied products | 3,531 | 2,614 | 1.35 | 3,235 | 3,727 | 0.87 | NA | NA | 0.72 |
| Petroleum refining and allied industries | 4,119 | 3,836 | 1.07 | NA | NA | NA | NA | NA | NA |
| Rubber and miscellaneous plastics | 1,798 | 910 | 1.98 | 2,325 | 1,117 | 2.08 | NA | NA | 1.41 |

| | | | | | | | | | | | |
|---|---|---|---|---|---|---|---|---|---|---|---|
| Leather and leather products | 1,203 | 634 | 1.90 | 1,491 | 638 | 2.34 | NA | NA | NA | NA | 2.09 |
| Stone, clay, and glass products | 1,871 | 976 | 1.92 | 1,979 | 1,370 | 1.45 | NA | NA | NA | NA | 1.33 |
| Iron and steel | 1,876 | 1,486 | 1.26 | 7,606 | 2,386 | 0.67 | NA | NA | NA | NA | 0.53 |
| Nonferrous metals | 1,998 | 1,394 | 1.43 | 3,106 | 1,217 | 2.55 | NA | NA | NA | NA | 1.36 |
| Fabricated metal products | 1,776 | 838 | 2.12 | 1,635 | 1,016 | 1.61 | NA | NA | NA | NA | 1.29 |
| Machinery (except electrical) | 1,884 | 1,023 | 1.84 | 2,272 | 1,572 | 1.45 | NA | NA | NA | NA | 1.00 |
| Electrical machinery | 1,764 | 1,013 | 1.74 | 2,428 | 1,982 | 1.23 | NA | NA | NA | NA | 0.93 |
| Transportation equipment (total): | 2,089 | 1,262 | 1.66 | 3,055 | 2,632 | 1.16 | NA | NA | NA | NA | 0.89 |
| Motor vehicles | 2,359 | 1,343 | 1.76 | 3,821 | 2,515 | 1.52 | NA | NA | NA | NA | 1.11 |
| All other | 1,884 | 918 | 2.05 | 2,542 | 2,176 | 1.17 | NA | NA | NA | NA | NA |
| Instruments | 2,267 | 769 | 2.95 | 2,115 | 1,408 | 1.50 | NA | NA | NA | NA | 0.82 |
| Miscellaneous | 1,523 | 752 | 2.03 | 2,089 | 1,195 | 1.75 | NA | NA | NA | NA | NA |
| All manufacturing (except tobacco products and military ordnance) | 1,911 | 971 | 1.97 | 2,328 | 1,530 | 1.52 | NA | NA | NA | NA | 1.34 |

NA = Not available.

Source: Japan Productivity Center Report on International Comparison on Labor Productivity (Tokyo: Nihon Seisansei Hombu, March 1981): Table 3.4, pp. 91–102.

dollar, a computed purchasing power parity for that year. The fine structure of the various industrial classifications differs between the two countries, and the U.S. data are not entirely comparable with those used for Table 4-1.[3] In addition, questions are raised about Japanese data on hours worked insofar as overtime is underreported in many companies.[4] Nevertheless, the picture is much like that presented in Table 4-1, with the United States remaining in the lead but by a decreasing margin. Relatively lower levels of productivity now exist in chemicals, iron and steel, electrical machinery, and transportation equipment. Some of these industries, most notably iron and steel, have become the focus of American protectionism.

A minority view, however, is that not only the growth rate but also the absolute level of Japanese productivity outpaced levels in the United States in the early 1970s. This view is represented in a controversial article by an American-Japanese team, Jorgenson and Nishimizu (1978), published in a British journal.[5] They fit a production function to both American and Japanese data, including both a time trend as a proxy for technical progress and a dummy variable to distinguish American from Japanese observations. They measure general-factor or multifactor productivity rather than labor productivity alone, and they allow for depreciation on capital. They also use dollar-yen exchange rates for capital and for output that vary over time.

In 1952 the Japanese level of technology was merely one-fourth of the corresponding U.S. level. During the period 1952–1959 the difference was reduced from 75 percent to 51 percent. Beginning in 1960 the level of Japanese technology moved up sharply relative to that of the United States, reaching nearly 90 percent of the U.S. level by 1968. Between 1968 and 1973 the level of Japanese technology actually overtook the U.S. level, so that by 1973 and 1974 the aggregate level of technology in Japan stood ahead of that in the United States. None of the remaining difference between U.S. and Japanese aggregate output in 1974 was the result of a difference in levels of technology.

For the period 1960–1974, the dramatic reduction in the difference between U.S. and Japanese total output was due to the substantial increase in Japanese capital input relative to U.S. capital input and to the closing of the gap between Japanese and U.S. technology. Japanese and U.S. labor input grew at almost the same rate, whereas the average annual growth rate of capital in Japan was nearly three times the U.S. rate, and Japanese productivity grew at a rate four times that in the United States on average during this period. While the gap between U.S. and Japanese technology had closed by 1973, there remains a substantial gap between U.S. and Japanese capital intensity of production. All the remaining difference between U.S. and Japanese output per unit of labor input is the result of differences in the capital intensity of production in the two countries.[6]

The appendix of this chapter presents a further explanation of the differences between the productivity concepts popular in Japan and those that have come to attract more attention in the United States, particularly the distinction between productivity per worker or labor-hour and multifactor or general-factor productivity.

Regarding productivity growth rates, as distinguished from levels, the different productivity concepts tell much the same story of Japan outrunning the United States. The data in Table 4-3 are based on the data in Table 4-1. The ubiquity of the Japanese advantage, which extends over almost all the principal sectors of the economy, suggests that the difference cannot easily be ascribed to differing patterns of structural shifts between high- and low-productivity sectors.

## A LAUNDRY LIST

A number of specialists on growth, productivity, and the American economy have prepared laundry lists of possible explanations or suspects for the post-1970 or post-1973 U.S. productivity slowdown. Among the fullest and most influential of such efforts have been those of Edward F. Denison, associate director of the Bureau of Economic Analysis, U.S. Department of Commerce, and former senior fellow at the Brookings Institution.[7] Table 4-4, Denison's basic table, shows the behavior of his national income per person employed (NIPPE) variant. Denison's list features an impressionistic and nonquantitative breakdown of his "residual" (line 14) among seventeen possible subdeterminants. We include in our own laundry list, presented in Table 4-5, certain factors that Denison was unable to treat quantitatively (lines 2–4 and 9–13) and impressions on the relative importance of each factor in Japan and the United States. From these comparisons we will argue that differences between Japanese and U.S. productivity performance can be explained by some combination of stimulating influences more important in Japan and inhibiting influences more important in America.

Denison concludes tentatively that the U.S. productivity slowdown is largely a chance phenomenon, an unhappy conjunction of numerous individually unimportant, unfavorable factors. At the same time, he recognizes the desirability of international comparisons. In Table 4-5, the prevalence of systematic "Yes-Yes" and "No-No" combinations[8] tends to oppose this conclusion, as, indeed, many other writers have done. There is

**Table 4-3. Index Numbers of Labor Productivity, United States and Japan, 1974 and 1978 (1970 = 100)**

| | 1974 | | 1978 | | Average Annual % Change 1974–1978 | |
|---|---|---|---|---|---|---|
| | United States | Japan | United States | Japan | United States | Japan |
| Agriculture | 104.1 | 148.2 | 113.5 | 151.4 | 2.2 | 0.5 |
| Mining and quarrying | 92.7 | 154.8 | 81.9 | 163.0 | -3.0 | 1.3 |
| Manufacturing | 112.0 | 125.8 | 127.1 | 171.0 | 3.2 | 8.0 |
| Electricity, gas, and water | 84.2 | 111.7 | 88.1 | 123.0 | 1.1 | 2.4 |
| Construction | 87.9 | 99.2 | 84.1 | 94.2 | -1.1 | -1.3 |
| Transportation, communication, storage | 112.4 | 124.8 | 129.4 | 129.3 | 3.6 | 0.9 |
| Commerce and services | 100.1 | 116.8 | 101.0 | 130.3 | 0.2 | 2.8 |

*Source:* Japan Productivity Center Report on International Comparison on Labor Productivity (Tokyo: Nihon Seisansei Hombu, March 1981): Table 4-3 was derived from data contained in this report.

**Table 4-4. National Income Per Person Employed in Nonresidential Business, Growth Rate and Source of Growth, United States 1948–1973 and 1973–1976**

|  | Contribution to Growth (percentage points) | | |
|---|---|---|---|
|  | 1948–1973 | 1973–1976 | Change |
| 1. Growth rate, total | 2.43 | −0.54 | −2.97 |
| Total-factor inputs | 0.46 | 0.33 | −0.13 |
| Changes in workers' hours and attitudes: |  |  |  |
| 2. Hours | −0.24 | −0.54 | −0.30 |
| 3. Age and sex composition | −0.17 | −0.25 | −0.08 |
| 4. Education | 0.52 | 0.88 | 0.36 |
| 5. Subtotal (lines 2–4) | 0.11 | 0.09 | −0.02 |
| Changes in capital and land per person employed: |  |  |  |
| 6. Inventories | 0.10 | 0.02 | −0.08 |
| 7. Nonresidential structures and equipment | 0.29 | 0.25 | −0.04 |
| 8. Land | −0.04 | −0.03 | 0.01 |
| 9. Subtotal (lines 6–8) | 0.35 | 0.24 | −0.11 |
| Output per unit of input: |  |  |  |
| 10. Improved allocation of resources | 0.37 | −0.01 | −0.38 |
| 11. Changes in legal and human environment | −0.04 | −0.44 | −0.40 |
| 12. Economies of scale | 0.41 | 0.24 | −0.17 |
| 13. Irregular factors | −0.18 | 0.09 | 0.27 |
| 14. Advances in knowledge and miscellaneous determinants (residual) | 1.41 | −0.75 | −2.16 |
| 15. Residual (line 1) minus the sum of lines 5 and 9 | 1.97 | −0.87 | −2.84 |

Source: E. F. Denison, "Explanations of Declining Productivity Growth," Survey of Current Business (August 1979): part ii, Table 1, p. 3.

much talk, not confined to Marxist circles, of the downward phase of a "long wave" of capitalist progress, marked not only by poor productivity performance but also by the persistence of a "great recession" since 1973.

Each item in our list calls for a certain amount of comment or expansion.

## Line 1: Hours of Work

Japan has shared in the worldwide postwar pattern of shorter work hours and longer vacations for both white-collar and blue-collar workers. A difficulty, as we have already indicated (in note 4), is that overtime is incompletely reported for those workers paid on a monthly basis.

**Table 4-5. Factors in U.S. Productivity Performance, Further Breakdown of Table 4-4**

| | Unfavorable to Productivity Growth? | Less Important in Japan? |
|---|---|---|
| **Included in Main Body of Table 4-4:** | | |
| 1. Shorter working day, week, and year | Yes | No? |
| 2. Change in age, sex, race composition of labor force | Yes | No? |
| 3. Change in level of education and on-the-job training | No | No |
| 4. Lower increase in capital and land per employee | Yes | Yes |
| 5. Labor already allotted to most productive uses | No | Yes? |
| 6. Greater burden of safety, health, and environmental regulations | Yes | No? |
| 7. Declining economies of scale | Yes | Yes? |
| 8. Cyclical irregularity of employment | Yes | Yes? |
| **Included in Residual of Table 4-4:** | | |
| 9. Declining importance of research and development | Yes | Yes |
| 10. Declining opportunity for scientific progress | Yes? | No |
| 11. Declining Yankee technological ingenuity | Yes? | No |

| | | |
|---|---|---|
| 12. Aging of capital stock | Yes? | Yes? |
| 13. Diversion of inputs to compliance with government regulation (general)[a] | Yes | Yes |
| 14. Government-imposed paperwork | Yes | Yes |
| 15. Regulation and taxation, diversion of executive attention | Yes | Yes |
| 16. Regulatory delay of new projects | Yes | Yes |
| 17. Regulation and taxation; misallocation of resources | Yes | Yes |
| 18. Increase in burden of taxation (general) | Yes | Yes |
| 19. Increase in burden of taxation (capital gains) | Yes | Yes? |
| 20. Increased worker preference for leisure | Yes? | Yes |
| 21. Impairment of efficiency by inflation | Yes? | Yes |
| 22. Lessening of competitive pressure, lower management quality | Yes | Yes |
| 23. Rise in energy prices | No | Yes |
| 24. Shift to services and similar structural changes | Yes | No? |
| 25. Possible errors in data | Yes | Yes? |

Source: Edward F. Denison, "Explanations of Declining Productivity Growth," *Survey of Current Business* Vol. 59, part ii (August 1979): 1–24.

[a] Other than already covered under line 6.

**Table 4-6. National Productivity Indexes, United States and Japan, with and without Allowance for Sectoral Shifts**

|  | Actual Data | | Contribution of Sectoral Shifts | | Hypothetical Data Without Sectoral Shifts | |
|---|---|---|---|---|---|---|
|  | United States | Japan | United States | Japan | United States | Japan |
| 1970 | 100.00 | 100.00 | 0.00 | 0.00 | 100.00 | 100.00 |
| 1974 | 103.05 | 124.23 | 0.11 | 3.03 | 102.94 | 121.20 |
| 1978 | 107.95 | 144.84 | −0.25 | 1.83 | 108.33 | 143.01 |

*Source*: Japan Productivity Center Report on International Comparison on Labor Productivity (Tokyo: Nihon Seisansei Hombu, March 1981): Table 1.1.5, p. 22.

## Line 2: Demographic Factors

Japan has not had the recent American problem of adapting large numbers of semiliterate rural workers to industrial disciplines and routines.[9] Like America, Japan has its racial minorities and prejudices,[10] but the numbers involved are much smaller than in the American case, and the American affirmative action policy has not been copied by Japan.

Japan sees its problem in labor demographics as an aging work force, including male workers who live longer, female workers who enter or reenter the work force after their youngest children are in school, the end of the postwar baby boom, and the rise of the school-leaving age for both young men and young women. Although reliable and disciplined, older workers are said to lack the physical strength and the flexibility required to learn new techniques. A typical older male worker is a permanent employee. His pay is relatively high, and his employer would like him to take early retirement, making way for better, younger, and cheaper workers, as well as for promotion all along the line. Early retirement is induced in individual cases by a variety of informal social pressures, and methods for expanding and formalizing this procedure and for separating the sheep from the goats among the older workers (without unnecessarily antagonizing the goats) are under study. In contrast, the typical older female worker is a labor force reentrant. She may or may not be a permanent worker, but if she becomes proficient at lower skill levels and not too insistent about promotions, she will not be let go or laid off in hard times.

## Line 3: Education and Training

Younger Japanese industrial workers, blue collar as well as white collar, are predominantly high school graduates. Most are from academic secondary schools, which are superior to American public high schools. Proposals to stream the academically less talented into purely technical or vocational training have been made repeatedly and represent a reaction in the direction of Japan's pre-1941 educational system. They are generally opposed by parents and teachers and do not seem destined for widespread success. (Technical and vocational high schools exist in considerable numbers, but prestigious employers hesitate to hire the graduates of vocational high schools for their main-line jobs.) Once employed, the male worker in the "good" company is assumed to be a permanent employee. It therefore pays the Japanese employer to make a larger investment in his technical and vocational training on the job than is the case in the United States. This is somewhat less true for the female worker, who is expected to quit after marriage or her first pregnancy. The American job-hopping problem does not exist in Japan. And a problem it most certainly is.

> How could anyone expect good teamwork, group loyalty, or a common interest in raising firm productivity when almost half the work force will either quit or be laid off within 12 months? Neither worker nor company has any interest in the economic success of the other. Workers, including managers, are not willing to sacrifice to help build the future prosperity of the company since they know that they will not be around to share in that prosperity. Conversely, the company is not willing to invest in the future success of the individual, since that person is apt to be somewhere else when the investment that goes into training him pays off. The result is gross underinvestment in creating the on-the-job skills necessary for industrial success. Blue-collar workers are traditionally trained on the job, but with today's high turnover rates no firm wants to invest in training its work force since there is a very high probability that the workers will soon leave for another job. For each firm it is cheaper to bid, with higher wages, a skilled worker away from other firms, but this obviously does not work for the economy as a whole. The result is a perpetual shortage of skilled blue-collar workers whenever the economy remotely begins to approach anything remotely resembling full employment.[11]

On the other hand, there is little firm evidence of long-term "shortages" of specific skills in the United States. Short-term "shortages" and "surpluses" are necessary features of the successful operating of labor markets. In addition, there are productivity returns to society when workers move to employment opportunities in which the workers' productivity is higher.

## Line 4: Capital per Worker

At this point, the higher Japanese propensity to save and the lower Japanese propensity to invest in private residential housing enter the picture. Much has been said on both points, but one aspect has been underemphasized: the slow development (some might say the underdevelopment) of Japanese consumer credit. This has meant, in the inflationary environment of the 1970s, increased saving to make ever-larger down payments, in contrast with the U.S. pattern of buying to beat the next price rise at the expense of saving and investment.

An additional capital-related problem appears to have developed in the United States during the 1970s: a decline in the intensity of capital use, particularly in periods of economic slack, which Foss (1981) treats as a decline in the workweek of fixed capital.[12] We have found no evidence of any similar tendency in Japan but assume that it exists to some slight degree.

## Line 5: Labor Reallocation

This is presumably a progrowth influence on productivity. Employment in the United States has been shifting from old-capital centers in the Snow Belt (the Northeast and Midwest) to new-capital centers in the Sun Belt (the South and Southwest), although the more basic movement from low-productivity subsistence agriculture and domestic service has largely ceased. The Japanese strategy has been to set up more small and midsized plants in small and midsized towns, chiefly along rail lines in the already developed Tokaido (Pacific coast) region. This has encouraged the holding of multiple jobs, for example, part-time agriculture and domestic industry (both piecework and minifactories in residential buildings). Our highly tentative position, supported by the work of the Japan Productivity Center, is that the American method may have been more effective on the whole, despite the immunity of piecework and home factories from labor organization or government regulation.[13] Former Prime Minister Kakuei Tanaka proposed, in 1971, a major restructuring of the Japanese economy, under government auspices, from the developed Pacific Ocean side of Japan to the less developed Japan Sea side. This would have been more drastic than the American Snow Belt–Sun Belt movement has ever been. It has not yet been carried out, however. The land speculators got there first, Tanaka lost his premiership in a series of corruption scandals, and none of his successors has revived the plan.

## Line 6: Safety, Health, and Environmental Regulations

Because of its dense population, Japan faced critical environmental problems earlier than the United States did, and with less warning. The volume and rate of improvement have also been more rapid. However, the Japanese tend to fight brush-fire wars, one crisis at a time, in preference to enacting blanket regulations and enforcing them literally nationwide. Moreover, government aid (abundant cheap credit) is available to private firms for safety, health, and environmental improvements. Japan is proud of its so-called polluter-pays principle, a graduated tax on the level of pollution caused by the firm. But, in practice, the short-run payer is the general taxpayer, not exclusively the polluting industry.

## Line 7: Declining Economies of Scale

This factor seems quite unimportant in Japan, where a great deal of small-scale activity remains, much of it apparently inefficient, in all phases of the economy, especially in distribution.[14] However, these areas seem to be retained as reservations for those workers and managers judged incapable of becoming productive participants in the larger-scale economy.

## Line 8: Cyclical Irregularity of Employment

This is blamed widely by prolabor writers for statistical declines in reported labor productivity, which they interpret as calls for speedups and harsher work rules.[15] (During slack periods, key workers are kept on the job full time despite the lack of work; the result is lower productivity.) Although the Japanese system appears more susceptible to this particular effect than the American, by reason of permanent employment (*shūshin koyō*), the figures hardly confirm this expectation.

The importance of the Japanese concept of permanent employment is often exaggerated. It is estimated that between 30 and 40 percent of the labor force has this type of employment status. Only government workers and males have any possibility of being employed under a permanent contract. Unless they work as civil servants, women, who now make up more than 40 percent of the labor force, are excluded and are usually in jobs classified as "temporary."

About 28 percent of the Japanese labor force is self-employed and obviously has no permanent employment guarantee. Another 40 percent has an employment contract, which means these people work for firms that are subcontractors to large firms; they do not, however, have permanent employment. Even among those with permanent employment status, almost all must retire at age 57, even though the majority remain in the labor force beyond the age of 60.

There is obviously some overlap between temporary women workers, contract workers, workers over age 57, and the self-employed. Nevertheless, it is reasonable to estimate that between 60 and 70 percent of the Japanese labor force does not have permanent job security. Indeed, even among those who have permanent contract status, the degree of employment security apparently varies, with those in large firms having the greatest protection.

Offsets to permanent employment therefore include layoffs of temporary workers, pressure for early retirements, compulsory vacations at reduced pay, widespread bankruptcies among smaller companies, and the reversal of labor reductions among students, homemakers, and workers over age 57 when a recovery develops. In practice, this labor force flexibility is not so different from the temporary and permanent layoff procedures that potentially affect the majority of U.S. workers.

## Line 9: Declining R&D Expenditures

One of the two or three most popular explanations for declining American productivity growth is the decreasing relative importance of research and development (R&D) expenditures in the private, nonmilitary economy. Such spending applies to both technical invention and the innovation process by which inventions move from the laboratory through the pilot plant and into general use. Moreover, an economic innovation need not embody an invention at all; the supermarket and the credit card are examples of innovations not based in any important way on anything classified as an invention.

Statistics indicate a decline in American civilian R&D expenditures as a percentage of the GNP.[16] In addition, an increasing proportion of outlays classified as R&D expenditures appear to be cosmetic rather than fundamental, the annual model change as distinguished from the new product or process.[17] The 1981 American tax legislation provides for special tax treatment of R&D expenditures in an attempt to reverse these trends.

Private Japanese R&D expenditures are rising as a proportion of GNP and exceed the American figures, which is not surprising. As Japan has progressed technically, it can only rely to a decreasing extent on buying licenses for products and processes developed elsewhere. But the combined advantages of an adaptable labor force, a permanent employment system, and the absence of craft unions may also continue to keep Japan the international second adopter of new processes from abroad, as well as the first adopter of new processes developed at home. By 1981, Japan became the world leader in the robotizing of assembly lines, although little of the basic research on robotics was originally done there.

"The Japanese Way" has not been to subsidize or otherwise favor as such research and development or to draw distinctions between fundamental and cosmetic aspects of reported R&D expenditures. The government, meaning primarily the Ministry of International Trade and Industry (MITI), always in consultation with business interests, has selected particular industries as comers or hot prospects in the world economy and then fostered, favored, and protected those industries and the leading firms in them through tax favors and easy credit. Because a new industry is R&D-intensive almost by definition, the consequences of

Japanese policy are obvious. Examples can be drawn from the automobile, television, and computer industries, although in many cases the present leaders in Japan have not been the firms originally favored by MITI.

## Line 10: Declining Scientific Opportunity

This argument relates primarily to invention rather than innovation. It is a hardy perennial, although all the historical evidence has been against it. We join Denison in discarding it.

## Line 11: Declining Yankee Technical Ingenuity

Denison may be too hasty in dismissing this argument out of hand. It has some plausibility, in that the technical ingenuity of the youngster may be blunted both by higher living standards and by urbanization. (Why fix or improve it yourself when there is a repair shop in the next block?) On the other hand, we have found no real evidence to support this proposition. Certainly, the record of "the Yankees of the East" is against it.

## Line 12: Aging of Capital Stock

Given the continued lag of the American saving and investment rates (line 4), it is understandable that the American capital stock is aging relative to the Japanese and that some American equipment now appears hopelessly obsolete to Japanese visitors. In addition, a good deal of the older Japanese capital stock still in use (often after being sold to smaller firms as secondhand machinery) may be somewhat more likely than its American equivalent to be maintained at close to its original productivity.

## Line 13: Diversion of Effort into Compliance with Regulation

This point is difficult to distinguish from the burden of regulations as such (line 6). The argument is that American managers' and executives' time and effort have become overly occupied with guessing what is coming next in the way of regulation and also what may be required for compliance, avoidance, or evasion by their firms. How important this marginal element of uncertainty in America may be we cannot say; there are, after all, so many other uncertainties to contend with. It is probably less important in Japan, however, because of the differences (line 6) in the two countries' regulatory philosophies.

## Line 14: Government-Imposed Paperwork

It is probably true that the paperwork burden of the Japanese firm is less than that of its American counterpart, especially with regard to taxation (line 18). In addition, Japanese workers are, on average, more fully literate and numerate than their American counterparts. Paperwork is, accordingly, somewhat less of a burden both for them and for their supervisors and superiors.

### Line 15: Regulation and Tax Compliance

The principal point to be made here is that the total burden of taxation, particularly direct taxation, remains substantially smaller in Japan than in the United States, despite post-1973 Japanese efforts to become what Japanese insiders call a welfare superpower. The primary reasons for this difference are probably the low level of Japanese defense expenditures (approximately 1 percent of GNP) and the high level of reliance on the American "nuclear umbrella." Moreover, many more regulation (and tax) cases are settled cheaply in Japan by direct negotiation and compromise than in the United States, and many fewer by expensive administrative or judicial litigation.

### Line 16: Regulatory Delay of New Projects

The wide-reaching environmental impact statement, with its subsequent meanderings through the bureaucracy and the courts, is a major problem in Japan only where nuclear power is involved. Japanese consumer and environmentalist groups are, however, strong. In addition to working for regulations to prevent nuclear accidents, they are actively opposed to noise pollution, the blocking of sunlight, the diminution of fish supplies, and the preemption of residential land. Japanese society is not litigious, however, and lawyers are few in number, so the issues have thus far been settled more economically and sometimes more expeditiously by compromise agreements than is possible under the U.S. pattern of legal action. However, there have been conspicuous exceptions, and their number can be expected to grow. Three such exceptions involved the fate of the nuclear-powered merchant ship *Mutsu* (whose engines developed radiation leaks), the garbage war in Tokyo (over the dumping of rich men's garbage in poor men's wards), and the development of the international airport at Narita.[18]

### Line 17: Resource Misallocation in Regulation and Taxation Controversy

This frequent American complaint has had no Japanese equivalent since the end of the Occupation (lines 6, 13, 14, and 15).

### Line 18: Tax Burdens

Over and above the lower defense burden (line 15), two features of the Japanese system should be mentioned: (1) its greater reliance on indirect taxes (property and excise taxes) for revenue and (2) the centralized Japanese government structure, which is still directed largely from Tokyo despite Occupation pressure for federalization. The Japanese prefecture, in particular, is much less important and costly than the American state. It is comparable in size to a large American county, and its degree of autonomy is correspondingly small. The difference between the Japanese and the American city is less marked, but education, relief, and public health remain national government concerns that a city can supplement if it so desires, but not replace.[19]

## Line 19: Capital Gains Taxation

Denison's concern in the area is with a number of special provisions of the U.S. Revenue Act of 1969 that have since been repealed or modified.

## Line 20: Worker Preference For Leisure

"They don't want to work anymore" has been, as Denison says, a perennial complaint of employers against workers, particularly the young and better educated. Because of rising levels of income and welfare-state provisions for the nonworker and the casual worker, we consider the complaint somewhat more reasonable and more important than Denison does. Japanese methods of employee selection and personnel management seem to be more successful than American ones in keeping the so-called loafer and troublemaker out of the industrial mainstream. (See the section " 'Miracle Management'?")

## Line 21: Impairment of Efficiency by Inflation

The main issue here is the inadequacy of the real deduction for capital depreciation. Funds needed for maintaining or upgrading capital are lost to the tax collector. In addition, the "money illusion" of constant price levels may confuse decision makers about which profit or loss prospects are genuine and which involve only temporary variations in inflation rates. The importance of such factors depends on the nature of the tax system and also on the rapidity of the inflation. The Japanese system has been generally easier on capital gains. Furthermore, in most years since 1971, the Japanese inflation rate has been lower than the American one.

## Line 22: Lower Competitiveness and Management Quality

Two principal charges against contemporary American business management are (1) that management is increasingly reluctant to face price competition, preferring collusion, market sharing, public regulation, and administrative protection against its rigors, both domestic and international, and (2) that management is increasingly practicing what business schools call end gaming, meaning concentrating on short-run profits during one's terms of service in successive posts and leaving one's successors to pick up the pieces or clean up the mess. Japanese managers seem little (if any) more price-competitive than their American counterparts and complain with equal bitterness about excessive competition when their customary margins are threatened. However, these margins are often lower than American ones because Japanese companies pride themselves on taking a longer-term economic view than foreigners do, sacrificing near-term profits for growth or market-share gains.

### Line 23: Rise in Energy Prices

The post-1973 rise in the prices of crude oil and its derivatives has hit Japan even harder than it has the United States because Japan is so much more dependent on energy imports, both in general and from the Middle East. Nevertheless, Japanese productivity continued to advance, although at a slower rate than was the case prior to the 1973 oil price hikes. This record suggests that those writers who (like Jorgenson)[20] blame the American productivity decline primarily on the relative price of energy may be guilty of some exaggeration.

### Line 24: The Shift to Services

It is increasingly pointed out that the postindustrial American economy employs more workers in its tertiary (service) sector than in its primary (agricultural) and secondary (manufacturing) sectors combined. Something similar, possibly with a time lag, is apparently occurring in Japan. It has also been an accepted view that productivity in the tertiary sector increases only slowly if at all, so that a shift to services would itself constitute a downward structural change in measured productivity.[21]

### Line 25: Statistical Artifacts and Anomalies

There seem to be four principal statistical artifacts and anomalies that affect the reported data: (1) imputation, the inclusion in value added of the imputed values of the services of land and capital instruments owned by the reporting firm; (2) depreciation of the value of capital goods inaccurately taken into account, especially in inflationary periods; (3) underreporting of labor time used; and (4) measurement of output value by input cost, a frequent practice in the service industries. Except perhaps in the case of underreporting of labor time used, there seems no a priori reason to expect these weaknesses to affect U.S.-Japanese comparisons in any systematic way.

## "MIRACLE MANAGEMENT"?

Japanese writers are less boastful and arrogant about their managerial successes than were their American predecessors in the immediate postwar generation and *Le Défi Américain*. They prefer to think of the American (and British) worker as overpaid and lazy and to warn of a spreading Anglo-American disease that threatens their own shores. Such notions as "miracle management" and "Theory Z" come from foreign observers.

Far from inviting or challenging the rest of the world to "do as we do, and as we will teach you to do," Japanese wonder whether Japanese management methods can be either fully understood or effectively applied by people unfamiliar with Japanese culture. "Japanese culture" in this context does not mean flower arrangement or the tea ceremony; rather, it refers to the Japanese ethical-religious background in Buddhism, Confucianism, and Shintoism, together with the "way of the merchant" (*shōnin-dō*), to which these philosophies gave rise during the early years of the Tokugawa shogunate (seventeenth century).[22]

If we try to be more precise, we find that there may be no specific Japanese pattern of personnel selection and training in the interest of high productivity. As Levine and Kawada (1980) have pointed out, patterns have varied from time to time, industry to industry, and firm to firm, as well as from blue-collar to white-collar workers.[23] Furthermore, selection and training standards are constantly evolving.

"*Shōin-dō* and all that" went into temporary eclipse as feudalistic during the first half of the modernizing Meiji era (roughly the last third of the nineteenth century), but a number of its fundamental institutions seem to have revived almost simultaneously during the first quarter of the present century. This revival was designed first to train and then to retain a core of skilled workers acquainted with the working and maintenance of the best European and American machinery of the day.

The characteristic features of what we now consider the general Japanese model of personnel management for high morale and high productivity include most (if not all) of the following seven items:

1. Lifetime employment, at least for male workers, until retirement age, with dismissal only for cause, granted after a brief trial period (often three months). This protects workers against layoffs in slack periods; it also protects workers whose special skills may become obsolete. Most firms, however, employ temporary as well as permanent workers.

2. Seniority wages, under which a worker's wage (over and above a base, and not usually inclusive of bonus or fringe benefits) is related more closely to the worker's seniority, family responsibilities, and prior educational record than to his on-the-job performance. (Even for salesmen,

salary is a more important part of compensation and commission a less important part, much to the annoyance of Western sales managers in companies with Japanese branches.) This system is under constant modification and appears to be weakening over time.

3. Loyalty of the worker to the company for providing training opportunities, good wages, and fringe benefits (also for keeping him off the breadline).[24] Workers are not expected to leave a company voluntarily unless remarkable opportunities arise elsewhere; labor pirating between firms is unethical behavior.

4. Great care in the selection of permanent employees. The agility and flexibility required to absorb frequent training and retraining are attributes in great demand and are judged by educational records (levels of examinations passed, quality of schools attended, and so on, often including public civil service examinations or company equivalents). Personal interviews are long and often even more important. They check the examination results, gauge how well the candidate will get along with people and absorb the company's mind and spirit, and estimate his tolerance of the inevitable intervals of dull work and slow promotion. They try to weed out potential militants and troublemakers. The non-Japanese and the religious enthusiast are also considered undesirable, along with the standard sorts of social deviants.

In many companies, the selection process formerly included investigation by private detectives to an extent conflicting with American notions of an applicant's right to privacy. Our informants disagree on the extent to which such investigations survive at the entry level. (They have become extremely expensive.) We believe that this practice is now moribund, if not completely dead.

5. Subjection of the employee to frequent training and retraining, rather than letting him rest on the laurels of techniques already mastered. The importance of this factor varies from company to company. In company A, training as an accountant leads to a series of bookkeeping, taxation, and auditing jobs in various plants and departments. The worker departs from the accounting track only if, in his early forties, he is looked on as top-management material and given a high-level tour of duty in other functional areas. In company B, the same budding accountant is not regarded as a specialized professional and expects to be rotated upward to become, perhaps, a section chief in finance or a department head in marketing. Shifts between white- and blue-collar jobs are rare; it is common but usually not advantageous[25] for the entrant with some specialized skill (an engineering degree, fluency in an important foreign language) to remain in jobs where that skill is important.

6. Foremanship and supervision are highly regarded and developed skills in the Japanese company. They are aimed at identifying the better

workers and combating boredom and alienation all along the line. The Japanese foreman or supervisor is less likely than the American to be a petty sadist of the army sergeant type and more likely to be a friendly teacher or scoutmaster.

7. In recessions or depressions, dividends, executive salaries, executive bonuses, and other executive perquisites are cut before workers' numbers or incomes are reduced. Even the social pressure for early retirement is applied to office deadwood before spreading to shop-floor deadwood; it is almost never applied to young male workers. One Japanese informant calls this feature "genuine economics-textbook capitalism" because owners and managers bear the initial risks of loss. American capitalism is allegedly a perversion, with the major risks falling on the worker who is laid of.

The American Occupation, encountering this system for the first time under the special circumstances of 1945–1950, regarded it with disdain and hostility. In the immediate postwar depression, Japanese-style management was taken to mean merely the retention of unneeded workers, resulting in high costs and low productivity. Occupation efforts to force the Japanese government, particularly the Japanese National Railways, to dismiss excess workers (including leftists in disproportionate numbers) led to a number of violent incidents, including the unsolved murder or suicide of the president of the national railway system. The Korean War (1950–1953) changed the picture permanently, and Japanese-style management has become a subject of interest, admiration, and even imitation. The feature most frequently imitated, often in isolation from the rest of the pattern, is the quality control circle (*jishū kanri*).[26]

## HUMAN BEINGS OR HUMAN CAPITAL?

Most of what one reads about Japanese docility, conformity, and robotization implies that the Japanese experience is impossible or at least difficult to replicate in more individualistic environments. But most of what one reads is also, in our opinion, considerably exaggerated. The Japanese worker is not born a "deferential workaholic automaton."

What happens, rather, seems to be this: With little more direct or overt conformist pressure than exists in most other societies, it becomes apparent to parents,[27] teachers,[28] and young people that the rewards for compliance with the established standards of the meritocracy are substantial in Japan; likewise the alternative costs of playing the free soul, hippie, or bum. The system works with carrots instead of sticks. What Thoreau termed "lives of quiet desperation" may be a little less desperate in Japan than elsewhere and marching to a different drummer a little more expensive, all without benefit of concentration camps, persecution of dissidents, or similar authoritarian paraphernalia. The productivity trends reflect the difference but do not in themselves answer any underlying ethical questions about which system is superior.

But what of those aspirants without family backing who fall behind in the fine arts of the examination and the interview? Some, of course, drop out into one or more of the several countercultures that exist in Japan as elsewhere; the proportion is probably smaller than in America, though perhaps not in white America. Most accept inferior jobs on farms, in family businesses, or with small firms in Japan's segmented labor market, for segmentation does survive in Japan, although, again, perhaps no more than in the United States.

For the less gifted aspirant with middle-class or upper-class connections, the rigors of the Japanese meritocracy are fairly easily, though expensively and incompletely, avoidable. The avoidance system, which constitutes a back door to high-productivity and high-paying jobs, is difficult to defend on ethical grounds. The individual goes to a private school, where reasonably good academic records ensure admission to the particular private university at the apex of that particular private school system.[29] On graduation, he competes for good jobs, if not for absolutely top jobs, on the basis of his and his family's connections. Once in a good company through this back door, he may have as good a chance to rise as anyone else. True, he may not be quite so bright as his competitors, but he may be better developed as a "whole man," without psychological scars from the "examination hells" and "narrow gates" of the meritocratic system.

## TRANSFERABLE ACROSS THE PACIFIC?

To what extent, if at all, can a Japanese firm or, for that matter, an American one (impressed with Japanese methods of productivity) practice these methods in the American environment? We have already taken a somewhat skeptical view of the quality circle (see note 26, p. 141) patterned on the Japanese *jishū kanri*. With regard to the entire body of techniques for personnel selection, training, motivation, and promotion, we take the somewhat dissident view that these are fundamental to everything else in "miracle management."

We begin with a conditional conclusion: If the assimilation of Japanese methods starts slowly and quietly in new plants, in places with relatively weak craft unions, relatively docile minorities, and relatively low executive salaries, it may well succeed and spread. If, however, the assimilation process takes the form of a big push with loud anti-union, anti-affirmative action, anti-overpaid management, or anti-educational democracy public- ity in strike-happy cities prone to racial violence and blessed with black- board jungle public schools, and if it encompasses many of these cities' prestigious employers, it will create a stone wall of opposition and quite probably fail.

A Japanese informant mentions a competitor in his industry that bought an operating American plant in a large city. This plant had previously been beset by labor troubles and low productivity. The Japanese purchaser tried to remedy these difficulties, using the same American labor force, by installing a Japanese top-management team to apply home-office methods to the fullest extent possible. The effort was a failure. Our informant's company, on the other hand, always starts new U.S. plants from scratch with an all-Japanese management (English-speaking, of course), which it replaces with Americans as soon as it can. (These Americans need not know Japanese; most Japanese multinationals conduct their international affairs in English.) This company also prefers to start plants far from industrial centers, in places where good land and willing, trainable labor are available and where there is no history of significant labor conflict.

Another Japanese informant adds that with good selection and training plus a longer probation period before final acceptance, rural Americans are good workers who can equal the Japanese in productivity. The foremen, he says, can equal Japanese in quality control, even when this includes taste testing to Japanese standards food products that these workers do not themselves consume. However, he goes on to say that Japanese methods can be applied more easily in distribution than in basic manufacturing. His company had been distributing Japanese products in the United States for approximately a decade, mainly on the Pacific Coast, before beginning to manufacture some of them in the Midwest.[30]

There seem to be four obstacles to successful application of Japanese-style management: (1) affirmative action in choosing and promoting workers, (2) craft unionism, (3) industrial unionism, and (4) executive retention.

**Affirmative Action**

The Japanese system of selection by school quality, school grades, and company examinations followed by in-depth interviews is likely under American conditions to yield a labor force, both blue and white collar, disproportionately white and perhaps also disproportionately male. This will be no problem for small companies in small towns and in industries not involved in government contracts. In some places, particularly the Southeast and Southwest, the problem can be finessed by giving examinations and interviews in Spanish as well as English and creaming the supply of Spanish-speaking labor. If circumstances require location in an area near a black ghetto, the interview procedure can be relied on to reject criminal and deviant elements, to weed out militants both political and religious, and to reserve desirable employment for the large proportion of minority workers whose main goals are integration into the work force and achievement of equality of opportunity.

## Craft Unionism

Craft unionism interferes, often fatally, with the training and retraining of individual workers as technology changes. When skilled jobs are downgraded and mechanized, craft unions typically demand that the machine operatives be union members, possess skills no longer necessary, and, of course, be paid skilled-labor wages. And when workers are to be trained for skilled jobs within their jurisdictions, craft unions seek to restrict training opportunities to their own members or to graduates of union-approved apprenticeship programs. Craft unionism also gives rise to jurisdictional disputes between unions over the control of borderline jobs. Such disputes can delay production while they are being arbitrated, or they may result in jurisdictional strikes. Obviously, also, the more unions the employer must bargain with simultaneously, never forgetting the rivalries between them, the more difficult the collective bargaining procedure is. If a plant is unionized, it should preferably have an independent union fairly close to the Japanese type, although American practice has not tended to include blue and white-collar workers in a single union. The second choice would be a local of an industrial union, without separate locals for skilled workers.

Within any union or union local, one expects to find workers with varying degrees of militance and of sympathy for the employer's position. In the case of permanent employees in Japan, it is a function of the interview procedure to keep the militants out; it is a function of the training program to co-opt or reconcile those militants who survive the interview; it is also a function of personnel management to prevent militance arising from unfairness within the firm after people are hired.

All these practices, singly or in combination, may be ineffective when U.S. management must deal with business agents and other union representatives sent down from national or regional headquarters, individuals who are not employees at all and might have been rejected had they applied for jobs. (Such intruders are largely avoided under the Japanese enterprise-union system.)[31]

## Industrial Unionism

Industrial unionism, apart from its skilled-craft enclaves, is less of a problem for Japanese-style management. It will, however, disrupt operations in case of a nationwide strike over nationwide issues if the "Japanese" firm sides with other employers against the union. If the company wishes to pay less than the union scale to any considerable body of its workers, making up the difference by permanence of employment and nontaxable fringe benefits, it can anticipate problems keeping the union out of its plants (if this is its desire) or in wage bargaining with any but an independent union. Promotion by seniority will have to be sacrificed or modified more quickly and substantially than in Japan if the company is to retain its most productive employees. Concessions also have to be made, of course, in the direction of the overtime-pay labor-relations institution in the United States.

### Executive Compensation

This aspect of "miracle management" has not been given the attention in America that some Japanese writers think it deserves, probably because the Japanese position seems one-sided to the outside observer. The theory is that high Japanese worker morale and productivity depend to some considerable extent on a closer approach to industrial democracy within the plant and also between the plant and the office. To a greater extent than in America, blue- and white-collar workers, regardless of rank and salary, eat lunch together and use the same facilities (cafeterias, washrooms, gymnasiums, and so on). Japanese executive salaries, in particular, are held to a smaller multiple of workers' wages (standardized for age and seniority) in the interests of industrial harmony than is the case in the United States.

This Japanese practice can be maintained for Japanese managers stationed temporarily in America and handicapped by residual linguistic deficiencies. Competitive pressures from American firms, both in its own industry and in other industries, may force modification of this practice, at whatever cost to labor morale, if the company is to retain its best American executives in the American environment. (Japanese companies themselves hope to solve this problem by appropriate combinations of nontaxable fringe benefits and intangible "loyalty" in both directions, company to employees and employees to company.)

### CONCLUSIONS

Japanese firms were more successful than their American competitors in raising labor and general productivity before the energy crisis and also in maintaining productivity growth after that crisis. In our opinion, six leading factors have been responsible for Japanese superiority.[32]

1. Higher Japanese net saving and investment ratios, primarily the latter
2. Lower Japanese burdens of taxation and regulation
3. Faster Japanese rates of innovation, although possibly not of invention in any technical sense
4. The meritocratic Japanese systems of selecting both blue- and white-collar workers for the commanding heights of the economy and of maintaining morale
5. Japanese indoctrination and training procedures, which seem effective in creating and maintaining company loyalty, mainly perhaps because so many problem children have been excluded by the meritocratic selection process
6. The weakness in Japan of such disruptive forces as racial conflict and craft unionism

In comparison with the other accounts that we have read and heard, we tend to place greater stress on factors 4, 5, and 6 and less on factors 1, 2, and 3.

We also believe, with Ezra Vogel,[33] that many Japanese methods, however imperfectly understood by non-Japanese, are gradually transportable across the Pacific as "lessons for America," but only if certain problems, particularly of racial diversity and of craft unionism, can be surmounted. It would be a mistake to propose Japanese-style management as part of a reaction against affirmative action, job consciousness, or democracy in education.

A final technical note: Although Japan leads America in productivity growth, comparative productivity levels are another matter except in individual industries such as steel and automobiles. There, the Japanese level seems higher than the American, a fact more than coincidentally related to the prominence of these industries in recent Japanese-American economic controversy.

## APPENDIX: MEASURING PRODUCTIVITY

In comparing Japanese and American productivity levels, the most important quantitative source of qualitative differences in results has been the difference between labor (or worker-hour) productivity and multifactor (or total-factor) productivity. Labor and worker-hour productivity measures are used almost exclusively in Japan; they show the Japanese productivity level still lower than the American in most branches of industry. Multifactor or total-factor productivity measures are becoming more common in the United States, thanks particularly to the work of John W. Kendrick.[34] They show that the Japanese productivity level has reached and surpassed the American.

When two or more distinct inputs, or factors of production, work together in producing a common output, it may be (and often is) misleading to concentrate on the productivity of one input to the neglect of the others. A high measured productivity of input $a$ (labor) in producing an output $x$ may result from wasteful overuse of one or more cooperant inputs $b$, $c$, ... (machine, land, ... ). What is sought is a productivity measure that cannot be misinterpreted so easily. Total-factor productivity has been the expedient adopted widely for this purpose in the United States, but it is unfamiliar in Japan.

Multifactor or total-factor productivity can be estimated in at least three ways.

1. We may estimate the amount of gross output or, more commonly, value added (in money terms) per money unit of all inputs taken together in what the employer considers the best proportion. If value added is $x$ units at a price $p_x$,[35] while units of various inputs $(a, b, c, \ldots)$ are used in the productive process at prices $(p_a, p_b, p_c, \ldots)$, total-factor productivity might be defined as:

$$\frac{xp_x}{ap_a + bp_b + cp_c + \cdots}$$

Using this measure over time, with the prices of inputs and outputs constantly changing, we ordinarily have recourse to index numbers that standardize the prices, usually at the levels of some base period. This procedure reduces the influence of price changes on what is conceived as a measure of physical productivity.

For capital goods, there are two special problems: (1) the so-called Wicksell effect, whereby a change in the price of capital services (rent on capital) is capitalized into a change in the amount of measured capital in money terms, and (2) progress in technology, through which the capital instruments of a late vintage are qualitatively different from those of an earlier period.[36]

These problems have led many economists, especially the so-called neo-Cambridge school in Britain, to deny the possibility of measuring capital at all. However, practicing statisticians believe (or at least hope) that deflation of money values by special index numbers of capital equipment prices provides an adequate approximation.

2. If output or value added $x$ is related to inputs $(a, b, c, \ldots)$ by a production function $f(a, b, c, \ldots)$ and also by a time trend $g(t)$, where $t$ is time, used as a proxy for technical progress, we can fit the combined function in physical terms as:

$$x = g(t) f(a, b, c, \ldots)$$

The change in total-factor productivity between, say, times $t_1$ and $t_2$ is then the derivative $dg/dt$, and its growth rate is $(dg/dt)/g(t)$.

3. We may estimate separate productivities for inputs $a$, $b$, $c$, ... and take a weighted average, the weights being the shares of the suppliers of the particular inputs in the total value added by the proportion process. If the individual input productivities are $x/a, x/b, x/c, \ldots$, and the respective income shares are $s_a, s_b, s_c, \ldots$, which add to unity, the total-factor productivity is computed as:

$$s_a \left(\frac{x}{a}\right) + s_b \left(\frac{x}{b}\right) + s_c \left(\frac{x}{c}\right)$$

There are unavoidable index-number problems when the relative shares change widely over time or across space.

Unfortunately for the aspiring statistician, these three methods cannot be guaranteed to yield the same or even very similar results. This is one reason for the reluctance to make greater use of total-factor productivity. There are two other objections, both stronger in Japan than in the United States.

1. When labor and capital (here $a$ and $b$) are predominantly complementary rather than competitive in production,[37] and when the capital-labor ratio is generally increasing over time, labor productivity $x/a$ can be expected to rise more rapidly than capital productivity $x/b$, with total-factor productivity in an intermediate position. Any serious consideration of a measure other than labor productivity weakens a common productivity argument used by trade union spokesmen in seeking wage increases.[38]

2. Labor productivity and its growth rate may be rising because workers have more and better machinery to assist them. But in this same situation, capital productivity and its growth rate may be falling because each machine is being operated by fewer or by less trained workers. Such declines in capital productivity or in its rate of increase are hard to explain to the Japanese public. In Japan, productivity (*seisan-ryoku*) is a value-loaded term, a good thing associated with training, skill, and industry.[39] How, then, can capital have been lazy, flunked examinations, suffered from too much *sake*, or taken too many days off?

## NOTES

*Author's note*: I am grateful to the Japan Productivity Center (particularly Mr. Tamisaburo Sasaki), to Keizai Doyukai, the Japan Committee for Economic Development (particularly Mr. Tadashi Shishido), and to Aoyama Gakuin University (particularly Chancellor Kinjiro Ohki and Professor Hiroshi Ohta) for cooperation, assistance, and logistic support during the preparation of this chapter.

1. In agriculture, it is equally common to measure output or value added per unit of land (acre or hectare).

2. GDP differs from the more common gross national product (GNP) in its treatment of international payments. If, for example, capital invested in country A pays dividends or interest to a capital owner in country B, these payments are included in the GNP of country A and in the GNP of country B.
3. U.S. data for Table 4-1 are from national income accounts; those for Table 4-2 are from the *Census of Manufacturers*. The first series includes imputed interest and rent on owned capital and land; the second series omits these items.
4. A Japanese informant who has worked with one of the automobile companies surmises that unpaid work or free labor may be an important source of high worker-hour productivity in the automobile industry because much preparation for work and cleaning up the workplace are done on the workers' own time. In the same way, Japanese elementary schools can report high labor productivity because many janitorial services and some building maintenance are done on a voluntary basis by students and their families.
5. Dale Jorgenson and Mieko Nishimizu, "U.S. and Japanese Economic Growth, 1952-74: An International Comparison," *Economic Journal* 88 (December 1978): 707-726.
6. Jorgenson and Nishimizu, "U.S. and Japanese Economic Growth, 1952-74: An International Comparison," *op. cit.*, p. 723.
7. Edward F. Denison, "Explanations of Declining Productivity Growth," *Survey of Current Business* (August 1979, Part ii). This is a preview of a longer Denison study, *Accounting for Slower Growth: The United States in the 1970s* (Washington, D.C.: Brookings Institution, 1980).
8. A "Yes-Yes" combination identifies a factor as both unfavorable to productivity growth and less important in Japan. A "No-No" combination identifies a factor in precisely the opposite way.
9. Japan passed through a problem of this kind, considerably more slowly, during the Meiji era (1868-1912).
10. These include Koreans, Chinese, Ainus (aborigines), *burakumin* (like India's untouchables), Eurasians, Afrasians, and aliens in general. The largest minority (Koreans) amounts to perhaps 600,000 people, slightly more than one-half of 1 percent of the resident population.
11. Lester Thurow, "A Plague of Job Hoppers," *Time*, 22 June 1981, p. 66. Reprinted by permission from *Time*.
12. Murray E. Foss, *Changes in the Workweek of Fixed Capital: U.S. Manufacturing, 1929 to 1976* (Washington, D.C.: American Enterprise Institute, 1981).
13. Worker-hour productivity in piecework and home factories is low, especially after allowance for crosshauling and other extra transportation. However, productivity per worker may be high because workers have several jobs and put in long hours.
14. On the Japanese distributive system, widely assailed as atavistically inefficient and unproductive, see Edward J. Lincoln, *The Japanese Distribution System*, U.S.-Japan Trade Council Report no. 18 (Washington, D.C., June 22, 1979), and Lincoln, "The Zebra's Stripes, *Distributus Japonicus* and the Economists" (U.S.-Japan Trade Council, 1980, Mimeographed).
15. Influential examples are Paul Sweezy and Harry Magdoff, "Productivity Slowdown: A False Alarm" *Monthly Review* 31 (June 1979): 1-12, and Sweezy and Magdoff, "The Uses and Abuses of Measuring Productivity," *Monthly Review* 32 (June 1980): 1-9.
16. Compare Michael Boretsky, "The Role of Innovation," *Challenge* 23 (November-December 1980): 9-15.
17. This topic is explored in Edwin Mansfield, "Basic Research and Productivity Increase in Manufacturing," *American Economic Review* 770 (December 1980): 863-873, for an American context. We have not found anything similar for Japan.

18. These problems were solved as follows: The *Mutsu* has not been permitted to leave her home port because of fear that her radiation will kill fish and interfere with fishermen's livelihood. After years of dispute, Suginami ward (the wealthier one) was required to incinerate its own garbage but was given special financial aid by Tokyo prefecture. The Narita Airport was opened, several years behind schedule and after considerable violence, despite arguments about the acquisition of farmland and the safety of the pipelines bringing jet fuel to Narita from the port of Cleiba.

19. Osaka, for example, has three large public universities: a national one, a prefectural one, and a municipal one.

20. Dale W. Jorgenson, "The Answer is Energy," *Challenge* (November-December 1980).

21. An early and influential article in this connection is William J. Baumol, "Macroeconomics of Unbalanced Growth: The Anatomy of Urban Crisis," *American Economic Review* 57, no. 3 (June 1967): 415–426.

22. Philosophical Japanese businessmen like to contrast American and European individualism with the "extended-family-ism" of *shōnin-dō*, which (together with its abuses) antedates the opening of Japan to the West by over two centuries. The term *shōnin-dō*, incidentally, is a precise analogue to the better-known *bushidō* ("way of the warrior").

23. Solomon B. Levine and Hisashi Kawada, *Human Resources in Japanese Industrial Development* (Princeton: Princeton University Press, 1980).

24. A secondary aspect of permanent employment is promotion from within. A man who has lost his job after acquiring seniority must start again at the bottom in a new firm. There his loyalty and morale cannot be expected to remain high, and so he is usually not hired at all.

25. Not advantageous, that is, for the employee's future career. In general, to be moved about with great frequency, but largely within the Tokyo or Osaka headquarters, is a sign that one is on the elite course to a top management position.

26. There is nothing either new or Japanese about the quality control circle (QC) idea. Groups of skilled workers, primarily blue-collar, meet at regular intervals and suggest methods of improving quality and/or productivity. Workers making usable suggestions are rewarded financially and considered for rapid promotions.

27. Particularly mothers. The Japanese "education-mama" (*kyōiku-mama*) has all but the religious connotations of the American "Jewish mother." If she can, she tutors her children (especially her sons) for the all-important entrance examinations to the better middle schools, high schools, and even universities. She also sends them to tutoring schools or hires private tutors for them, finances permitting.

28. The Japan Teachers Union plays an ambiguous role in this connection. Officially, this is a leftist union, struggling against the processing of innocent schoolchildren into complacent human capital for the Establishment. In practice, at the local level, it has carried on a losing battle against competition from private schools and pressures from parents and from the Ministry of Education. Most individual teachers in most individual schools ignore union ideology and are comfortably conformist, pushing as many students as they can past the most prestigious examinations.

29. For young women, private junior college is often the highest educational level attained. It costs less than a full university course but qualifies the recipient for a somewhat lower entry-level white-collar job.

30. Readers should note that these impressionistic references have been only to Japanese firms with U.S. branches. We could find no American firms that have

copied Japanese practices beyond the QC level in their U.S. operations, although most of them run their Japanese branches Japanese-style. Will G. Ouchi's *Theory Z* (Reading, Mass: Addison-Wesley, 1981) mentions a few prominent U.S. firms that he believes have developed quasi-Japanese methods on their own. A few other companies also have statements of company philosophy that Ouchi finds entirely compatible with the quasi-Japanese Theory Z.

31. Enterprise unions can, of course, hire outsiders to represent them. In unions of government workers, particularly the Japanese National Railways, these outside representatives are often militants who have been dismissed for illegal strikes and slowdowns.

32. As this chapter was being written, four recent articles crossed my desk with which these conclusions may be compared, and there are doubtless many more: Hideo Ishida, "Japanese-Style Human Resource Management: Can It Be Exported?" *Sumitomo Quarterly* (April 1981); "How Japanese Manage in the U.S." *Fortune*, 15 June 1981, pp. 97–103; an unsigned United Press International dispatch from Dearborn, Michigan, entitled, "Nissan's U.S. Truck Plant Will Be Closely Patterned on Japanese Models," *Japan Times*, 23 July 1981; Amanda Bennett, "Davy Datsun: A Pioneer from Japan Helps to Clear the Way for Nissan's U.S. Plant," *Wall Street Journal*, 4 August 1981.

33. Ezra Vogel, *Japan as No. 1* (Cambridge, Mass: Harvard University Press, 1979).

34. John W. Kendrick, *Productivity Trends: Capital and Labor*, National Bureau of Economic Research Occasional Paper no. 53 (New York, 1956); Kendrick, *Productivity Trends in the U.S.* (Princeton, N.J.: Princeton University Press, National Bureau of Economic Research, 1961); Kendrick and Elliott S. Grossman, *Productivity in the United States: Trends and Cycles* (Baltimore: John Hopkins Press, 1980).

Kendrick, however, credits Hiram S. Davis with keynoting the movement to measure productivity in terms of all inputs simultaneously (*Productivity Trends: Capital and Labor*, *op cit.*, note 1, p. 2f).

35. The price $p_x$, interpreted as the unit price of value added, is the unit price of output *minus* allowances for purchased raw materials, intermediate products, fuel and light, and so on (per unit of output) and also minus allowances for business taxes and for depreciation charges on fixed capital equipment from whatever source derived (and likewise per unit of output).

36. Something similar may also be true for some types of labor that embody increasing amounts of human capital over time, resulting from the availability of formal education and on-the-job training.

37. This means that the productivity of any given quantity of labor *rises* when more and better capital instruments are available to work with. If labor and capital were *competitive* in production, as in "technological unemployment" cases, the productivity of labor would still rise with more and better capital, but the quantity of labor employed would fall. (In the competitive cases, either productivity or employment of labor, and conceivably both, fall when capital is increased.)

38. When unionists demand wage increases without productivity justification, however, they are quick to blame inadequate or outmoded equipment for their poor showing. This is especially true when their employers are concentrating their current investments abroad or in luxury housing or when they are not investing at all.

39. This conception of productivity as a good thing is by no means confined to Japan. And certainly productivity is a good thing in the sense that more is better than less—if the increment costs nothing. But productivity is an

economic service or, rather, an umbrella for a number of economic services. Like other goods or services, its provision involves costs. Some of these fall within the traditional purview of economics; others do not. The benefits of increased productivity may or may not exceed the associated costs—economic, social, psychological, medical, environmental, or what have you. For a full-dress treatment of this problem, see Moses Abramovitz, "Welfare Quandaries and Productivity Concerns," *American Economic Review* vol. 71, no. 1 (March 1981): 1–17.

If one believes as we do, and as we believe Abramovitz does, that the benefits of increased productivity are likely to exceed the sum of these costs at the margin, one may legitimately treat productivity as a good thing. But if one believes the opposite, he or she may with equal legitimacy regard productivity as a bad thing. The term itself should settle nothing. In practice, alas, it sometimes does settle things in theoretical argument, as Gunnar Myrdal among others has complained for years.

# 5

# Responding
# to the Productivity Crisis:
# A Plant-Level Approach
# to Labor Policy

J. R. NORSWORTHY and C. A. ZABALA

The productivity crisis has led to a new trend in labor relations. Union representatives and corporate managers have negotiated highly visible wage and benefit reductions or freeze concessions in national contracts. At the plant level, local union representatives have accepted work rule and production standards concessions. Factory workers have conceded certain seniority rules that determine rehiring rights of laid-off workers. Also, some skilled workers have conceded craft rules that limit management's flexibility to assign them to different jobs. Truck drivers have accepted changes that require them to handle certain freight so that companies can lay off semi-skilled warehouse workers. Airline pilots have extended the hours they will fly.[1]

In the beleaguered auto industry, for example, new contracts have recently been reached well in advance of the scheduled date for talks with the United Auto Workers (UAW). Chrysler achieved a package of special concessions as part of a federal rescue mission in 1980. Ford and General Motors have written separate agreements with the UAW that exchange wage concessions for greater job security. Significantly, the Ford agreement also contains provisions for new formal arrangements for continuing labor-management dialogue at the national and local levels. International Harvester, also in early discussions with the UAW, has opened its books to the union. The UAW agreed to begin early talks after examining the financial data provided. In the trucking industry, the International Brotherhood of Teamsters is entering negotiations with some 600 companies that want a cheaper contract than the master freight agreement signed in January 1983. A separate agreement with United Parcel Service is also in the works.

Freedman and Fulmer (1982) predict that unions and companies will move away from setting wage agreements to conventional automatic escalation clauses and from the pattern bargaining cycle of the postwar era. Instead, they believe, wages will be linked to competitive conditions for specific industries and even specific products at both the firm and the plant levels. In contrast, Dunlop (1977, 1982) suggests that automatic escalation clauses in multiyear wage agreements have provided for relatively stable collective bargaining relationships in the postwar era and that the wave of compensation and local bargaining concessions simply represents a short-term shift in the balance of power. Clark (1980) argues that labor-management systems, such as quality-of-work-life programs, which aim to reduce adversary bargaining and promote consensual labor relations, improve productivity. However, this literature is not supported by strong empirical evidence. Furthermore, a recent Harris poll of American executives indicates a polarization within management ranks regarding their future plans for bargaining with unions:

> The split is most apparent in the answers executives gave when they were asked which way they would like to see their own companies' collective bargaining go in the future—toward a return to traditional negotiation or toward forcing concessions from labor, "even to the point of eliminating the unions." Among executives of companies that are heavily organized and accustomed to dealing with entrenched and sophisticated unions, there is little sentiment for pressing current gains. By a margin of 66 percent to 23 percent, these executives are anxious to return to traditional collective bargaining practices.... As Harris comments: "These people don't expect to get rid of unions and figure that they might as well work with them." But executives in companies with relatively little unionization split almost equally on whether to return to an adversary relationship.[2]

There is recent evidence that labor policy research is more susceptible to quantification than is common in the industrial relations literature. Zabala (1983) has examined the sociological and economic factors that influence industrial relations performance at the plant level. Norsworthy and Zabala (1983) have found a quantitative link between worker performance and total-factor productivity in the industry. In this chapter, we provide an analytic framework to link labor policy to worker performance and then to total-factor productivity and total unit cost of production at the plant level. This framework offers an alternative to pattern bargaining.

Pattern bargaining, as it developed in the United States, takes place primarily at the national union and corporate levels in one industry and does not involve workers and managers in the plant. Wages and benefits are determined between the national union and a *target* company. Then, the union and each remaining company use this model compensation package in their respective negotiations. In this way, similar compensation agreements are obtained. The breakdown in pattern bargaining is the result of current general problems in the U.S. economy, which have tended to draw attention to interfirm and interplant differences. For example, when productivity growth is reasonably good throughout an industry and its major firms are enjoying success in varying degrees, the costs of pattern bargaining are lower; high-performance plants generate a kind of surplus that can compensate for marginal performance elsewhere. However, when productivity growth is low and markets are shrinking because of import penetration, the high-performance firms and plants do little more than cover costs, and lower-performance units are closed down to reduce losses. Under these circumstances, which are widespread in the steel and auto industries and common throughout much of manufacturing, wages, fringe benefits, and other conditions determined in pattern bargaining create special problems in particular firms or plants.

Investment for higher productivity in general and in robotics in particular is not likely to provide the answer to such economic difficulties, certainly not in the near or intermediate future. The huge investment program that would be required to achieve a rapid rise in productivity cannot be financed from low or negative profit streams, and high interest rates make it difficult to raise capital from outside the enterprise. Moreover, even if the investment funds were available, sufficient capacity to produce large quantities of new capital goods is simply not available. Without considerable expansion of its own productive capacity, the capital goods industry cannot support a massive modernization program. For these reasons, at least through the 1980s and early 1990s, a large fraction of domestic production will take place in industrial plants similar to those of today. Consequently, the success of American industry will in large measure depend on the success of American managers and American workers operating domestic plants.

We suggest that this new trend has been characterized by deviations in pattern contracts and the negotiation of firm agreements with particular firms to improve productivity and profits. Our analytic model also departs from pattern bargaining and links industrial relations practices to labor policy and then to productivity performance at the plant. We offer empirical evidence and list the data requirements for a data information and analysis system that connects the shop floor to the multiplant corporation. Quantifying the impact of labor policy on worker performance and linking policy formation to worker and plant performance and its implementation at the plant are the next stages in the research agenda for corporate labor relations.

## THE RESPONSE: A NEW APPROACH TO LABOR POLICY

A labor policy for the 1980s must take into account a far wider range of information than has commonly been considered: information about worker and plant performance at the local level and about key factors that influence worker and plant performance. Such a policy will make systematic use of this information and formulate local labor policy on the basis of the expected effects of the elements of that policy on performance. A feedback process based on total plant performance, including not only labor but other inputs as well, will then link corporate and union policy making to shop-floor activity. The basis for this feedback is physical and financial plant performance measures that correspond to productivity and costs, respectively.

Central to this new approach is the concept of *worker performance*: the measurable, behavioral manifestation of worker attitudes, a term that is difficult to use as a judgment-free concept. Worker performance is influenced by the economic and sociological aspects of measurable variables such as wages and fringe benefits, performance standards, job security, and health and safety conditions. These variables are *labor policy elements* and are the constituents of industrial relations policy (which, for brevity, we will also refer to as *labor policy*).

Worker performance is also influenced by other measurable elements in the worker's environment: for example, the composition of the labor force in terms of age, sex, seniority, race, and ethnic group and the technology of production, which is broadly construed as the capital-materials-labor configuration of production.

In addition, the worker is influenced by relationships on the shop floor: with the union and its representatives, with the line supervisor, and with co-workers. These elements, which play an important role in the formation of worker attitudes and hence in the determination of worker performance, are more difficult to measure.

Worker performance is measured in terms of such variables as grievance actions, authorized and unauthorized strikes, absenteeism, and sabotage incidents. In this way, worker performance can be taken to result from two sets of forces: labor policy elements and environmental variables. In turn, worker performance affects worker productivity, labor cost, and overall plant performance.

Plant performance is measured in terms of productivity and costs. The key concepts in plant performance are *total-factor productivity* and its financial counterpart, *total unit cost of production*. Measures of the productivity of individual factors—labor, capital, and materials (a shorthand term encompassing all other purchased inputs) combine into total-factor productivity. In the same way, unit labor cost, unit capital cost, and unit materials cost combine into the total unit cost of production.

These concepts provide the basis for a practical model of industrial relations at the plant. The model constructed here has three components: The first component describes the effects on worker performance of environmental and labor policy elements. The second component examines the effect of worker performance on plant performance and on productivity and costs. The third component is the feedback from plant performance to the formation and modification of labor policy.

## A Measure of Worker Performance

The authors have constructed an analytic representation of the determination of worker attitude, worker performance, and plant performance to show how the link between labor policy and productivity and costs can be measured statistically.[3] Because measurement of worker performance lies at the heart of the plant-level approach to labor policy, it is important to describe the concept in some detail.

First, the measure must be *objective and reproducible*. The survey approach cannot consistently meet these criteria, although it may be useful in supplemental activities.

Second, it must be *relevant to productivity and costs*. In a technical sense, it must be possible to find a statistical relationship between worker performance and productivity and the cost of production. In particular, the method of measurement must permit us to assign two kinds of valuation to worker performance: a physical valuation representing the effect on productivity, and a dollar valuation representing the effect on the cost of production. Furthermore, these valuations must be consistent with one another.

Third, the measure must take *technology into account*. An important observation in industrial relations is that changes in technology have direct effects (labor displacement or changes in job skill requirements) as well as indirect effects. The latter often take subterranean forms such as sabotage, slowdown, or absenteeism. (The direct effects of technology are represented in the description of plant performance.)

Fourth, it must allow for the *effect of the composition of the plant labor force*. Industrial relations studies have shown that seniority, age, sex, race, and ethnic origin influence worker performance. In order to sort out the other determinants of worker performance, it must be possible to control for the effects of labor force composition.

Fifth, the worker performance measure must take into account the *effects of labor policy* because labor policy is the instrument for improving plant performance. Labor policy is described in terms of job security; compensation, leave, and other benefits; and production and safety standards. The first two categories of variables can be quantified readily. The third requires some experimentation; direct enumeration from the local plant contract provides a starting point.

In summary, three categories of factors create the environment in which worker attitude and, hence, worker performance are determined: labor force composition, current and past labor policy, and the technology of production. Current labor policy is the active instrument by which worker performance is influenced. Figure 5-1 illustrates the relationship of the elements of a statistical model of worker performance determination at the plant level. Quantification of the local industrial relations performance in terms of past labor policy elements is an important step in creating a model of worker performance.

**Measures of Worker and Plant Performance**

Worker performance (as measured by the process just described) determines the character of labor input, and labor input enters the model of the production process—that is, the model of plant performance (see Figure 5-2). Although this is a single model, it has two aspects: physical and financial. On the physical (left-hand) side of the diagram, the worker's input enters the production process with materials to be processed and with technological support in the form of capital. The physical output of production is related to worker performance through worker input. An important feature of this approach is that the plant performance model

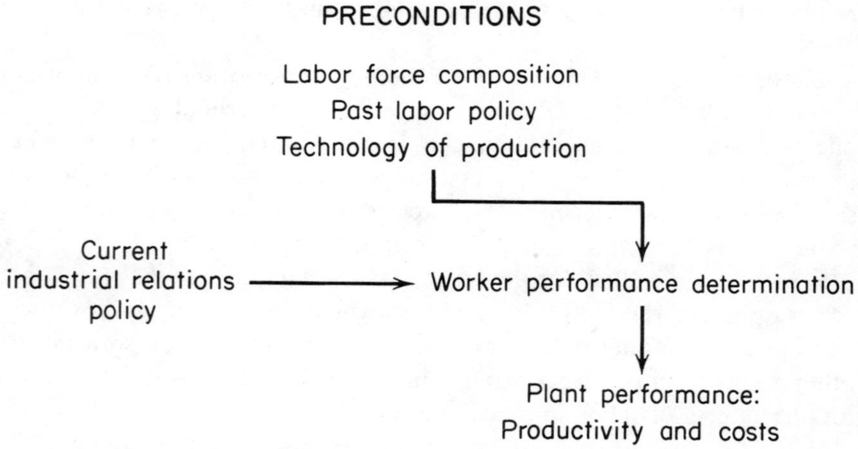

## PRECONDITIONS

Labor force composition
Past labor policy
Technology of production

Current industrial relations policy ⟶ Worker performance determination

Plant performance:
Productivity and costs

Figure 5-1. Determination of worker performance in the plant.

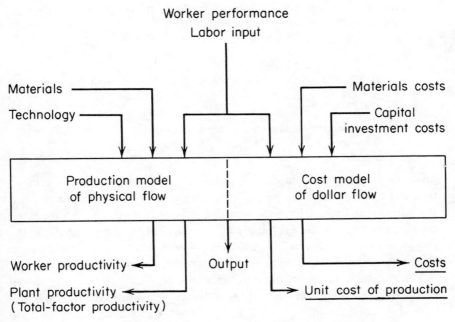

Figure 5-2. Effects of worker performance on plant performance.

does not focus on worker productivity alone; it is the productivity of all factors combined that describes plant performance. This more complete view, which takes into account all inputs to the production process (summarized here as labor input, materials, and technology embodied in capital goods), is called *total-factor productivity* (see Table 5-1).

Historically (as Table 5-1 shows), total-factor productivity has grown less rapidly than labor productivity, largely because capital and other inputs have been substituted for labor. But although these substitutions reduce labor input and labor cost, they increase other inputs and their associated costs. For this reason, total-factor productivity provides a more appropriate guide to the unit cost of production and product price than the productivity of any single input alone.

The production process has another aspect: the cost model (or cost function). The cost model takes account of the dollar costs represented by the physical flow of materials and the cost of capital, as well as worker compensation. Corresponding to the physical productivity of labor is unit labor cost, which is the labor cost embodied in a single unit of output. Similarly, corresponding to plant or total-factor productivity is the unit cost of production, which is based on the costs of all inputs to the production process. Just as total-factor productivity is the appropriate basis for

**Table 5-1. Average Annual Rates of Productivity Growth in the U.S. Auto Industry (percent)**

|           | Total-Factor Productivity | Labor Productivity |
|-----------|---------------------------|--------------------|
| 1959–1965 | 1.90                      | 4.66               |
| 1965–1973 | 0.90                      | 1.30               |
| 1973–1976 | 1.99                      | 3.12               |

*Source*: Norsworthy and Zabala, "Output Measurement and Productivity Growth in the U.S. Auto Industry" (1982).

measuring plant performance in a physical sense, the unit cost of production is a measure of plant performance in dollar terms. Accordingly, it is the unit cost of production based on *all* purchased inputs, not just the labor cost, that is appropriate for the pricing of output. In the same way, it is the productivity of *all* factors combined, not just worker productivity, that is the appropriate basis for gauging plant performance.

The statistical model of plant performance is based on the quantities of labor, materials, and capital and the measure of worker performance that enter into production, as well as their prices. A model of the production process that will adequately describe the various inputs and their interactions calls for the use of advanced econometric techniques. These tools are available and need only be applied to the task at hand. Very simple models of the production process—limited in scope to, say, labor productivity—cannot represent the production process adequately for measurement of the effect of worker performance on worker productivity and plant performance. In particular, it is possible to raise worker productivity by substituting other inputs for labor that cost more than the labor which is replaced, thus raising labor productivity and the total cost of production.

The key to the process outlined is the representation of worker performance in the model of production at the plant. (The technical aspects of this problem are discussed in the section "Empirical Results.") The major point is that the plant performance model measures productivity and cost effects of worker performance and takes account of changes in worker performance resulting from labor policy, as well as the environmental elements that affect worker performance (technology, labor force composition, and past industrial relations practices at the plant).

**Feedback from Performance to Labor Policy**

At this point, we have forged the two critical links in the chain connecting local plant conditions and local labor policy to productivity and costs through worker performance. The remaining task is to create a feedback link from plant performance to the formation of labor policy. Figure 5-3 illustrates the feedback process. Recall that local conditions and plant labor policies influence worker performance (Figure 5-1). Worker performance, in turn, is an important determinant of plant performance, and its effect is measured in that way (Figure 5-2). Measures of plant performance feed back into labor policy formation, at both the corporate and the plant levels; specific measures of the effects of labor policies go into the formation of current labor policy as it is carried out at the plant. The quantification and feedback of labor policy through worker and plant performance to policy modification makes possible the systematic use of information derived from past successes and failures in the formulation of current labor policy.

This characteristic of the new approach is crucial. Few (if any) companies examine the sources and results of labor policy failure; the typical response is to try in plant B the approach that appears to have worked in plant A. The decision is often made without carefully examining the situation at plant A and the key elements of the successful policy applied there. Similarly, there is seldom a serious effort to identify those conditions at plant B that may have contributed to labor policy failure there. Multiple plant observations may be required to sort out the local conditions and policy elements that contribute to success or failure in a particular plant. But negative results constitute information that can be helpful in formulating subsequent policies. This modeling approach provides a framework for sorting out the local plant conditions that contribute to the success or failure of particular labor policies and for quantification of their beneficial and detrimental impacts on plant performance.

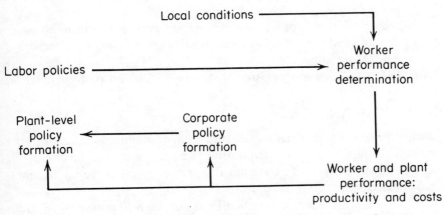

Figure 5-3. Feedback from productivity and costs to labor policy formation.

**The Framework**

1. Data Preparation
   a. Labor relations history for the plant is distilled into quantitative elements.
   b. Technological history is quantified for the production cost model and for worker performance model.
   c. Worker performance indicators are identified and collected on a regular basis.
   d. Production and cost information is collected on a regular basis.
2. Statistical Analysis
   a. Worker performance determination model is constructed on the basis of historical labor policies, technology, and labor force composition.
   b. Worker performance model is expanded to encompass multiple plants.
   c. Plant performance model is derived for each plant.
   d. Worker performance measures are incorporated in plant performance model.
3. Policy Analysis: Historical
   a. Labor policy influences on workers' performance are measured on the basis of worker performance model.
   b. Worker performance influences on productivity and cost performance are measured on the basis of plant model.
   c. Labor policy influences on productivity and cost performance are measured through integration of statistical models.
4. Policy Analysis: Current
   a. Potential labor relations policies are screened for each plant on the basis of local conditions and predicted worker and plant performance.
   b. Labor relations policies are carried out and their effects noted.
   c. Worker and plant performance models are updated to incorporate new information.
   d. Labor policies are adjusted to achieve improved performance.

## EMPIRICAL RESULTS

Although this set of activities constitutes a substantial undertaking, the individual stages can be carried out using currently applied techniques of analysis. No new scientific tools must be created to make the implementation of such a program feasible.

What is the evidence that a plant-level approach to industrial relations will prove practical? This empirical issue has been partially addressed in the auto industry by the authors.[4] The existence of a strong relationship between indicators of worker performance in part of that industry and overall industry performance is shown in Table 5-2. The measure of worker performance was determined as part of a cost function estimation and analysis. The measure was based on four industrial relations variables—grievance rates, unresolved grievance rates, quits, and unauthorized strikes. Four input factors were included in the cost function estimation process: capital, production worker labor, nonproduction worker labor, and materials (i.e., all other inputs). The resulting worker performance measure, $W$, has strong correlations with both total-factor productivity and labor productivity, the measures of performance in this summary application; thus, it measures negative performance. In addition, there is a strong relationship between total unit cost and the worker performance measure that is negative on average; a 1 percent change in $W$ leads to a 0.3 to 0.5 percent change in total unit cost.

The existence of such a relationship in highly aggregated data is particularly encouraging because it is easy to imagine why this relationship might be found at the plant level and yet be lost in the process of aggregating inputs and output to the industry level. Although these results should merely be considered illustrative, they indicate the feasibility of the approach.

Table 5-2 shows productivity, output, and worker performance for the industry examined. The relationship between productivity growth and growth in output in short periods is evident. There is also a reasonable correspondence between total-factor productivity and worker performance

Table 5-2. Productivity, Output, and Worker Performance Indexes
(1967 = 1000)

|  | Total-Factor Productivity | Output | Worker Performance (W) |
|---|---|---|---|
| 1967 | 100.0 | 100.0 | 100.0 |
| 1968 | 105.5 | 119.1 | 86.1 |
| 1969 | 106.2 | 119.8 | 94.9 |
| 1970 | 99.0 | 95.6 | 94.3 |
| 1971 | 108.8 | 123.7 | 106.8 |
| 1972 | 108.3 | 131.8 | 98.8 |
| 1973 | 113.2 | 153.1 | 89.5 |
| 1974 | 111.6 | 127.8 | 105.8 |
| 1975 | 112.4 | 115.3 | 131.1 |
| 1976 | 119.9 | 149.4 | 110.3 |

Source: Norsworthy and Zabala, "Worker Attitudes, Worker Performance, and Productivity" (1983).

as determined from analysis of the cost function of the industry (see Table 5-3). Perhaps most notable, however, is the countercyclical movement in worker performance.[5] This is most evident in the recession of 1974–1975. Even with the very sharp drop in output from the 1973 peak, total-factor productivity is sustained by a sharp increase in worker performance. Of course, plant closings would have removed the less efficient plants from production, but those plants remained in the capital stock measure for 1974–1975. This bears out the industrial relations tenet that under the pressure of layoffs and plant closings, worker performance improves. The fact that the older, more experienced workers are a larger share of the work force may also contribute to improved performance.

With regard to the worker performance index, $W$, the countercyclical influence of the grievance rate is very strong in this model. On the average, for the 1967–1976 period, a 1 percent increase in the index of worker performance results in a 0.3 increase in total-factor productivity and a 0.3 percent decrease in the total unit cost of production. The objective of the plant-level approach presented here is to seek to transfer the productivity-enhancing improvement in worker performance to more normal production conditions.

Again, it is important to bear in mind the very limited purpose of this example: Actual plant performance, as distinct from aggregate industry performance, may result in different relationships between indicators of worker attitude and worker performance. And the effect of worker performance on overall productivity and costs may differ. However, it must be regarded as significant that even when such highly aggregated and limited data are used, the results are consistent with the important outlines of our basic approach.

Table 5-3. Correlation Matrix for Average Year-to-Year Percentage Changes in Variables, 1959 to 1976 (percent)

|  | Worker Performance Index | Total-Factor Productivity | Labor Production | Total Unit Cost of Production |
|---|---|---|---|---|
| Worker performance index | 1.00 | −0.30 | −0.62 | 0.24 |
| Total-factor productivity | −0.30 | 1.00 | 0.61 | −0.52 |
| Labor production | −0.62 | 0.61 | 1.00 | −0.73 |
| Total unit cost of production | 0.24 | −0.52 | −0.73 | 1.00 |

Source: Norsworthy and Zabala, "Worker Attitudes, Worker Performance, and Productivity" (1983).

## EFFECTS OF DECENTRALIZED FORMATION OF LABOR POLICY

The broad-based innovation in the development and implementation of labor policy tailored to local conditions that we have described can be expected to have substantial effects on management practices and labor-management relations. Even a pilot study focusing on a few plants would require broad-based collection and analysis of historical data to sort out the influences of local conditions in terms of labor force composition and technology and thus would have implications beyond the plants where the decentralized policy was carried out. This brief report cannot analyze all important aspects of the new policy approach in detail, but it can provide a useful look at some of the major effects on management, the work force, and labor-management relations.

The new approach to labor policy can be employed in a variety of institutional circumstances. We believe, however, that the framework provided by plant- and company-level labor-management committees offers the kind of interaction that can yield good results.

### Labor-Management Committees

The new approach is a systematic measurement tool, but it is also far more than that. It explicitly introduces plant-level conditions into labor policy determination; indeed, the local labor-management committee is the focus of the method. It also makes possible systematic consideration of local plant conditions through these committees, which aim to reduce the differences in perception of local conditions between corporate headquarters and local management and workers.

Our system is highly analogous to the theory of consumer behavior constructed on the basis of revealed preferences by Paul Samuelson and others: Worker preferences with respect to labor policy are revealed by responses in worker performance in the context of local plant conditions.[6] The basing of labor policy on the preferences of workers revealed in this way represents a substantial departure in industrial relations.

In considering the emphasis on labor-management committees and plant-level productivity performance, it must be remembered that *decentralization of the basis on which decisions are made is not the same as decentralizing the power to decide*. The approach we propose carries the potential for centralizing *or* decentralizing the authority of companies and unions to make labor policy decisions, with, in either case, greater and more systematic consideration of local conditions. What the decentralized approach to labor policy provides, however, is the opportunity to develop a broad range of solutions to plant-specific labor relations problems. The labor-management committee utilizes the plant-level data on the local conditions that contribute to industrial relations performance and thus to the plant's productivity performance.

The major focus of the labor-management committee is twofold: (1) It provides quantitative assessments of labor relations problems that affect production costs. (2) It assesses the costs and benefits of proposed solutions to these problems: quality-of-work-life initiatives, flextime, profit sharing, leave and benefits options, job security guarantees, product quality programs, absenteeism reduction targets, and other experiments such as plant-level productivity programs aimed at setting local or national wage rates. Thus, the labor-management committee can be the vehicle for identifying and resolving labor relations problems that reduce the plant's productivity performance.

The quality of information in the local histories of labor relations and technological change can be improved in many cases by use of worker inputs in their preparation. Furthermore, frequent contact and interchange at the plant level can facilitate the introduction of new technology and new labor policies and permit an early fine tuning of the policies, leading to higher worker and plant performance. Local labor-management committees have worked well in several cases to create such an interchange. For example, these concepts of labor-management interaction appear prominently in the UAW-Ford agreement.

Although such an initiative in industrial relations is obviously beneficial to workers, it is clearly in the interest of management as well; both sides of the bargaining table stand to capture real gains from decentralized and democratized labor policy. In this context, the labor-management committee may be thought of as the transmission belt between shop-floor activity and labor policy.

The information systems for worker and plant performance data described here provide an important basis for reconciliation of labor and management views of many of the problems and constraints facing the local plant. Although shared information cannot itself produce agreement between the two parties, it can eliminate some of the causes of disagreement and identify a wider range of solutions to local conflicts.


## SUMMARY

The plant-level approach to industrial relations that we advocate here is much more than just another new wrinkle. It represents a new perspective on labor policy, one that is performance-oriented. It provides a new objective for labor policy: improving worker and plant performance where performance is clearly defined. It focuses on day-to-day performance on the shop floor in light of local plant conditions, which is where workers and many managers spend their working lives.

In an important sense, this approach represents a new paradigm for labor relations, a dramatic shift in perspective, with associated new concepts for measurement and decision making. This new paradigm takes a more detached view of human behavior: It *accepts* worker responses to various conditions, labor policies among them, as they *are* and attempts to alter those conditions through industrial relations policies designed to achieve the goals of the workers and the enterprise. This perspective contrasts with the adversary approach that *deplores* worker responses to local conditions and tries to persuade the worker to respond differently in order to achieve the firm's goals.

Viewed in this broader perspective, the goals of the enterprise may change. For example, once it is accepted that a particular worker objective—say, job security—pays off in measurably improved industrial relations performance, the company can quantify the trade-off between added costs and job security and can make its long-run decisions on that basis. In the absence of quantification of the performance effects of the policy, such issues as job security may be decided on the basis of managerial prerogative as viewed in the adversary collective bargaining framework.

Greater consideration of local conditions in labor policy determination argues for labor-management contact and interchange that is both wider in scope and greater in frequency than is the rule in many U.S. industrial plants. There is an even stronger case to be made where there is greater local autonomy in deciding labor policy; local labor-management committees may provide a forum for that interchange. But the most important aspect of our approach is its breadth: It draws on the fields of industrial sociology, economics, and cost accounting. The complete system of production and cost measurement facilitates evaluation of labor policy effects on worker and plant performance.

## NOTES

*Authors' Note*:   The conclusions and opinions expressed are the authors' alone and do not necessarily reflect those of the Bureau of the Census or its staff. The authors gratefully acknowledge the helpful comments by Professor Paul Lawrence, Dr. Christian van Schayk, and Dr. Paul Adler during the preparation of this chapter.

1. *Wall Street Journal*, 22 March 1983, p. 35; *Los Angeles Times*, 18 February 1983, pp. 1d–3d.
2. "A Management Split Over Labor Relations," *Business Week*, 14 June 1982, p. 19. Used with permission.
3. See Norsworthy and Zabala, "On Introducing a Measure of Worker Attitude in Cost Function Estimation" (1982).
4. Norsworthy and Zabala, "Worker Attitudes, Worker Performance, and Productivity" (1983).

5. See, for example, W. Michell, *Business Cycles* (Berkeley: University of California Press, 1913); J. Schumpeter, *The Theory of Economic Development* (Cambridge: Harvard University Press, 1934); J. Kendrick, *Understanding Productivity: An Introduction to the Dynamics of Productivity Change* (Baltimore: Johns Hopkins University Press, 1977). These writers maintain that labor-management conflict rises during business expansions and reaches its lowest levels during business recessions.
6. See Paul A. Samuelson, "The Theory of Revealed Preference and Other Topics in Nonstochastic Consumption Theory," in *The Collected Scientific Papers of Paul A. Samuelson*, Part I, ed. Joseph E. Stiglitz (Cambridge: MIT Press, 1966), pp. 1–114.

## REFERENCES

Clark, K. "The Impact of Unionization on Productivity: A Case Study." *Industrial and Labor Relations Review* 33 (July 1980): 451–469.

Dunlop, John T. "Reply." *Industrial and Labor Relations Review* 31 (October 1977): 14–17.

———. "Moderation's Chance to Survive." *Business Week*, 19 April 1982, pp. 123–126.

Freedman, A., and W. Fulmer. "Last Rites for Pattern Bargaining." *Harvard Business Review* 60 (March–April 1982): 30–48.

Kendrick, J. 1977. *Understanding Productivity: An Introduction to the Dynamics of Productivity Change* (Baltimore: Johns Hopkins University Press).

Mitchell, W. 1913. *Business Cycles* (Berkeley: University of California Press).

Norsworthy, J. R., and C. A. Zabala. "On Introducing a Measure of Worker Attitude in Cost Function Estimation." *Economics Letters* 10 (1982): 185–191.

———. 1982. "Output Measurement and Productivity Growth in the U.S. Automobile Industry."

———. 1983. "Worker Attitudes, Worker Performance, and Productivity."

Samuelson, Paul A. 1966. "The Theory of Revealed Preference and Other Topics in Nonstochastic Consumption Theory." In *The Collected Scientific Papers of Paul A. Samuelson*, Part I, edited by Joseph E. Stiglitz, 1–114 (Cambridge: MIT Press).

Schumpeter, J. 1934. *The Theory of Economic Development* (Cambridge: Harvard University Press).

Zabala, C. A. 1983. "Collective Bargaining at UAW Local 645, General Motors Assembly Division, Van Nuys, California, 1976–1981." Ph.D. dissertation, University of California.

# 6

# Productivity: The Industrial Relations Connection

ROBERT B. MCKERSIE and JANICE A. KLEIN

The "labor problem" has been listed as one of the prime culprits behind declining productivity in the United States. What part have industrial relations practices and procedures played in this arena? This chapter will address this question by exploring the linkages between productivity and industrial relations arrangements in this country.

As a starting point, about 40 Committee for Economic Development member organizations were surveyed to identify current managerial beliefs and actions concerning work force and industrial relations issues. The survey was administered at two levels within each corporation. First, corporate staff personnel were asked to provide a general overview of the corporation's industrial relations policies and practices and a list of productivity programs used within the organization. Second, to better understand the productivity process at the operating level, plant personnel were asked to identify restraints to increased productivity in the workplace.

These responses, coupled with field interviews and an extensive review of information from other sources, provided the basis for the following analyses and conclusions. This chapter is divided into three major sections: the problem or restraint side of the subject, positive programs used by companies to improve productivity, and a discussion of several strategies for tackling the challenging task of increasing productivity on a comprehensive and continuing basis.

## AN ANALYSIS OF PRODUCTIVITY RESTRAINTS

There are various ways to organize the extensive list of productivity restraints cited over the years in the literature and the popular press. It is

**Table 6-1. Productivity Restraints Identified by Survey Respondents**

| | Number of Times Identified as a Restraint |
|---|---|
| *Resistance to change* | |
| Worker or supervisor resistance to change[a] | 43 |
| First-line supervisory resistance | 2 |
| Adapting to change | 1 |
| Uncertainty of change | 1 |
| *Motivation* | |
| Absenteeism[a] | 37 |
| Attitudes | 4 |
| Work ethic | 1 |
| Union-management relationship | 1 |
| *Work rules* | |
| Subcontracting[a] | 21 |
| Crew size[a] | 19 |
| Seniority[a] | 30 |
| Contractual restraints or work rules | 11 |
| *Paid time off* | |
| Paid time off[a] | 34 |
| *Government regulations* | |
| OSHA regulations[a] | 25 |
| Other government regulations | 5 |
| *Business conditions* | |
| Limited resource dollars | 8 |
| Volume | 2 |
| Lack of sufficient information systems | 1 |
| Product complexity | 1 |
| Behind in technical improvements or equipment design | 3 |
| *Training* | |
| Insufficient training programs | 5 |
| Lack of technical personnel | 2 |
| *Other* | |
| Outdated incentive pay systems | 1 |
| Inability to perform time studies | 2 |
| Job security | 1 |
| Work stoppages | 1 |
| Overtime | 1 |
| Turnover | 1 |

[a] Restraints listed on questionnaire.

important to remember that many restraints have been around for some time and that therefore unless a particular condition has intensified, it cannot by itself explain the recent downward trend in productivity.

As part of our data-gathering program, we asked management at the plant or operating level to describe and rank the various inhibitors or restraints on greater productivity. Because of the manner in which we framed the questions about productivity at the operating level and the fact that the questionnaire was completed by management concerned with day-to-day results, the responses focused primarily on the short run. Table 6-1 summarizes the types of productivity inhibitors cited by the respondents.

Our survey identified three major areas that concern today's manager: motivational problems, resistance to change, and work rules.[1] Motivational issues usually affect the individual directly, whereas resistance to change and work rules more often affect the group or organization. Actually, resistance to change and work rules are two sides of the same coin. For a variety of reasons, workers develop norms and customary practices (work rules) to increase predictability. One of their roles is to put into concrete form the desire of the work group to maintain the status quo—in other words, to resist change.

**Resistance to Change**

Our survey respondents ranked resistance to change as the number-one restraint. This was true for almost all demographic groups (e.g., large and small, unorganized and unionized plants). Although outright opposition to new technology appears to have declined from about 30 percent of responses in a 1976 Conference Board survey[2] to approximately 5 percent of our respondents, workers and their union representatives are still cautious about accepting new technology. The establishment of new classifications, duties, shift arrangements, and the like required by new technology arouses substantially more opposition and even outright resistance to change. In other words, the new technology itself is not resisted, but it is difficult to bring the social organization into line with its requirements. This appears to be the case for both supervisory and nonexempt employees.

*Aggravating Factors*
Among possible explanations for the inability of organizations to realize their full production potential because of resistance to change, we found several factors especially significant:

- The technical requirements have moved ahead of the human capabilities of the organization. It has been suggested that as more technology has been introduced into different industries, the ability of the work force to operate and maintain these sophisticated pieces of equipment has not kept pace.[3]

- Management has lost some of its effectiveness. This is especially true of the front-line supervisor, who plays a crucial role in keeping a system operating efficiently. This problem involves training and the shift in authority away from the supervisor to staff groups and, in some instances, to autonomous work groups. Hence, there is a conflict between the advantages of involving workers in the solving of problems and the role and competence of the supervisor achieving and maintaining performance throughout the system.

- The measurement and reward systems used by American corporations overemphasize short-run competitiveness. This often leads to conflict or competition within a company. This lack of coordination and communication can prove costly to both the firm and the economy.

## Motivational Issues

Motivation, or its absence, is a subject often associated with an alleged decline in the American work ethic. When comparing American and Japanese workers, many writers assert that there is a difference in commitment or loyalty to the job or firm. It is believed by many that today's worker represents a new breed that brings a different mix of needs and expectations to the workplace.

Labor economists use the concept of *withdrawal of supply*, not just in the form of quitting but also in the form of absenteeism and low commitment (i.e., a reduction of energy and effort applied to the task at hand). One form of behavior most frequently cited as a symptom of motivational problems is excessive absenteeism. As can be seen in Table 6-1, absenteeism was the second most frequently mentioned productivity inhibitor. There is no firm evidence that absenteeism has increased over the past decade, although a number of industries indicate that their rates are in the double-digit range, whereas rates that have historically been considered normal were around 3 or 4 percent. Because absenteeism is unplanned, it makes it difficult for management to make preparations to keep operations running smoothly.

Quality problems are another manifestation of low commitment. Indeed, quality needs to be emphasized as a dimension of the productivity problem because it is not reasonable to emphasize mere quantity of output if quality is thereby sacrificed.

Research about the connection between motivation and productivity has produced a wide range of conclusions, and many authorities maintain there is no relationship. That is, they believe that high productivity can be achieved even where motivation is poor if management can extract performance either through its choice of technology or through close supervision. However, it is our feeling that there is a direct connection between motivation and absenteeism and also between motivation and the dedication of workers to quality.

*Causes of the Motivational Problem*
If the motivational restraint has contributed to the recent productivity slowdown, in what sense has it intensified? One answer may be a weakening of the links between performance and pay. The hypothesis is that when more pay is awarded on a basis unrelated to performance, the motivation to apply oneself is weakened. A major contributing factor is inflation; nominal wages and salaries are raised by cost-of-living clauses and other arrangements, such as annual adjustment programs, that, for the most part, award pay increases on an across-the-board basis. In addition, compression of wage differentials between skilled and unskilled jobs has lessened the recognition and pride associated with craft occupations.

Another possibility involves so-called new values. It is asserted by many people that more weight is now put on leisure and on enjoying the "good life." To the extent that this is true, there may be a conflict between the values that emphasize leisure and activities outside work and the requirements coming from new technology that make it imperative to have a work force available on a three-shift basis and, in some instances, on weekends as well.

**Work Rules**

Time and time again, company respondents indicated that one of the serious productivity inhibitors is the way in which work is organized and the difficulties encountered in deploying workers effectively throughout the enterprise. This very broad subject can be broken into at least three categories: first, the quantity of labor that is utilized, sometimes referred to as the crew-size problem or the featherbedding question; second, the division of work into the separate classifications or craft lines; and third, the deployment of labor among the range of occupations and classifications, which involves the conditions under which workers can be transferred, how overtime is allocated, whether extra shifts are utilized, and how workers are assigned to these opportunities.

*Industry Pattern of Restraints*
Certain industries, primarily those in which unions have been successful in organizing and where craft traditions have been strong, have been characterized by work-rule difficulties. Other industries, especially in

manufacturing, have not experienced the same dramatic productivity problems as the "craft" industries but still have work-rule problems. In these cases, the difficulties are not excess manning or rigid classification lines but, instead, deployment of labor.

*Magnitude of the Problem*

How great, in an economic sense, is the work-rules problem? Estimates for the construction industry range from a negative number (i.e., productivity is reportedly higher in the unionized than in the unorganized sector) to a high of about 25 percent of labor costs. A midrange estimate is a productivity loss of about 10 to 20 percent.[4]

It is our impression that there is less of a work-rule problem with respect to featherbedding and jurisdictional issues than was the case in the 1950s and 1960s. Respondents to the 1976 Conference Board survey ranked excessive manning as the number-one problem 41 percent of the time;[5] in our sample, the frequency had dropped to 31 percent. However, flexible deployment of labor appears to be much more of a problem today. Work rules guiding the deployment of labor were not much of a problem as long as the technology and production levels remained steady. However, with considerable economic and technical restructuring and fluctuating levels of activity, the rules that govern the human resource side of the organization eventually require revision. Most of the restrictions that are being modified in newly negotiated agreements involve the transfer of workers and the shifting of human resources to meet changing production requirements.

**Other Restraints**

One additional restraint, paid time off, also ranked high among our respondents. However, the distinction between this subject and absenteeism is rather ambiguous. Because of lack of questionnaire specificity, it is difficult to know whether respondents citing this restraint are referring to holidays, vacations, illness, or other personal paid time off. Therefore, we have assumed that many of the factors leading to increased absenteeism are also at play in increased paid time off.

The only other topic listed with some regularity was Occupational Safety and Health Administration (OSHA) regulations. However, this restraint is associated more with the increased cost of government regulations than with traditional industrial relations arrangements and therefore is outside the scope of this chapter.

**POSITIVE PROGRAMS**

Our survey revealed a multitude of efforts (see Table 6-2) but left us wondering whether there is any real focus to them. Are the programs really

**Table 6-2. Number of Times Specific Productivity Improvement Programs Were Mentioned by Survey Respondents**

| | Used by Corporation | Three Most Effective | Three Least Effective |
|---|---|---|---|
| Management methods | | | |
| Practices/tools | 13 | 8 | 1 |
| Job/organization redesign | 21 | 6 | 3 |
| Absenteeism control/employee assistance | 23 | 3 | 11 |
| Flexible hours | 16 | — | 8 |
| Training | 28 | 12 | — |
| Involvement | | | |
| Quality circles | 19 | 3 | 3 |
| Labor-management committees | 12 | 3 | 2 |
| Opinion survey | 17 | 1 | 8 |
| Communications program | 5 | 1 | — |
| Employee involvement | 6 | 4 | — |
| Reward systems | | | |
| Wage payment system | 14 | 6 | 2 |
| Awards/suggestion programs | 10 | 3 | 3 |
| Productivity bargaining | 8 | 2 | 2 |
| Technology | | | |
| Office automation | 25 | 4 | 5 |
| Manufacturing automation | 18 | 12 | — |
| Other new systems | 7 | 6 | — |

addressing those issues that have been identified as the major inhibitors of productivity growth? Or are they simply scattershot efforts to fix short-term crises? Within the range of productivity improvement programs, some are quite traditional (management methods); others, relatively new (quality of work). Some are results-oriented (productivity bargaining); others emphasize process (communication).

**Management Methods, Measurements, and Analyses**

The programs most frequently mentioned by our survey respondents can be grouped under the heading of management methods, measurement, and analyses. We have chosen to look only at those we believe to be new trends that appear to play a role in improving productivity.

*Productivity Coordination*
One of the most visible areas of emphasis is productivity measurement and control. Over the past several years, many large corporations have established a position of "productivity czar," a person responsible for

monitoring overall productivity growth for the corporation and instilling productivity awareness throughout it.

There is also widespread introduction or revision of corporate productivity measurements. Several corporations are using or developing multifactor techniques that may be described as *total-factor productivity measurements*. However, most continue to use traditional forms of labor productivity measurement, such as worker-hours per unit, units per employee, or revenue per employee. Whatever the measurement, increased emphasis and extensive communication campaigns have led to an enhanced sensitivity to productivity.

*Extension of Scientific Management to New Areas*

A number of white-collar industries have begun to utilize scientific management techniques previously used only in blue-collar areas. For example, the office industries, especially insurance and other large clerical companies, are extending the use of techniques such as work simplification and the establishment of time standards. This emphasis on traditional techniques involves some new labels and slants. For example, methods analysis, which also includes job simplification, is now approached with the philosophy of "work smarter, not harder." Rather than stressing only the techniques of scientific management, there is more emphasis on a harmonization of technical and social systems.

*Organizational Effectiveness*

In effectiveness analysis, staff people move through the organization asking such questions as: Should we be carrying out this particular function? Do we need to fill out these reports or send these letters? The second step of this process—namely, measuring standards and indicating how much work should be done by a particular person in a particular period of time—is now labeled *goal setting*, *management by objectives*, and *feedback of results*. Considerable behavioral knowledge is being applied to the process of setting goals, involving people, and providing them with "knowledge of results," which is believed to strengthen their motivation.

*Head-Count Management*

As a result of shrinking or stabilization of output levels in many industries, human resources management has shifted to emphasize reduction of the number of employees. Various techniques are brought to bear on this task. One common label is *head-count* management. It is often the function of methods analysis and work measurement to establish staffing levels needed by the organization for the relevant time period.

*Absenteeism Control*

Most of the survey respondents said they had programs to control absenteeism, yet many listed them as their *least* effective effort. Some would argue that this problem is a sign of soft management practices, but its magnitude seems to indicate other underlying issues, such as changing work values and increased emphasis on leisure or family time.

Some companies are addressing the problem by improving or updating traditional systems, such as record keeping. Others are emphasizing assistance to employees with physical or emotional problems, such as alcoholism, that affect job performance.

*Flexible Schedules*
The traditional configuration of employee work hours is giving way to flexible work patterns or schedules. It is estimated that at least 6 percent of the labor force is covered by some aspect of flextime.[6] However, our respondents were not particularly enthusiastic about the benefits of flexible hours. When mentioned, it was usually included as one of the three least effective productivity programs. Other variations on this theme are the three- or four-day workweek and weekend shifts.

## Human Resource Development

From an industrial relations perspective, there has been a major change in the structure and importance of the activities related to relations with people. In the past this was viewed primarily as a maintenance task, assisting in union relations and the recruitment and compensation of the work force. However, many of these tasks now are classed under a new title, *human resource management*, which has been elevated to the top of the organizational hierarchy.

A major emphasis in this new activity is training and development. Twenty-eight of the twenty-nine corporations responding to our survey identified training as one of their productivity improvement programs, and twelve listed it as one of their three most effective programs. However, actual cost-benefit analyses of these efforts are difficult to conduct. The consensus is that training is important and that only through increased knowledge and awareness of the basics of the business on the part of the work force will organizations be able to improve productivity.

Several factors have focused attention on training: First, increasingly sophisticated technology requires more highly trained workers. Second, the Japanese have shown how important this critical ingredient is in achieving high productivity and high quality in manufacturing operations. Third, changing demographics of the American work force have put an additional strain on the education and assimilation of many of its new members.

In many respects, training can be viewed as a socialization process to educate new and current members of an organization in its particular way of doing things and helping to assure a desired level of organizational efficiency and productivity. Companies have found it necessary to institute special training programs and, in effect, to develop their own advanced apprenticeship programs. In a conceptual sense, the internal labor market is playing a much greater role relative to institutions of the external labor market, which have historically supplied talent through formal arrangements and craft referral systems. Such training comes in various forms: skills or apprentice training, short refresher courses, and entry or orientation programs.

*Skills Training*

Probably the most common type of training focuses on the acquisition of new skills to perform specific tasks in different areas or functions of an organization. In addition, many corporations are developing systemwide programs to update their employees' skills. There has also been a renewed interest in management development training seminars for middle- and executive-level managers to update their quantitative and analytic skills.

*Orientation and Cultural Training*

Another type of training is commonly described as "learning the company politics or culture." This is specifically important for new members of an organization, especially for minorities and women entering companies that have been traditionally all white and male, in order to be quickly accepted by the current employees and to be able to understand the jargon and ways of doing things within the organization.

This type of training often focuses on improving the quality of work life and enhancing employee participation. Most organizational development consultants stress the need for intensive training at all levels of the management hierarchy in order to change the culture or management style of an organization.

## Employee Involvement to Improve Productivity

Although empirical researchers have long argued about whether increased job satisfaction will lead to greater productivity, most practitioners believe intuitively that more involved workers are more productive workers. In many respects, this belief is helping to fuel the current efforts to enhance quality of work life and thereby the commitment of the work force. The responses to our survey mirror this growing interest.

Although a number of firms initially embarked on a quality-of-work-life program for reasons other than productivity (e.g., to improve employee-management relations or quality), they readily admit now that increased productivity has been a welcome by-product. Nevertheless, many of these

quality-of-work-life programs are still in their infancy, and serious evaluation of their effectiveness has just begun.

*Communications*
Although improved communications may be an end in itself, it is also a
prerequisite for more elaborate forms of involvement. Better-informed
employees are more knowledgeable. This, in turn, can result in greater
congruence of worker and organization goals, enhanced quality, and
improved productivity.

*Participation*
Many managers are beginning to recognize that their workers may know
more about some areas of shop-floor (or office) practices and procedures
than the engineers who initially designed the work or put it into place.
Various types of participation programs are being instituted to draw on this
knowledge: labor-management committees, technology agreements, quality control circles, and autonomous work groups.

*Labor-Management Committees.* A commonly used approach is a labor-
management committee that operates outside the adversarial atmosphere
of normal negotiations. Although this method dates back to the 1920s,
there has been limited enthusiasm for it in this country except in times of
national crisis such as World War II. Indeed, the establishment of
labor-management committees in the steel and automobile industries may
be attributed to their adverse economic environments. The hypothesis
underlying the committees is that through understanding the other's
problems, labor and management will increase goal congruence, reduce
grievances and work disruptions, and increase productivity. Where trade
unions are involved, both sides must agree to keep issues of conflict (e.g.,
wages and benefits) separate from those areas where the parties can work
together to create a better work environment and improve productivity.

*Technology Agreements.* The joining of labor and management efforts in
meeting the challenge of new technology has not gone as far in this country
as it has in some others, where labor and management have formulated
and agreed on principles governing how new technology will be introduced. Nevertheless, there are several important examples of cooperation
in this area. For instance, both General Motors and Ford Motor Company,
in conjunction with the United Auto Workers (UAW), have established
technological change committees. The purpose of such committees is to
ensure that the introduction of technology enhances the quality of work life
and that the unions and the workers are sufficiently informed and given a
chance to discuss the new technology's impact. With increased competitive
pressures in many industries, there is a greater awareness among union
leaders that technological change is necessary.

*Quality Control Circles.* Probably one of the most talked-about new programs is the quality control circle. The main reasons for the recent interest in these programs are their low cost and the ease with which managers can put them into practice. Quality circles were introduced in Japan after World War II to heighten the quality consciousness of the work force and train employees in statistical quality control analysis. In the United States, quality control circles have been adopted to increase participation of workers and to focus attention on increased quality and productivity.

Popular literature abounds with stories about companies that have obtained significant cost savings with the aid of such circles. Lockheed has claimed a savings of almost $3 million in two years, or a six-to-one return on investment.[7] A sample review of several companies cited in recent articles reveals that average annual savings were $56,700 per circle.[8] But these figures are quite misleading and ignore the short-term nature of the returns that have been achieved. Few companies have been able to sustain these returns for more than a year or so at best. In addition, several companies have invested heavily in starting a quality circle program and found they had to abort their efforts because of employee or union resistance. Unless there is a sincere commitment by management to listen to and follow through on employee suggestions as well as a high level of trust between employees and management, many employees will view the program as one more attempt at squeezing additional work out of them. In addition, many may fear a loss of job security for suggesting work improvements if no complementary employment guarantees are adopted.

*Autonomous Work Groups.* Probably the most revolutionary of the quality-of-work-life interventions are the autonomous or self-managing work groups. Their roots date back to the human relations school, which held that if jobs are enriched vertically, employees will be more satisfied and therefore more productive.

Success in the use of autonomous work groups requires significant changes in management style and practices, not only in work organizations but also in the delegation of responsibility and authority. Because many employees and managers have difficulty in such a transition, it is not surprising that many of the major successes in this area have occurred in new plants.

Establishment of autonomous work groups has caused a problem for American trade unions in that they eliminate many of the grievance issues arising out of management of the work force. There have been questions about the legality of such efforts in light of the loss of the distinction between managerial and nonmanagerial employees.[9] However, severe

economic pressures in many industries have led several unions to cooper-
ate in several such experiments.

### Guidelines for Quality-of-Work-Life Programs

Do quality-of-work-life programs produce truly long-term productivity
improvements or merely temporary ones? Any real success requires a
genuine change in management philosophy or style and a climate of trust
and respect between management and employees. Organizational development specialists who have designed such programs stress the need for
gradual change over the long term. Unfortunately, the pattern has more
often been a sequence of immediate short-term improvements, followed by
a tapering off and a return to previous states.

For a quality-of-work-life program to succeed, a number of key elements
are necessary:

- Management must relinquish its monopoly on knowledge. This may
  mean a loss of power and control, and the diffusion process will take
  time.

- Decisions will take longer to reach. This will be a function of both the
  added time needed to convey information to all decision makers and the
  slower process of group decision making.

- Considerable training and education will be required at all levels of the
  organization. This will cost both time and money.

- Top management must be prepared for the resistance that is likely to
  develop. It may become necessary to replace middle- or lower-level
  managers who are unable or unwilling to adopt the more participatory
  supervisory style.

All in all, this sort of activity is probably the fastest-growing of all
productivity enhancement efforts and the one receiving the most favorable
comments from employees. It will take time, though, because of the
long-term nature of programs, for anyone to be able to evaluate its total
benefits adequately.

To date, the most successful programs have focused on individual work
groups or specific projects (as opposed to the entire work force) in order to
create more immediate personal involvement. However, there still remains
the challenge of finding the right balance between traditional controls
(rules, policies, lines of authority, and ultimate responsibility for decision
making) and individual involvement and autonomy. Improving the work
environment by dressing up the workplace, providing a more benevolent
boss, or the adoption of prefabricated, "quick-fix" package programs will
not automatically lead to increased productivity. The key is the creation of

an environment in which all employees are motivated to do a more efficient and effective job.

## Wage Payment Systems

The way in which payment is related to performance has always been at the center of the productivity challenge. It seems clear that the future will bring more arrangements in which compensation is contingent on performance and results. This movement toward some increase in payment by results comes after several decades in which traditional incentive systems declined in use. In industry after industry, management, where it could, abandoned individual and small group incentives in favor of measured daywork.

But in the steady movement away from traditional incentives, some of the impetus and discipline that comes with any such system was lost. In effect, management found itself always looking over the shoulder of the worker. In many instances, measured day work has represented a coercive system with substantial reliance on discipline to ensure a fair day's work.

An often overlooked advantage of traditional incentive systems is that they foster a type of mutuality. Management and workers must agree on the methods and the price for the job; once this agreement is reached, the system can usually run itself. Indeed, the autonomy that is present with piecework incentives is in some ways similar to the autonomy that management is reaching for through teams and other group emphases.

The current picture of the use of various incentives rather than measured daywork is quite complicated. Some industries, such as steel, continue to make extensive use of traditional incentives and, if anything, appear to be applying them to all operations. Other industries are installing incentives for the first time.

### Gain Sharing

Most of the increased emphasis on contingency compensation is being focused on *gain-sharing* plans. Usually, the achieving unit adopted is the entire plant to emphasize teamwork and coordination. Often, rather than setting precise time standards, historical data are used, and the group is rewarded if it improves on past performance.

Although gain-sharing programs have received a lot of publicity, they have not yet been widely installed. Our best estimate is that there are between 500 and 1,000 large group productivity schemes installed at the plant level in the United States. Those who have used Scanlon, Rucker, and Improshare Plans tout their effectiveness, and there appears to be considerable interest in them. Recently, a fairly comprehensive study by the General Accounting Office concluded that, on average, they increased productivity about 17 percent, a healthy result.[10] However, given the dynamics of group efforts, if it appears that a decent bonus will not be forthcoming, the plan will not have any impact.

It is difficult to identify any pattern of utilization of gain-sharing plans. In some cases, they are installed in existing plants that have not used incentive systems before. In others, they replace traditional incentives and play the crucial role of picking up the slack after individual incentive systems have been abandoned.

### Profit Sharing

Conceptually, profit sharing has much to recommend it. It meets the test of market performance because bonuses are shared only if improved productivity has contributed to profits (which means that productivity growth in the company has exceeded that of the industry). Another advantage is that the standard for rewards is constantly adjusted by the test of the market.

Of course, profit sharing presents its own problems. Profits are affected by many things beyond the control of workers inside the organization, and consequently, such a plan may not meet the test of reliability or equity— namely, that additional worker contributions are rewarded with additional bonuses.

### Suggestion Systems

Suggestion systems have been on the scene for a long time, albeit in a quiet way. But with the growth of quality control circles, they are in the limelight. Although these two programs are conceptually different, some companies are combining them in an effort to stimulate worker motivation and ideas. More often, companies are just revitalizing their existing programs.

Approximately one-third of our survey companies have some type of formal, companywide suggestion program. However, only three companies listed suggestion systems as one of their three most effective productivity programs. For those companies that provided result information, the savings per employee averaged about $50 a year. Obviously, suggestion systems help but do not have big payoffs.

A recent study of Japanese suggestion systems indicated that in 1980, they experienced a suggestion rate of 12.8 suggestions per employee.[11] On a very limited comparison base, our survey indicated a yearly rate of approximately 0.125 suggestions per employee. However, select success stories in this country can be found to surpass the Japanese rates. Consider an illustration from the IBM Corporation that has taken methods-improvement training one step further than most companies. At its Lexington, Kentucky, office products plant, it undertook to train all employees in methods improvement. The results were impressive. The number of suggestions accepted by the company increased from 500 in the base year to 2,600 three years later. Three out of four employees turned in suggestions, and the employees received $270,000 in awards for savings produced of over $1 million. The facility has been regarded as one of their most productive.[12]

Indeed, there is nothing resembling consensus on the effectiveness of suggestion systems. A significant number (one-third) of survey respondents did not have formal programs, and the decision not to have a program was, in several cases, based on experience or research.

## Productivity Bargaining

Although productivity bargaining was not mentioned by a large number of our respondents, we believe it deserves some discussion, especially in light of the current economic environment.

The essence of productivity bargaining is the realignment of the work organization with technology and operating requirements. Often a firm's internal organization remains intact while external circumstances change. Productivity bargaining helps achieve a better match between the work organization, the deployment of the workers, and the technological requirements of the operation.

The history of work organizations appears to be an ebb and flow between specialization and flexibility. Productivity bargaining is a means for helping the shift from one to the other. In some respects, the important event is change itself, rather than the particular work organization being introduced, because it gives the company an opportunity to sweep out the old.

In view of the current attention to "give-backs" and other efforts to save jobs through concession bargaining, it is not surprising that a number of the agreements contain significant changes in work rules aimed at improving productivity. One of the clearest indications that productivity bargaining is being practiced on a reasonably wide basis is the fact that the recent settlements in the automobile industry have major provisions dealing with changes in work rules. A variety of studies also indicate that workers and their union representatives are now quite receptive to use of the collective bargaining process to discuss the subject of productivity, which would have been unthinkable a few years ago.[13] About a quarter of the corporations that we surveyed have made use of productivity bargaining.

It is useful to compare productivity bargaining with other methods for adaptation of the work organization. Certainly, technological change by itself provides an opportunity to sweep out the old and bring in the new. When a new generation of technology is involved, management may not need productivity bargaining to rearrange the work organization. However, in most situations, the magnitude of technological change at any one time is not sufficiently dramatic to provide the basis for completely redesigning the work organization. For example, in the case of automobiles, even with the introduction of robots and other new technology, such things as craft demarcation, limitations on transferring workers across department lines, and inappropriate shift arrangements remain in place and can be changed only through mutual consent. Thus, in most cases, management is required to bargain to achieve changes rather than using new technology or a major reorganization.

Productivity bargaining tends to be more specific than quality-of-work-life programs and tends to focus on changes that can be identified in negotiations. In this sense, it is focused in time and is not an open-ended agenda for change. It involves two phases: first, the identification of and (with relevant parties) agreement on the desired changes and, second, the adoption of these changes.

### Types of Changes
Several categories of changes in work rules are dealt with in productivity bargaining: crew size or manning decisions, work jurisdiction (e.g., craft lines), and the deployment of labor (overtime, transfer, and seniority rights). Since crew size problems are not as prevalent today as they were ten or fifteen years ago, for the most part, the changes reached through productivity bargaining fall into the second and third categories.

*Work jurisdiction* often involves craft demarcation lines. Several examples from our survey capture the flavor of the changes being made in this area.

• A large oil company has introduced the concept of *zone operator*, a person who is responsible for all the operations as well as maintenance. When maintenance activities are necessary, they are performed by a refinery mechanic, a person possessing a range of skills, rather than a traditional set of craft skills.

• A large auto parts company has achieved one classification for all craftsmen.

• A company in the electrical equipment industry commented: "We have combined all trade crafts, such as bricklayer, carpenter, heavy equipment operator, into a single job description. Thereby, we eliminated the need for several crafts in order to complete a project."

*Deployment of workers* involves flexibility in the assignment of workers in terms of both space and time. With respect to space, several agreements have enhanced management's ability to shift workers, as the Japanese do, to operating areas where their services are needed. The emphasis is on increasing the ability of management to deploy labor at its discretion and to reduce worker-initiated moves such as requests for transfer.

The ability to move workers to different operations is enhanced by simplifying the classification systems that have grown up in many organizations. One company commented that it had reduced 125 job promotion steps to 39 and correspondingly had reduced the number of job descriptions from 480 to 169 jobs. Because the job classifications carry more components, there is a greater likelihood that workers can be assigned to different tasks.

Another aspect of work force flexibility is scheduling overtime. More companies are insisting on mandatory overtime and flexibility in deciding who works the extra hours (i.e., they are abandoning the strict use of seniority in allocating overtime). Some changes in hours and scheduling are quite minor; others can have significant productivity implications. For example, a large electronics company indicated that it has arranged shifts so that they overlap by ten minutes, thereby substantially increasing contact and coordination.

## EMPLOYMENT CONTINUITY

The effect of job insecurity on productivity is not as observable as those of other inhibitors,[14] such as lack of motivation and restrictive work rules, but it is pervasive—a fundamental force either dragging productivity down or enabling it to reach its natural level. Over time, workers develop expectations about the degree of job security inherent in a given employment relationship. Unemployment may be part of the situation, as is the case in craft industries and many manufacturing operations, where workers are laid off subject to recall. That kind of insecurity can be taken in stride, with no serious consequences for productivity. Indeed, some workers may prefer this alternation of work and respite. The labor market can be viewed as offering jobs with different patterns of income and leisure and workers with different preferences. The workers and the job characteristics sort themselves out, so that a given pattern of work and unemployment may be quite acceptable to a particular group of workers. Thus, layoffs in and of themselves are not dysfunctional.

The problem develops when expectations change for the worse, usually as a result of market developments. If workers believe that their plant may be shut down, or if a large group of workers feels vulnerable to permanent layoff, productivity will be adversely affected. Under such circumstances, certain costs and problems arise. Turnover usually increases substantially. The people who leave voluntarily tend to be the younger workers with more job opportunities. There is a substantial drop in morale throughout the organization. The workers do not know just who will be selected, and there is great uncertainty and malaise during the period of waiting and wondering. Greenhalgh and McKersie found that the announcement of impending cutbacks reduces productivity by a minimum of 2 percent.[15]

Analysis of our survey responses indicates that when corporate policies for handling excess workers are correlated with restraints on a plant-by-plant basis, a strong relationship is found between use of layoffs (in contrast with attrition) and impediments to productivity such as resistance to change and absenteeism. The implication is that if a company could modify its policies to avoid layoffs, some of these detrimental effects would be reduced.

When unions are involved, the rule of seniority serves to protect most workers against layoffs; and in this sense, it is a device that helps to immunize senior workers from the fear that they will be affected by partial shutdowns. However, if the specter of a total shutdown looms (as is the case in a number of industries today), a change in expectations will affect all workers.

### Guidelines for Program Principles

Management can take advantage of the insecurity involved in any employment relationship and use it as a constructive force for improvement of productivity, thereby enhancing the job security of the enterprise. An approach that acknowledges the existence of some job insecurity informs and motivates everyone to improve the viability of the enterprise over the longer run. The objective is to take an *offensive* position, rather than to react defensively and possibly retaining jobs in the short run but in the long run jeopardizing the very viability of the enterprise.

It is better to reduce the size of the work force by attrition than by layoffs, so long as the cutback is not large and the transition period is no longer than a year. Of course, the principle of attrition has to be reconciled with economic realities. If the displacement of workers is of such magnitude that the carrying time and costs would be prohibitive, attrition is not a reasonable policy.

Another principle, and one that facilitates the attrition strategy, is the active redeployment of workers from declining divisions to divisions that have openings. For this to succeed, workers must be willing to undergo training, to acquire new skills, and possibly even to be transferred geographically. The worker is not guaranteed a particular job, but is assured of employment with the company or, more specifically, an opportunity or an alternative if the current position must be terminated.

Several arrangements can facilitate redeployment. There may be periods when the size of the excess complement is such that some type of *work sharing* is needed until attrition takes up the slack or an increase in volume of operations occurs. Redeployment is also made easier by the absence of the sharp jurisdictional lines that may arise under craft unions. For example, German companies have been able to manage work force transitions more easily than U.S. companies because of the prevalence of industrial unions that represent all workers rather than multiple unions at the plant level, as is very much the case in Britain and to some extent in the United States.

These programs and principles require considerable expertise in human resource management. Unfortunately, too many companies lack the technical knowledge about the human side of the enterprise and move ahead with changes only to find they are faced with substantial costs they never anticipated. The role of human resource planning management is critical in minimizing the disruption and deterioration of productivity during periods of economic change.

It is also important to recognize that an occasional separation of workers may have a very beneficial effect on the organization, increasing productivity to the extent that the employees who have been let go are marginal. If seniority rules do not have to be strictly adhered to, it may be possible for a company to weed out the weak members.

**A Balanced Perspective**

The objective of employment security is much more feasible as a facilitating condition for productivity bargaining or quality-of-work-life programs than it is for a major restructuring involving a substantial shift of production facilities. Employment security needs to be kept in perspective; if it becomes a primary objective, it can prevent economic restructuring and the changes that will lead to much greater productivity in the long run. What is needed is a proper balance between economic change and cushioning of the consequences for the workers involved.

The balance to be achieved depends on the extent and pace of economic restructuring. If the restructuring is selective and can be accomplished over a period of several years, the German approach makes considerable sense. However, if the change is widespread and rapid, as has been the case in several U.S. manufacturing industries, the U.S. system of severing workers may be preferable, even though there are substantial short-run costs.

**STRATEGIC PERSPECTIVES**

A very fundamental mismatch appears to exist between the restraints identified by our survey respondents as key reasons for the productivity problem (Table 6-1) and the programs (Table 6-2) that they indicated are proving most effective. The major contributory influences to the productivity slowdown are all connected with change and restructuring. The motivational problem, as exemplified by increased absenteeism, can be attributed to changed work force demographics and values. Similarly, the pervasiveness of work-rule problems stems from the fact that most industries are undergoing important changes in organization and technology. Work rules that may not be especially troublesome in a stable situation are very troublesome when updating and modernizing become necessary. Resistance to change is the best example of the fact that productivity problems emerge from the inability of an organization to adapt to a new environment. This is true whether we are talking about the impact of economic pressures or the labor market and a new breed of employees.

It is important, therefore, to ponder the mismatch between these themes of change on the problem side and the oft-mentioned business-as-usual programs on the action side. The prevalence of such productivity improvement programs as management methods and wage-payment systems suggests that in many organizations management is resorting preponderantly to traditional means. The emphasis on technology and training suggests that programs that help the organization adapt *are* in the picture. Nevertheless, the overall impression on the action side of the survey is that the programs are not responsive to the basic needs of most organizations. This is best illustrated by absenteeism, which ranked as a top restraint but among the least effective programs. Companies are experiencing increased absenteeism because of a changed milieu and work force; yet their response is to use fairly traditional carrot-and-stick arrangements, and these are not proving very helpful.

One of the reasons for this mismatch is the tendency of U.S. business to respond to a crisis by looking for ready-made solutions, such as quality circle programs, rather than probing more deeply into structure, strategy, and process. The productivity problem has been a long time in the making and consequently programmatic responses here and there are unlikely to make very much of a difference. We believe that fundamental changes in outlook, policy, and strategy are required.

## Levels of Analysis

In this section, we look at three levels of organization—the industry, the plant, and the work group—and at three issues—technology and investment (rationalization), the design of work structures (harmonization), and the development of high commitment (intensification) (Table 6-3).

### Productivity Payoffs

The question of what the potential payoffs are at the different levels of

**Table 6-3. Levels of Strategic Analysis**

|  | Industry | Plant | Individual or Small Group |
|---|---|---|---|
| Theme | Rationalization of capital resources | Harmonization of work structure | Intensification of human resources |
| Major options | Green-field versus retrofit | Productivity bargaining, buy-out, or organizational change | Involvement programs versus administrative change |
| Impetus | Changes in technology, world-wide economic changes | Competitive factors | New values and demographics |
| Productivity potential | Large; shift in capital-labor ratio | Moderate; elimination of inefficiency | Moderate; elimination of $x$-inefficiency |
| Model system | Germany | United States | Japan |

analysis is not easy to answer. A whole host of factors come into play, including the rate of technological change, availability of investment, and cultural characteristics. We believe that the greatest promise in the long run lies in industry-wide developments in the form of new capital investment, especially in those industries that have a heavy technological base. In some industries, a whole new generation of technology has been introduced within five or six years, and productivity has improved several-fold. Next in order of importance is the design of the appropriate work organization so that over a period of several years, productivity may be improved between 30 and 40 percent. (This estimate is derived by comparing the effect of different work organizations with similar technology among comparable plants.)[16] At the individual and small-group level, the contribution is smallest, in the range of 10 or 20 percent, which is the margin usually assumed to be available if workers can be motivated to the utmost through some type of incentive or gain-sharing system.

Of course, the fact that a payoff is possible does not mean that it is easily obtainable. If sufficient capital is not available to permit new technology to be exploited, the expected value from the highest level of decision making with respect to new plants and new technology may be relatively low compared with that from eliminating outmoded work rules or installing a program for the involvement of workers. In other words, when the feasibility side is taken into consideration, it is not clear without specifying other particulars which strategic level of action will yield the most cost-effective results.

**Distinctive Connection of Industrial Relations**

We see more and more labor-management relationships moving in the collaborative direction under the influence of the Japanese model and as a result of the pressures of the current economic environment. One of the concepts that links a collaborative relationship with work rules and investment strategy is *job investment bargaining*. Through a process of labor management consultation (generally not formal bargaining), the parties agree on a package committing additional investment to the existing operation in exchange for improvements in productivity such as the elimination of onerous work rules or ineffective incentives and employment of labor on a round-the-clock basis in order to utilize fully the capital involved. The approach is not full-fledged codetermination, but unions are very much involved in discussing investment decisions and their implications for employment and the long-run survival of the firm.

Employment continuity facilitates the integrative linkage. Here, the broad alternatives are the view of labor as a variable cost to be hired and let go as needed or, instead, as an asset to be recruited, trained, and redeployed within the enterprise. Given the stimulus of the Japanese model, more firms have been considering the concept of career employment and enhancing job security for their workers. Such an approach can eliminate some of the resistance to change that is inevitable when workers worry about their jobs in the face of new technology. In turn, the new technology and a commitment to invest in the operations (especially at existing locations) can enhance the economic viability of the enterprise and, consequently, job security.

## Rationalization

*Rationalization* is a term frequently used in Europe to describe the process of restructuring the physical facilities of a business. The process usually sweeps through an entire industry because of technological developments or cost influences that lead to a shift in the worldwide deployment of manufacturing facilities. This broad subject involves many different kinds of investment decisions. We will consider only the movement of facilities to a new location instead of the modernization of existing facilities and the relationship of these two options to industrial relations considerations.

### New Is Better

Resistance to change, a fundamental problem, is a function of the age of facilities. Apparently, an aging or ossification process takes place in most enterprises, so that over time the organization loses its adaptability. This may be attributable to the accumulation of tradition or the aging of the work force or some combination of these factors. This process takes place regardless of whether a union is on the scene.

An obvious response to this fact of life is for companies to abandon the old and to emphasize the new. The establishment of a new plant also gives a company the opportunity to choose the type of social system (i.e., organization and job structure) it would like to institute. Many companies are installing participative, open systems in their new plants and deriving impressive results.

Considerable publicity has been given to the advantages of moving to a green-field site, and a number of studies document the higher productivity achieved when a plant is started from scratch with the latest technology and a brand-new work force. Here are a few examples.

- A large tobacco company has parallel operations, one in a large urban area and another in a rural area of the South. The southern operation is just several years old while the urban operation has been at its location for decades. Productivity at the southern operation is about twice what it is at the older, urban location. Some of the differences are explained by very modern equipment, some by worker flexibility—operators at the southern plant do much more adjustment work to operating equipment and craftsmen perform as "all-around" mechanics at the new plant. However, state-of-the-art machinery and the need to keep this sophisticated equipment operating smoothly does require a higher ratio of supervisors and technicians to operators.

- For a large company in the electrical equipment industry, the productivity advantage of a new plant is 20 percent over its "mother" plant. In this case, both are located in the North, with one (the older plant) in a heavily industrialized area and the new plant in a rural location.

- In an example from an automobile company, the productivity difference between a newer plant in the South and one in the North (older operation) is approximately 20 percent. The newer plant is using team concepts, as well as exploiting the latest in advanced technology.

- A large company engaged in the manufacture of aircraft engines has compared productivity between an older, urban operation and a newer rural operation. The first is unionized and the second is not. In this case, productivity is 16 percent better in the nonunion operation, primarily because absenteeism is only 3 to 4 percent, whereas it is double that level at the older operation. There is also a difference in capital and technology, so that it is not a straightforward matter to credit the motivational factor as the sole influence responsible for the productivity difference.

*Advantages of Mature Plants*
The experience inherent in an old plant may facilitate better system performance than that in a new plant because the "teething period" of a new plant may be quite long, especially if sophisticated new technology is required. Here are two examples.

- A large semi conductor company calculates that its productivity is as good as that of its competitors that have been on the scene for only the past decade. This company is heavily unionized, while its competitors generally are nonunion. It achieves its good performance through very sophisticated manufacturing engineering that makes the production process very reliable. The work force is quite senior, very sophisticated, and very well trained.

- One of our case studies revealed a very interesting comparison between a new operation in the South, unorganized, and an older operation in the North, unionized, both producing similar products. In this instance, productivity is higher in the North. This is explained by an older, well-seasoned work force; whereas in the South the work force is inexperienced, and there is considerable turnover (in some years) amounting to 50 percent. The manufacturing facility in the North would be characterized as *low-motivation* (there is substantial absenteeism)—however, there is high attachment (only about 5 percent turnover; and after a long strike virtually every worker returned to his job) and many *work rules* for the deployment of labor (no mandatory overtime and rigid application of seniority for transfers). By contrast, the operation in the South involves much more flexible deployment of labor (there are no union rules), but the advantages of flexibility are not enough to offset the human capital disadvantages of a very transient work force that is not highly trained.

## *Summary of the Alternatives*

There are both advantages and disadvantages to each of the two alternatives—construction of a new plant and retrofitting of an old one. Certainly, the establishment of a new operation may result in higher productivity, precisely because it puts new arrangements into place and squeezes out much of the old. The opportunity for new beginnings will always be salutary, and it will be especially invigorating if motivation and work-rule problems can be shed along with the old plant.

The two alternatives involve different cultures. The established system is running, the work force trained, and it has a certain momentum going for it. In contrast, the new plant provides the opportunity to shape a new culture and to generate the enthusiasm that comes with new beginnings. Whether the new culture will gradually evolve so that in fifteen or twenty years it will have some of the same characteristics as the culture of existing plants is difficult to determine (and a question to which research should be directed).

A number of other considerations and developments play a part in choosing the strategically better alternative.

*Technology.*    Clearly, technology exerts an important influence on the choice in two areas: site flexibility and the nature of the new generation of technology. For some types of technology (e.g., in the steel industry) the reinvestment needs to be carried out at existing locations;[17] for others (e.g., in the electronics industry), the green-field alternative is feasible. In between (e.g., in the automobile and rubber industries), there may be advantages to locating plants adjacent to existing plants but they are not decisive.[18] When new technology is limited to existing facilities because of former investment, these capital decisions are made without regard to the industrial relations situation at a particular site. In some cases, the relationship may actually be perverse. One of the companies we surveyed recently decided on a major expansion of one of its large Chicago-area chemical plants, despite very bad labor relations, because of the asset base already in place and the need for greater capacity for the Midwest market.

If the nature of the new technology is very different from the existing technology, that fact may dictate the choice of the green-field alternative. However, if the new technology represents refinements of the existing equipment, that leads in the direction of the retrofit option.

*Availability of Funds.*   The choice between a new site and the upgrading of an existing site is not so one-sided as it was for most of the 1960s and 1970s. Given the high cost of capital (and assuming a new site requires more capital), corporations are looking much more carefully at what portion of existing operations can be upgraded. Quite significantly, a number of respondents volunteered the information that limited capital resources were holding back productivity. The ideas were available, but the funds were not forthcoming from corporate capital budgets. In such cases, the retrofit choice is preferable to the green-field option.

*Industrial Relations Considerations.*   The development of concession bargaining (and the linkage of work-rule changes to new investment) has introduced a new element into the picture. In a number of situations recently, a direct link has been established between changes in operating practices and the willingness of a company to invest a substantial sum of money to enhance the competitive position of the plant (job-investment bargaining). Given the shockwaves that have gone through the manufacturing sector, there appears to be a much greater willingness to get rid of old arrangements and freshen up the atmosphere via productivity bargaining, quality-of-work-life programs, and labor-management committees. An existing operation has many assets, not the least of which are an experienced work force and routines that are familiar and easily maintained.

*Avoiding the Status Quo*
The option of allowing operations to drift should be avoided. The age range of many of the plants in our survey was between fifteen and forty years. As we just noted, a number of these plants reported that they were unable to secure needed resources from corporate capital budgeting programs to modernize their operations. It would appear that many plants in manufacturing have been allowed to deteriorate slowly. The plant and equipment are fully amortized, and as long as there is demand for the product, the establishment is kept in existence. The work force may also be aging along with the equipment because new hiring has ceased.

This strategy produces two problems for productivity: First, it suffers directly because plant and equipment are not modernized and the establishment does not derive any benefits from a new generation of equipment. Second, the work force, aware of the gradual deterioration, often adopts a fatalistic attitude and coasts until retirement or until the plant is finally shut down.

**Harmonization**

The strategy of putting up-to-date plant and equipment in place creates circumstances conducive to the design of an appropriate work structure. Harmonizing the work organization with the technological and organizational environment of a plant involves the heart of what most people perceive as the major connection between industrial relations and productivity: the work-rule problem.

Certainly, rules and traditions develop regardless of whether a union is present. For example, a rule for deciding how to deploy workers often emerges in a nonunion plant; one large electronics company said that it used seniority for overtime allocation in filling jobs even in its nonunion plants. Although the principle of seniority often prevails in a nonunion operation, it is usually easier for management to make exceptions. Another consideration is that even if work rules and the division of labor are fairly well developed in a nonunion operation, these rules are probably easier to alter as conditions change.

To some extent, the claims by management that nonunion plants are more efficient than their union plants overestimates the true effect. Management attempts to relate productivity results to the absence of unions, but these plants also happen to be new plants with newly recruited (often from rural labor markets) and newly trained workers. All these influences enhance productivity, and the presence or absence of a union may actually be a minor consideration. Other important questions are pertinent. What would productivity be like if the new plant were located in an urban area? What will productivity be like in some of these plants in fifteen or twenty years, after the inevitable aging process has taken place?

Fortunately, we can disentangle the effects of age and union status that are associated with the establishment of a new plant. On the basis of our statistical analysis of the survey data, we have concluded that the productivity benefit derived from a new plant (unionized or not) is two or three times greater than the effect of eliminating formal work rules. The restraint that is most closely associated with age is resistance to change, which occurs uniformly among plants, regardless of union representation.

Resistance to change has a substantial effect on productivity because it holds up the introduction of new technology. Work rules impede productivity, but the effect amounts to only about 15 or 20 percent at any one time, and it is not of the magnitude of twofold or threefold increases that can be obtained with a new generation of equipment. Thus, we conclude that the effect of unions on productivity is not so detrimental as management assumes.

## Conclusions

Our general conclusion about the productivity effect is that it is possibly detrimental but varies greatly with the particular context and the imperatives of change. The possibly adverse (minor) effect of unions on productivity must be viewed from other perspectives. First, in many situations, a company is not able to do very much about the issue of union representation because this is ultimately an employee decision. Second, the adverse effect of collective bargaining on productivity can be reversed. The possibility that collective bargaining can benefit productivity is receiving substantial testing as a result of concession bargaining, labor-management committees, and joint economic forums.

## Intensification

At the level of the individual and the small group, many companies face the strategic necessity of increasing the intensification of human resources, that is, the commitment of the work force. In a very basic way, the human side of the organization can be thought of as an asset that can be developed and enhanced, achieving, in effect, an increase in social capital. The problem or restraint side is lack of commitment (e.g., absenteeism). On the program or positive side are the strategies of involvement and stimulation of the organization's capacity to handle change.

### Strategy of Involvement

It is helpful at this point to trace the evolution of the worker involvement movement. The industrial relations system and its legal framework are based on a belief that managers make decisions and direct the work force, and workers follow those directions. If the workers disagree, they can initiate grievance proceedings after they have performed the assignment. This framework fits well with the growth of scientific management because it was assumed that managers and professional engineers knew best how work should be done. But recent Japanese and European successes with participative management programs have led American managers to take a second look at this rigid distinction between the managers and the managed. In addition, the new work force demographics and values are forcing managers to question the worth of autocratic decision making.

These developments have introduced industrial democracy in the form of employee involvement. The underlying logic is that increased involvement will lead to increased commitment or identification with the company and personal pride in the product. Although this is really not a new approach in terms of eliciting good managerial attitudes and behavior, it is revolutionary in that it is pushing this belief down through the organization to involve nonmanagerial employees. It can be viewed as a basic philosophical realignment in American industry toward a belief in *human* capital instead of labor; that is, investment in the quality of labor, not only devoted to a worker's skill, but also in the worker's knowledge and understanding of the product, process, and workplace. In its purest sense, it is a return to the basics of talking and listening and improved communication between employers and employees.

This involvement has taken a variety of forms. Initial experiments involved from-the-top-down humanization by managers in the form of changing management style or the design of jobs to enrich or enlarge them. More recently, there has been more of a move toward an emphasis on from-the-bottom-up or jointly initiated and designed programs.

The interest in quality-of-life programs and other devices for involving workers must be seen as an attempt to reverse the poor industrial relations/poor bottom line combination. The fact that most of the quality-of-work-life effort has not made much of an impact only reflects the difficulty of changing a culture that strongly reinforces itself.

Another reason involvement does not take readily is that the new industrial relations system is viewed by many as a direct attack on managerial authority and status. Even the reward system is questioned. It used to be that hard work led to a promotion, which meant more dollars, more authority and control, and a higher position in the hierarchy. But today, authority or control must be shared extensively with subordinates.

*The Adaptable Organization*

Essentially, the purpose of increasing commitment or the intensification of the labor supply is not just to eliminate $x$-inefficiency but to set in motion a process through which change and adaptation occur on a continuing basis.[19] Ultimately, the successful introduction of new technology and new methods and the elimination of work rules occur only when individuals and small groups at the operating level agree to accept these new arrangements.

Certainly, in principle workers may be willing to be reassigned and to accept new work arrangements; but when the changes become specific and the issues of security, equity, and the fabric of economic and social relations are involved, resistance may develop. We consider several strategies for overcoming this resistance.

*An Economic Approach.*   A worker (or, indeed, management) will resist change because the expected costs are higher than the expected gains; this can be further complicated by the tendency of workers to be risk-averse. In other words, the uncertainty of a new operation magnifies the possible costs compared with the known gains and advantages of existing circumstances.

How, then, does the organization reduce costs? A number of possibilities suggest themselves: guaranteeing the job, training workers so that the new responsibilities can be taken in stride, and creating an atmosphere of growth so that people feel that they are part of a progressing operation. Similarly, there are ways to deal with uncertainty. This is where communication and participation, as well as exposure to operations that are organized along similar lines, fit into the picture.

On the gain side, bonuses and learning-curve incentives may be very effective. Another program, which we call *contingency compensation*, can tie the economic interests of workers much more closely to the fortunes of the enterprise. The Japanese model is relevant here: Each year, four or five months' compensation is received in semiannual bonus payments. The magnitude of this sum creates a very close economic identification between workers and the enterprise.

*A Social Approach.*   Social or group resistance to change is much more crucial than economic resistance. Basically, change places a social structure under threat because it directly challenges the survival of the existing pattern of associations. Almost any change that moves workers to another department or shifts them to another line of work will alter their pattern of social interaction.

It is not as easy to think through programs to deal with the possibility of social disintegration as in the case of economic threat. This difficulty in itself suggests why resistance to change is not easy to overcome; often it is not possible to leave the work group intact.

The fundamental premise of sociotechnical analysis is the need to harmonize social structure with technical requirements. Another perspective on administering change identifies culture as the key concept; in effect, it is the culture that is preserving the status quo and making new arrangements difficult.

Without question, one of the most difficult undertakings facing management today is the need to change the culture of an existing plant. If the business profile of a plant or office involves stagnation, it is unlikely that any change can be made in the outlook of the organization without more fundamental changes in the underlying material conditions. Hence, a prerequisite for a change may be new investment that convinces the organization it has a future. The next step would involve the challenging task of seeking to change values and moving the establishment in the direction of participation, openness, communication, equality, security, and mutual responsibility—all attributes of the Japanese method. All this represents extensive social restructuring and can take the better part of a decade to accomplish.

*Specific Mechanisms.*   Programs aimed at paving the way for change involve a number of dimensions. Certainly, emphasizing job tenure and career employment incentives can help. To the extent that people are reluctant to go along with change because it may mean that their jobs will be eliminated, the provision of job tenure can help remove this resistance.

A second mechanism is the provision of information on plans and consequences. Generally speaking, people go along with new arrangements when they have had time to rehearse the new situation in their minds and when they have some basis for understanding the rationale and overall plan for the change. Communication works best when it provides workers with information they can use to change their behavior. General information about the direction of the industry or the economy will be of some use as background but will not provide guidance about doing something differently within the enterprise. However, if the information is about the company's market share, and if the cost and quality of the product have something to do with market share, the work force is presented with an opportunity and an incentive. In many large U.S. corporations, workers are insulated from the vicissitudes of the external market. This is a function of size and, until recently, of economic success. Communication cuts through this barrier and confronts the worker with economic realities.

Communication prevents two kinds of errors that often occur in industry: The first is the error of ignorance, when the firm is gradually losing out economically but the workers are in the dark about this decline. The second error, which now occurs more frequently, is one in which the workers try very hard, but the economic situation in beyond repair. This explains why union leaders sometimes argue against concessions but workers at the local level are willing to do anything in an effort to save their jobs.

Certainly, methods that enhance participation and involvement of workers through quality-of-work-life programs, opinion surveys, and the like, help to get the attention of the organization and develop a sense of mutual purpose and commitment in management and the work force. Several other devices of a more immediate nature can encourage change. An organization may consider paying a one-shot performance bonus to shorten the learning curve involved in introducing new machinery or moving over to any new system. Such an arrangement is common practice under defense contracts. The idea is for a one-shot bonus to be paid to the workers involved if it is successful in shortening the start-up time.

Formal gain-sharing programs such as the Scanlon Plan and profit sharing can help in promoting continuing adaptation. If handled correctly, and if accompanied by an adequate communication program, these programs can keep the activities of an organization focused on competition and on the internal changes that are needed to meet external challenges and developments.

Another very specific and powerful technique for helping people cope with the uncertainty that always accompanies change is to use experimental and pilot projects before installing new equipment or a new method on an organizationwide basis. Side-by-side operations, one with the new arrangement and one using the traditional methods, can teach very powerful lessons. This technique also makes it clear to workers that if the new method does not succeed, they will continue to use their accustomed machinery and procedures.

The use of pilot operations is well established in industry for research and development work, but it is not as institutionalized as part of a learning system in which workers from other plants come to observe and participate. The pilot project can be used not just to solve technical problems but also to deal with motivational and social problems.

## INDUSTRIAL RELATIONS AND PRODUCTIVITY IMPROVEMENT STRATEGIES

Industrial relations involves the structuring of the relationship between the employer and the workers. Thus, when a union is present, labor-management relations is the institutionalization of the employment relationship.[20]

### Connection Between Collective Bargaining Activities and Productivity

If the consequences of collective bargaining are measured via such items as grievances, number of strikes, and time spent in solving grievances and negotiating contracts, there is strong evidence that as these activities intensify, productivity decreases. It is not clear that a direct cause-and-effect relationship exists, but it is clear that there is a reinforcing effect between the labor-management relationship and the economic performance of the enterprise.[21]

The character of the labor-management relationship has a direct bearing on the productivity achieved in a given situation. When the labor-management relationship is very adversarial, there is clearly a detrimental effect on productivity. In other words, good industrial relations can be thought of as a prerequisite for productivity, a necessary but not a sufficient condition for increasing productivity. But what really holds productivity back when the labor-management relationship is poor? A poor labor-management relationship is a system-type condition, and such events as grievance proceedings (with supervisory time spent in arguments) and strikes are bound to have an adverse influence. One of the plants in our survey listed illegal work stoppages as its number-one productivity restraint.

Can good industrial relations alone make much of a direct contribution to good productivity? The answer is not clear. There are many examples of plants where industrial relations appear to be good, but where productivity is not up to the desired levels. It is not clear whether labor peace has been "bought" at a price of lower productivity or whether the explanation is more complicated and rests with the other factors that are needed for good productivity such as sound management, adequate capital, and positive programs for coordination of the factors of production to achieve good results. We lean toward the latter explanation.

Of course, positive industrial relations cannot be maintained over the long run if productivity is not satisfactory. The viability of the labor-management relationship depends on the viability of the enterprise over the long run, and no labor-management relationship can remain healthy if the plant is in trouble in terms of its market position.

This emphasis on the long-run relationship for both the position of the firm and the nature of the labor-management relationship puts the movement toward collaborative labor-management relations in a new perspective. The long-run emphasis focuses attention on the range of mutual dependence or what might be called *mutual advantage.* Any employment relationship has to possess mutual advantage for the parties to remain committed to it.

It is fashionable these days to say that labor-management relations in the United States are too adversarial, but this label leaves out an important part of the story. The parties can afford to deal with each other on an adversarial basis only so long as it is mutually advantageous for them to remain in the relationship.

While it is the case that when grievances are higher, productivity is lower, the remedy is not simple. A decrease in grievances may require a change in management style, an alteration of the technology or the work structure, and/or the hiring of different kinds of workers. Grievances and productivity are both outcomes, and their roots stem from very complicated interactions. A culture reinforces itself and is not amenable to change in a mechanical fashion.

The subject of absenteeism provides a specific illustration. Katz, Kochan, and Gobeille found that absenteeism correlates positively with the other measures of an industrial relations system and negatively with economic performance on a cross-sectional basis. However, at plants that have undertaken intensive quality-of-work-life programs, there was little (if any) improvement in absenteeism as a result of the intervention.[22] The message is that if the industrial relations–productivity equation is going to be changed, a very comprehensive strategy of new policies and structures is required.

*The Industrial Relations Connection to the Different Strategic Levels*
How can industrial relations make a positive contribution or at least not play a negative role at the three levels of strategic analysis?

*Intensification of Human Resources.*   At the level of the individual or the small work group and the strategic assignment of intensification of human resources, the model industrial relations system is that of Japan. This presents somewhat of an anomaly for the U.S. labor movement because the role of unions at the plant level in Japan is quite minimal; Japanese management enjoys considerable freedom in transferring workers among assignments, and work rules appear not to exist. Hence, there is some support for the general proposition that the more powerful a union is at the shop-floor level, the greater its ability to enforce work-rule arrangements and the greater its prospective drag on productivity.

However, strong trade unions can exist without exercising extensive control over shop-level decisions. In both Sweden and Germany, trade unions are strong at the national level, but management enjoys much more flexibility in the assignment of workers than is the case in the United States. Layoffs are very rare in these two countries; consequently, adherence to work rules in order to enhance job security is unnecessary. Also, firms recruit, develop, and advance workers much more from within. Employees are hired for entry-level positions and trained within the establishment or industry. Finally, unions exercise their influence at the central level of the industry or economy, such as through the German network of codetermination arrangements where unions participate in strategic decision making at the Board of Director's level. The point is that a different industrial relations system can accommodate a strong trade union without imposing restrictions at the shop-floor level.

These examples of industrial relations systems provide guidance for the long run. But for the short run, what role does collective bargaining play in influencing the behavior of individuals and small groups? To be blunt, we do not believe that a union plays a significant role in improving productivity at this level. There is some evidence to support management's contention that good productivity can be achieved if there is intelligent supervision and if the workers are involved directly. The role for a union at this lowest level is, therefore, to minimize the drag that comes from excessive grievances, proceedings, unnecessary strikes, and the like.

*Harmonization of Work Organization.*   The middle or plant level, where the collective bargaining agreement takes form, is the heart of the U.S. industrial relations system. The plant agreement and the structuring of a relationship at the local level between management and the representatives of the workers are the essence of this system. The many rules that emanate from the contract and from customary practice that often inhibit productivity also have their greatest impact here. For this level, there is no preferred model from another country; instead, the model guiding the design of work organizations comes directly from U.S. experience.

We can distinguish two major species of industrial relations systems. On the one hand, there are companies that have instituted new operations with the array of techniques that have been referred to as *comprehensive personnel policies*. These facilities are for the most part unorganized, and case studies suggest that motivation and enthusiasm are very high. On the other hand, there are established plants, usually unionized, that are undergoing dramatic change through productivity bargaining, concession bargaining, quality-of-work-life programs, and labor-management committees—measures that have been referred to as the *new industrial relations* or the *cooperative economy*. The dust has not settled, and it is too early to tell the extent to which these developments will really change the culture of established operations and have a dramatic effect on productivity. But considerable experimentation and change are under way.

Our survey included dramatic examples of both systems. We found steel plants that are engaging in participative endeavors and plants in other industries that are practicing the sociotechnical ideas that are often adopted in unorganized plants. It is clear that more experience with integrative bargaining or problem solving is being acquired. The emphasis is on accommodation rather than conflict.

Productivity bargaining can be the first step toward collaborative labor-management relations. A type of reinforcement takes place between the specific activity and the general labor-management strategy. Quite often, parties in an adversarial relationship have embarked on productivity bargaining as a way of dealing with certain operating problems and, as a result of a successful agreement and the recognition that costs can be lowered and jobs made more secure, have become willing to deal with each other in an accommodative manner.

A good example of this reinforcement can be seen in the experience at Goodyear in establishing new capacity for the production of radial tires.

The company indicated that it was willing to place the facility at an existing location, either Topeka, Kansas, or Gadsten, Alabama. At Topeka, the rank and file voted down productivity changes; as a result, Gadsten got a chance to compete for the new plant. At Gadsten the union voted 100 to 1 in favor of adopting a labor agreement that guaranteed new productivity levels as a result of abandonment of incentives, instituting round-the-clock shift operations, and restricting the use of seniority (for transfer and bumping) to the new plant.

### Rationalization of Investment

At the highest level, the level of the corporation or industry where the basic business decisions about the deployment of capital assets are made, the German model is the most efficient.

For U.S. unions, involvement at this level has been relatively infrequent. Indeed, most unions have said that they prefer to leave business decisions to management. However, given the worldwide movement of capital and vital stakes for employment of their members, greater involvement seems to be imperative. At the lowest level good results can be obtained without the presence of the union, but we believe that a balancing of the stakes cannot take place without some representation of worker interests at the highest level.

When fundamental restructuring is involved, it is possible that the unionized operation can adjust more rapidly than the unorganized facility. Union leaders are often aware of the basic economic realities facing the industry and recognize that some plants have to be closed and that modernization has to take place in order to maintain the viability of the industry.

Moreover, we believe that such involvement on the part of unions also can be in the best interests of management and stockholders. If the concerns of workers are brought into key business decisions, those decisions will be qualitatively better, to the long-run benefit of all concerned. For example, a union participating in a discussion about the shift of capital from one location to another can propose a transition timetable that minimizes disruption for the workers involved, thereby enhancing operating effectiveness and producing a win-win solution. Why can't management on its own balance such interests and achieve an optimal course of action? One answer is that pressures to achieve short-run gains often lead to a drastic shifting of resources that produces the desired immediate results but in the long run destroys the human capability of the organization.

Some persuasive examples from Germany show that the participation of unions has served to achieve gains for all sides. The best examples come from the experiences of Volkswagen and a number of German steel companies during the mid-1970s. The unions involved helped shape programs for achieving economic change. In the case of Volkswagen, some production was shifted from Germany to the United States. In the steel industry, the impact of regearing facilities from bulk to specialty steels was minimized for workers through gradual realignment, retraining, and early retirement programs.

The process that we envision involves the presence and participation of the union. When unions have been brought in on business decisions in this country, they have generally not tried to block these decisions but have concentrated on modifying them to reflect worker concerns. Clearly, these kinds of discussions fall within the nonmandatory sphere of U.S. collective bargaining. This is just as well because mandatory bargaining over business decisions would embroil the parties in considerable posturing and power confrontation.[23] We see substantial movement in this direction. Recently agreements in the meat-packing and automobile industries, for example, have spelled out ways in which the investment decisions of the companies will be reconciled with the interests of the workers. In some instances, forums and other means of discussion and communication have been set in motion to link business decisions to the stakes of workers and unions in the shape of the enterprise over the long run.

General Motors refers to its consultation program as the "forum for the competitive edge." This is appropriate because it focuses attention on the viability of the enterprise and the steps that need to be taken at the highest levels. Information about market share and the status of new technology are pieces of the picture that affect the employment security of all employees, the profitability of the enterprise, and the interests of others who have a stake in the business.

### The Concept of Industrial Relations as a Bottom Line

When productivity or economic performance is the bottom line, there is considerable connection between the character of industrial relations and economic performance. For example, Schemenner found that the character of industrial relations is a very important element in management's decision to expand an existing operation or to move to a green-field site.[24] At least half a dozen firms in our survey indicated that they will direct investment in a way that depends on industrial relations factors. Usually, the sequence is one of committing new investment to green-field sites or to plants that have a good labor relations atmosphere. A troublesome plant may be phased out slowly; it will be kept in operation as long as cash flow is positive. Obviously, industrial relations factors have an effect, albeit slowly and behind the scenes.

We are also convinced that investment decisions and many of the other important management strategies have a direct effect on industrial relations. The difficulty is that we do not have adequate ways of measuring the quality of the bottom-line nature of industrial relations. We can measure detrimental elements such as grievances, strikes, and absenteeism. But if the industrial relations system and, more broadly, the organizational arrangements are viewed as part of technology, we lack the tools for measuring the capacity and effectiveness of this human technology. We have the concept of human capital, which involves the skills and education acquired by individuals, and we know effective organizations when we see them, but we do not have good ways of measuring *human assets as a discrete input*.

Japanese companies place considerable emphasis on maintaining the growth and vitality of the organization. Many large and successful high-technology firms in the United States have the same outlook. Certainly a positive labor-management relationship cannot hurt productivity. Although such a relationship may not be a factor that will in and of itself guarantee productivity, it certainly will not be an impediment. For this reason, many corporations, especially in the United States, are emphasizing this strategic direction. According to a survey by the Sentry Insurance Company, 61 percent of U.S. business executives feel that there is too little cooperation between business and unions, in comparison with only 15 percent of Japanese businessmen.[25] Japanese companies have been able to develop a substantial amount of organizational and social capital. It is appropriate for U.S. companies to meet this challenge. One step would be to view industrial relations as a bottom line and to institute policies and programs to enhance industrial relations performance.[26]

This chapter began by identifying restraints on improved productivity in the workplace and then reviewing the various types of programs being used within U.S. corporations to increase productivity. Unfortunately, what we found was a mismatch between the themes of change on the problem side and the programs, often emphasizing business as usual, on the action side.

Many organizations have taken to improving productivity through piecemeal, faddish, and, often, superficial means. What is needed is a more integrated approach and one that incorporates industrial relations themes into overall corporate strategy. The strategies we have proposed start first with the context or the investment arrangement for the enterprise, then move to the work organization and the process by which technology and workers are combined, and then lastly, to the level of the individual workers and the need to intensify their motivation and commitment.

## NOTES

1. By focusing on these three types of restraints, we do not want to imply that the many others mentioned by the survey respondents are less important in particular situations. However, these three appeared to apply in all industries.
2. David C. Hershfield, "Barriers to Increased Labor Productivity," *The Conference Board Record* (July 1976), pp. 38–41.
3. *Wall Street Journal*, 8 January 1981.
4. *Business Week*, "Building Trades Lose Ground," 9 November 1982, p. 103.
5. D. Hershfield, "Barriers to Increased Labor Productivity," *op. cit.*, p. 39.
6. Stanley Nollen, "Does Flextime Improve Productivity?" *Harvard Business Review* 57, no. 5 (September-October 1979), p. 12. It should be noted that Nollen's findings are not consensual; other researchers have found little (if any) productivity improvement.
7. William F. Schleicher, "Quality Control Circles Save Lockheed Nearly $3 Million in Two Years," *Quality* (May 1977), pp. 14–17.
8. List of citations available on request.
9. Harold J. Krent, "Collective Authority and Technical Expertise: Reexamining the Managerial Employee Exclusion," *New York University Law Review* 56 (October 1981), pp. 694–741.
10. U.S. General Accounting Office, "Productivity Sharing Programs: Can They Contribute to Productivity Improvement?" GAO Report AFMD-81-22 (Gaithersburg, Md.: U.S. General Accounting Office, March 3, 1981), p. 15.
11. "Quality Control Circle Activities and the Suggestion System," *Japan Labor Bulletin*, January 1, 1982.
12. Lawrence M. Baytos, "Nine Strategies for Productivity Improvement," *Personnel Journal* 58, no. 7 (July 1979), pp. 449–456.
13. Peter Cappelli, "Concession Bargaining and the National Economy," *Industrial Relations Research Association Proceedings*, 1982 (Madison, Wisc.), pp. 362–371.
14. The difficulty of observing the effect of job insecurity may explain why none of the respondent firms mentioned this as a constraint on productivity improvement.
15. Leonard Greenhalgh and Robert McKersie, "Cost Effectiveness of Alternative Strategies for Cutback Management," *Public Administration Review* (November-December 1980), pp. 575–584.
16. Harry Katz, Thomas A. Kochan, and Kenneth R. Gobeille, "Industrial Relations Performance, Economic Performance and the Effects of Quality of Working Life: An Inter-Plant Analysis," *Industrial and Labor Relations Review* 37 (October 1983), pp. 3–17.
17. It is significant that it is the large integrated steel mills that commit the firm to its site, but the smaller mills have been able to achieve the advantages of a clean start. See John Savage, "Incentive Programs at Nucor Corporation Boost Productivity," *Personnel Administration* 26, no. 8 (August 1981).
18. Some companies in the automobile and rubber industries have decided to locate new plants in the same labor market areas as plants being terminated. This makes it possible for workers to be carried over but also makes it more difficult to change the social system of the new plant because there is a strong carryover of the old culture when workers are transferred from existing plants.
19. The term *x-inefficiency* refers to the slack that exists in an organization. It is the headroom between the operating efficiency that an organization has reached and the higher state of efficiency that can be realized through better management, better programs, better motivation, and a wide range of other improve-

ments. See Harvey Leibenstein, "Allocative Efficiency vs. 'X-Efficiency,'" *American Economic Review* 56 (June 1966), pp. 392–415.

20. The government can also be introduced as an actor; over the past several decades, the employment relationship has been shaped in some very fundamental ways by legislation and regulatory agencies.

21. Katz, Kochan, and Gobeille found a strong connection between the overall climate of labor management relations (as measured by number of grievances, unresolved local issues, and time to settle local contracts) and a variety of economic performance measures. Katz, Kochan, and Gobeille, *op. cit.*

22. Katz, Kochan, and Gobeille, *op. cit.*

23. It should be noted that the legal framework governing labor-management relations in the United States does not provide for consultation. Instead, the approach is to identify mandatory subjects of bargaining, including wages, hours, and working conditions. Such subjects as productivity, investment plans, and participation fall in the permissible area.

24. Roger Schmenner, *The Location Decisions of Large Multi-Plant Companies* (Cambridge, Mass.: MIT Press, Joint Center for Urban Studies, 1980).

25. *A Sentry Study, Perspectives on Productivity: A Global View* conducted by Louis Harris and Associates, Inc., and Dr. Amitai Etzioni, Director, Center for Policy Research (Stevens Point, Wisc., Sentry Insurance Company, 1981), p. xii.

26. The concept of industrial relations as a bottom line has been emphasized in several speeches by Donald Petersen, president of the Ford Motor Company.

# 7

# Analysis of the Productivity Slowdown: Evidence for a Sector-Biased or Sector-Neutral Industrial Strategy

FRANK M. GOLLOP

The decline in U.S. productivity growth has been a central issue indicating the need for a national industrial policy, a strategy to revitalize the U.S. economy. Most agree that improved productivity is a key element in any long-run solution to inflation, unemployment, and the declining international competitiveness of U.S. business. At this point, however, agreement stops, and the industrial strategy debate begins.

Proponents of sector-targeted action claim that public policy should be designed to identify and stimulate winning industries, providing them with direct federal financial assistance, tax incentives, and loan guarantees. For support, this school cites economic studies claiming that much (if not most) of the slowdown in aggregate productivity growth is due to a postwar shift of industrial activity from high- to low-productivity-growth sectors. If the studies are correct, the implication is that a sector-targeted strategy could have a sizable impact on aggregate productivity performance.

In contrast, advocates of an economy-wide or general industrial strategy refer to studies concluding that activity reallocations explain little of the economy's disappointing performance, and that the productivity slowdown is widespread across sectors. The implication is that industrial stimulants should be applied broadly; no constraints should be imposed on the ability of the market system to allocate resources to their most productive uses. Policy should be sector-neutral, not sector-biased.

The proper economic interpretation of the recent productivity slowdown is central to the industrial strategy debate. Unfortunately, past research does not offer unanimity of approach. Some studies rely on sectoral models of labor productivity; others define productivity in terms of labor and capital inputs. Still others include material and energy inputs. Some are concerned only with shifts in labor input; a few focus on capital inputs. Many define sectoral shifts in terms of output. As one might expect, these choices should not be arbitrary. Economic theory is clear with regard to the principles that should underlie both the proper definitions of aggregate and sectoral productivity and the concept of sectoral shifts. An important objective of this chapter is to define the proper economic framework within which the competing industrial strategy arguments can be evaluated.

The analysis decomposes the economy's aggregate rate of productivity growth into three sources: (1) changes in sectoral productivity, (2) sectoral shifts in economic activity, and (3) the effects of resource reallocations. Changes in sectoral productivity growth clearly affect aggregate performance. Productivity gains in individual sectors are transmitted to consumers both directly through deliveries to final demand and indirectly through deliveries to intermediate demand. The first source component captures the overall importance of changes in productivity *within* sectors. The sectoral shift component is concerned with the productivity consequences of shifts in economic activity *among* sectors with differing rates of productivity growth. The resource reallocation term monitors how well the market system allocates resources to their most productive uses.

Each component is relevant to the industrial strategy debate. If the recent slowdown in aggregate performance is due largely to a widespread decline in sectoral productivity, a sector-neutral policy is indicated. If the market has failed to allocate resources to their most productive uses or, worse, has reallocated them to less productive uses, a sector-neutral policy relying on the market system loses its appeal, and sector-targeted intervention finds support. The sectoral shift component warrants careful interpretation. Unlike declines in sectoral productivity or resource misallocations, sectoral shifts do not necessarily reflect economic failure. Shifts result from a number of causes, including simple changes in consumer tastes (the decline in the use of tobacco), the introduction of new products (computers), and basic changes in economic institutions (the rise of services). If these shifts are the productivity culprits, it is not obvious that public policy should reverse the trends, nor is such a reversal advocated by proponents of a sector-biased strategy; it only would suggest, given history, that forces shifting economic activity among sectors can have a significant effect on the performance of the economy as a whole.

The magnitude of each source contribution can be quantified. In the "Past Research" section, we review the evidence in the economics literature. The results of past studies are reconciled with the economic model presented in the section "Productivity Growth and Resource Reallocation." The model is then applied to an examination of aggregate and sectoral productivity in the postwar United States. The results are reported in the section "The Story of Postwar Economic Growth." We begin with the model.

The important conclusions are:

 (i) Although sectoral shifts in economic activity have occurred over the postwar period, they are unimportant in explaining the recent slowdown in aggregate productivity growth.
 (ii) The decline in sectoral productivity growth has been substantial and widespread across sectors, lending support to a sector-neutral industrial policy.
(iii) The market has responded by reallocating inputs to more productive uses, arguing against the adoption of a sector-biased industrial policy.

## PRODUCTIVITY GROWTH AND RESOURCE ALLOCATION

Output per hour worked, or labor productivity, is the traditional productivity measure. However, during the 1950s, the increasing capital intensity of U.S. business forced economists to restructure their measure of productivity growth to incorporate both labor and capital inputs. A value-added measure emerged. The events of the past decade urged a further restructuring; energy and material inputs no longer could be ignored. A measure of total-factor productivity evolved.

Labor, value added, and total-factor productivity models offer fundamentally different descriptions of productivity growth. The important question is: Which model forms a more appropriate basis for measuring productivity growth?

The answer follows directly from economic principles. Productivity growth is a measure of economic performance. It serves as a barometer, sensitive to the economy's and each sector's success in solving the economic problem: the allocation of scarce resources to satisfy human wants.

What makes this an *economic* problem is the notion of scarcity, a concept no more appropriate to any one primary input than to any other. In short, the efficient solution to society's economic problem involves all inputs. It follows that well-defined indexes of productivity growth must measure how well the economy allocates and sectors use *all* scarce resources.

This principle has important implications for measuring productivity growth at both the aggregate and the sectoral levels. Primary inputs for the overall economy include labor and capital. Intermediate goods can be viewed as internal, offsetting transfers. Sectoral deliveries to intermediate demand (steel produced for the automobile industry) and intermediate input purchases (steel consumed by the automobile industry) are self-canceling transactions within the economy. In contrast, studies of sectoral productivity must consider all labor, capital, and material inputs, including energy. Steel is as primary to the automobile industry as labor or capital is. At the sectoral level, transactions in material inputs are not self-canceling.

It follows that the formal specification of productivity growth differs depending on whether the focus is on the economy as a whole or on individual sectors. The two models are developed separately below. (Formal derivations are provided in the Appendix.)

## The Aggregate Economy

Economists have long recognized that society's economic objective is to satisfy human wants through deliveries to end users. Consequently, the proper measure of aggregate output is the sum of deliveries to final demand—personal consumption expenditures, gross private domestic investment, government purchases, and net exports[1]—or, as conventionally described, aggregate value added.[2] As we have already indicated, labor and capital are the primary inputs available to the macro economy.

The definition of aggregate productivity growth is derived from production theory. After all, aggregate productivity is concerned with how well the economy transforms inputs into output. The relevant production relation for the macro economy expresses aggregate output or value added, $V$, in terms of labor, $L$, and capital, $K$, inputs and time, $T$:

$$V = f(L, K, T) \tag{7-1}$$

As demonstrated in the Appendix, the rate of aggregate productivity growth, $G$, is defined as the growth in value added minus the income-share-weighted growth rates of labor and capital inputs:

$$G \equiv \frac{d \ln V}{dT} - \frac{p_L L}{q_v V} \cdot \frac{d \ln L}{dT} - \frac{p_K K}{q_V V} \cdot \frac{d \ln K}{dT} \tag{7-2}$$

where the logarithmic derivatives indicate growth rates, and $q_V$, $p_L$, and $p_K$ represent the prices of aggregate output, labor, and capital, respectively.

Equation 7-2 provides the proper definition of aggregate productivity growth; both labor and capital inputs are treated symmetrically. The formula was popularized by Kendrick (1961) and Denison (1962) and is currently the basis for official measures published by the Bureau of Labor Statistics.

## The Individual Sectors

The characterization of sectoral productivity growth differs importantly from its aggregate counterpart. Whereas the macro economy is concerned with maximizing value added, individual sectors satisfy human wants through the production of gross output (bushels of wheat, tons of coal, and so on). Each sector transmits the benefits of its productivity growth to consumers both directly through deliveries to final demand and indirectly through deliveries to intermediate demand. The proper measure of a sector's output is its total production, the sum of its deliveries to intermediate and final demands.

Moreover, analyses of sectoral productivity cannot focus narrowly on labor and capital inputs. These inputs are no more primary to a producing sector than materials and energy are; they certainly are no more important. In manufacturing, material and energy inputs account for as much as 70 percent of input costs. Given market prices, a firm chooses a particular combination of capital, labor, material, and energy inputs. As prices change, the firm rationally adjusts its input mix. As a measure of sectoral performance, productivity growth must treat all inputs symmetrically.

The importance of including material goods and services in a model of sectoral productivity is easily demonstrated. A supermarket manager, for example, can choose to have an employee display ice-cream products in the frozen foods cabinet or contract with the "raw materials" supplier to have its delivery person display the product. The first is a direct labor cost to the supermarket; the second is an expense related to material input. Presumably, the store manager makes this choice on the basis of the relative productivities and prices of the employee and the delivery person. Assume that the manager first uses the delivery person. Later, if the productivity of employees increases, it may be possible to produce the same output for less cost by hiring an additional employee and substituting this laborer for the material input of the delivery person. Costs will be lowered, and productivity will be enhanced. Measured total-factor productivity will increase; measured labor productivity will decline. Excluding material inputs from the measure of productivity growth not only presents a distorted characterization of the manager's rational behavior but also biases any subsequent analysis of the trend and sources of the industry's productivity growth.

The microeconomic theory of production provides the basis for the measurement of sectoral productivity growth. Sectoral productivity is concerned with how efficiently managers convert inputs under their control into outputs:

$$Q_j = h^j (L_j, K_j, M_j, E_j, T) \tag{7-3}$$

where $Q_j$ is the gross output of the $j$th sector and $L_j$, $K_j$, $M_j$, and $E_j$ are the sector's labor, capital, material, and energy inputs, respectively. As demonstrated in the Appendix, the sectoral measure of total-factor productivity growth, $e_j$, is defined as the growth in output less the income-share-weighted growth rates of all inputs:

$$e_j \equiv \frac{d \ln Q_j}{dT} - \frac{p_{Lj}L_j}{q_jQ_j} \cdot \frac{d \ln L_j}{dT} - \frac{p_{Kj}K_j}{q_jQ_j} \cdot \frac{d \ln K_j}{dT}$$

$$- \frac{p_{Mj}M_j}{q_jQ_j} \cdot \frac{d \ln M_j}{dT} - \frac{p_{Ej}E_j}{q_jQ_j} \cdot \frac{d \ln E_j}{dT} \tag{7-4}$$

where $q_j$ is the price of output and $p_{Lj}, p_{Kj}, p_{Mj}$, and $p_{Ej}$ are the input prices paid by the $j$th sector.

Equation 7-4 is the proper formula for measuring sectoral productivity growth. Because it treats all primary inputs symmetrically, it is a correct model of any manager's ultimate productivity concern: how well the manager is utilizing all the inputs under his or her control. Moreover, unlike sectoral labor and value-added models, the total-factor productivity model places all sectors on an equal footing. Some sectors, such as retail trade, are labor-intensive; others, such as electric utilities, are capital-intensive. Still others, such as food and related products, are materials-intensive. Equation 7-4 evaluates how well all scarce resources are used to produce output.

## Aggregating Over Sectors

Recent events have impressed us with the importance of the microeconomic foundations of aggregate productivity growth. Long-term economic trends can be understood and projected only by relating economy-wide developments to changes in economic activity at the level of industrial sectors. Stated more formally, the link between the aggregate rate of productivity growth defined in Equation 7-2 and the sectoral rates defined in Equation 7-4 is the key to understanding the sources of the economy's recent productivity performance.

That link (developed formally in the Appendix) begins with the recognition that the aggregate economy is simply the sum of its parts. If accounting

identities are used and Equation 7-4 is substituted into Equation 7-2, the
following expression results:

$$G = \sum_j \frac{q_j Q_j}{q_v V} \cdot e_j + \sum_j \frac{q_v - q_j^v}{q_v V} \cdot \frac{dV_j}{dT}$$

$$+ \sum_j \frac{p_{Kj} - p_K}{q_v V} \cdot \frac{dK_j}{dT} + \sum_j \frac{p_{Lj} - p_L}{q_v V} \cdot \frac{dL_j}{dT} \qquad (7\text{-}5)$$

where $q_j^v$ is the price of the value added produced in the $j$th sector.

The aggregate rate of productivity growth, $G$, can be expressed as the
sum of four components: a weighted sum of the sectoral rates of productivity growth and three terms reflecting the reallocation of value added, labor,
and capital among sectors. Each of the four components identifies an
important potential source of productivity growth in the macro economy.
The first component captures the contribution of changes in productivity in
the individual sectors. Each sector's rate of productivity growth, $e_j$, is
weighted by the ratio of the value of that sector's gross output to the value
of the total economy's net output (defined as value added or aggregate
deliveries to final demand).

A formal argument is developed in the Appendix; a heuristic but equally
persuasive case can be developed for the weights associated with $e_j$ in
Equation 7-5. Consider an individual sector that experiences an advance in
its rate of productivity growth. If all primary and intermediate outputs are
held constant, the sector can provide the economy with increased output.
The objective of creating the appropriate weight for this sector's technological advance is to correctly assign causal responsibility to the sector for
any effect on aggregate productivity growth. Since the ultimate macroeconomic concern is the effect of this technical change on aggregate output,
the appropriate denominator in the weight is aggregate value added.
Because the individual sector transmits the benefits of its productivity
growth to final consumers both directly (through deliveries to final
demand) and indirectly (through deliveries to intermediate demand), the
appropriate numerator in the weight is the sector's total output (the sum of
its deliveries to final and intermediate demands).[3]

The three reallocation components in Equation 7-5 identify additional,
independent sources of aggregate productivity growth. Collectively, these
terms provide the basis for the quantitative evaluation of the importance of
resource reallocations over the postwar period.

The labor and capital components identify the productivity consequences resulting from any sectoral reallocation of the economy's primary
inputs. Each component has a straightforward interpretation. Consider the

reallocation term corresponding to capital. The variable $p_K$ refers to the average price of capital input in the aggregate economy; $p_{Kj}$ represents the return on capital input in the $j$th sector. Aggregate productivity growth is affected by the reallocation of capital among sectors with varying rates of return. For example, if capital input moves from a sector with a relatively low rate of return $(p_{Kj} < p_K)$ to a sector with a high rate of return $(p_{Kj} > p_K)$, the quantity of capital input for the economy as a whole is unchanged, but the level of output is increased; that is, aggregate productivity is enhanced.[4] In this example, the capital reallocation component has a positive value. Similarly, sectoral shifts in labor resources are monitored by the labor reallocation term. If labor input moves from a sector where it has relatively low marginal productivity to a sector where it has relatively high marginal productivity, economy-wide labor input is unchanged, but aggregate productivity is improved.

The reallocation term corresponding to value added has a perfectly symmetrical interpretation; the only difference is that it refers to shifts in the sectoral composition of aggregate value added rather than aggregate inputs. In a competitive economy, relative prices of sectoral value added reflect relative differences in marginal costs. If the sectoral allocation of labor and capital inputs is held constant, and if the composition of aggregate value added shifts from relatively high marginal cost $(q_j^v > q_v)$ to relatively low marginal cost $(q_j^v < q_v)$ sectors, social product increases; aggregate productivity improves.

It is important to emphasize that the three reallocation terms concern all the variables central to the definition of aggregate productivity growth (Equation 7-2). Value added, labor input, and capital input are treated symmetrically. Clearly, the overall productivity effects of resource reallocations cannot be interpreted by focusing exclusively on any one or even two components. If the sum of the three reallocation terms is positive, resource reallocations have spurred aggregate productivity growth. If the sum is negative, resource reallocations have contributed to the productivity decline.

Resource reallocations may be accompanied by sectoral shifts in economic activity. The productivity consequences of these shifts are revealed through the first term in Equation 7-5, the weighted sum of the sectoral rates of productivity growth. Changes in either the weights or the sectoral rates affect macroeconomic performance. At one extreme, relative sectoral activity (the weights) may not have changed; any change in aggregate $G$ would be explained by movements in the sectoral $e_j$. At the other extreme, sectoral productivity may not have changed; as a result, changes in the distribution of economic activity determine the change in aggregate productivity. The two separable effects can be identified quantitatively by simply adding and subtracting a base-period-weighted sum of the $e_j$ to Equation 7-5:

$$G = \sum_j \left(\frac{q_j Q_j}{q_v V}\right)_B e_j + \sum_j \left[\left(\frac{q_j Q_j}{q_v V}\right) - \left(\frac{q_j Q_j}{q_v V}\right)_B\right] e_j$$

$$+ \sum_j \frac{q_v - q_j^v}{q_v V} \frac{dV_j}{dT}$$

$$+ \sum_j \frac{p_{Kj} - p_K}{q_v V} \cdot \frac{dK_j}{dT} + \sum_j \frac{p_{Lj} - p_L}{q_v V} \frac{dL_j}{dT} \tag{7-6}$$

where $B$ weights identify the sectoral distribution of economic activity in some prior base period of interest.

The first term in Equation 7-5 is decomposed into the first two terms in Equation 7-6. The first identifies the pure contribution of changing sectoral productivity *within* sectors. Base-period weights are used; the distribution of economic activity across sectors is held fixed. The second captures the effect of shifts in economic activity *among* sectors. If present weights equal base-period weights, the component takes a zero value. If activity weights associated with high-productivity-growth sectors have increased (decreased), the component takes a positive (negative) value. Taken together, the first two terms in Equation 7-6 provide the structure for evaluating the sectoral shift argument central to the industrial strategy debate.

It is important to emphasize that the sectoral shift and resource reallocation terms address distinct, independent effects. The former is concerned only with shifts in economic activity resulting largely from changes in demand. The latter focuses on whether the market is effective in reallocating resources to their most productive uses.

Equation 7-5 provides a focus and a structure for evaluating the economic hypothesis underlying the industrial strategy debate. By linking the proper definitions of aggregate and sectoral productivity growth, Equation 7-6 clearly demonstrates that the specification and interpretation of both sectoral shift and resource reallocation effects are not arbitrary but, rather, follow directly from the underlying definitions of productivity growth.

The derivation of Equation 7-6 illustrates a number of important principles. (1) The productivity model used to examine shift and reallocation effects must treat all primary inputs symmetrically. Labor and capital are primary to the aggregate economy; these plus energy and materials are primary to each sector. (2) The model for evaluating the industrial strategy hypotheses must recognize that the economy does not consist of horizontally independent sectors. It is, instead, a set of vertically interdependent sectors, each dependent on intersectoral transactions. If productivity measures are to serve as meaningful barometers of society's success in solving its economic problem, neither material inputs nor intersectoral linkages can be ignored. (3) Each sector transmits the benefits of its productivity growth to consumers directly through deliveries to final demand and indirectly through deliveries to intermediate demand. The sectoral weights used in formulating the effect of sectoral shifts must capture these two roles. (4) The resource reallocation terms must monitor how well the price-signaling marketplace allocates resources to their most productive uses. This requires consideration of reallocations of labor, capital, and value added, the three variables that define aggregate productivity growth.

## PAST RESEARCH

In an important 1967 paper, William Baumol was the first to describe the aggregate productivity consequences of unbalanced growth among sectors with differing rates of productivity growth.[5] The theoretical structure of that paper is very restrictive. All inputs other than labor are ignored. Wages are assumed identical across sectors. Full employment is critical to the development of the argument. Nonetheless, that paper and the emerging productivity slowdown stimulated a number of economists to study the importance of resource reallocations and sectoral shifts as factors in the disappointing productivity performance of the aggregate economy. Estimates of the percentage of the decline in aggregate productivity growth attributable to overall shift effects range from less than 10 percent (Denison, 1973) to more than 80 percent (Nordhaus, 1972).[6]

This section is not an exhaustive survey of the details and results of studies examining shift hypotheses; that lengthy task is left for others.[7] Our objective is to interpret past research in light of the economic principles developed in the preceding section. Existing studies are grouped according to their treatment of two fundamental conceptual issues: (1) the scope of productive inputs considered in the definition of sectoral productivity growth and (2) the choice of modeling sectoral differences in terms of productivity levels or rates of productivity growth.

### Sectoral Productivity

Differences in both measured productivity growth across sectors and the aggregate effect of sectoral shifts depend importantly on the inputs included in the definition of sectoral productivity. The scope of this definition varies considerably. Labor is the sole input considered in the studies by Baumol (1967), Denison (1973, 1979), Kutscher, Mark, and

Norsworthy (1977), Mark (1978), Nordhaus (1972), Norsworthy and Fulco (1974), and Thurow (1979). Although concerned with movements in labor productivity, Norsworthy, Harper, and Kunze (1979) also consider the productivity effect of intersectoral shifts in both labor and capital inputs. Wolff (1981a) examines two measures of sectoral productivity growth, one based on labor and material inputs and a second based on these plus capital inputs.

As we have demonstrated, proper measures of sectoral productivity and any subsequent analysis of shift effects must be evaluated in the context of total-factor productivity. All labor, capital, and material inputs are equally primary to sectoral producers. Intersectoral linkages cannot be ignored. Intermediate inputs affect both measured productivity growth and the sectoral weights used to determine the effect of sectoral shifts in economic activity. The remaining important question is: If everything else is held constant, can the simple change from a partial- to a total-factor productivity context have a significant effect on empirical conclusions regarding the importance of shift effects in explaining the slowdown in aggregate productivity growth?

Wolff's work (1981a) presents a test case. Beginning from common data sources, focusing on identical time periods, and proceeding from a consistent set of assumptions, he constructs two measures of sectoral productivity growth. When defined in terms of his partial (labor and materials) indexes of sectoral productivity growth, Wolff's "output composition" effect indicates that changes in the composition of final demand between the 1947–1967 period and 1976 accounted for 1.32 percentage points (about 50 percent) of the 2.68-percentage-point decline in aggregate productivity. When evaluated in terms of his total-factor productivity measures, sectoral shifts accounted for 0.10 percentage points (less than 4 percent) of the slowdown between 1947–1967 and 1976. In fact, Wolff's analysis of partial indexes of sectoral productivity indicates that changes in the composition of final demand from 1967 to 1976 *decreased* aggregate productivity growth by 0.24 percentage points a year. His analysis of his total-factor productivity indexes implies that the same shifts in final demand *increased* aggregate productivity performance by 0.75 percentage points a year.[8]

The implication is that the definition of sectoral productivity growth cannot be arbitrary.

## The Fallacy of Levels Comparisons

Resource reallocations and sectoral shifts in economic activity are interesting phenomena only if sectors exhibit productivity differences. In theory, sectors can differ in productivity levels and/or rates of productivity growth. Shifts in economic activity among sectors with different levels of productivity can affect the level of aggregate productivity; shifts among sectors with different rates of productivity growth can affect the rate of aggregate productivity growth. Unfortunately, sectoral patterns of productivity levels have no necessary implications for sectoral patterns of productivity growth rates. The converse also holds. Consequently, studies of sectoral shifts that examine productivity levels and those that evaluate productivity growth rates are addressing quite different shift hypotheses.

Kutscher, Mark, and Norsworthy (1977), Mark (1978), Norsworthy and Fulco (1974), and Thurow (1979) are concerned with differing productivity levels. Sectoral rates of productivity growth are the subject matter for Baumol (1967), Baumol and Wolff (1982), Denison (1973, 1979), Norsworthy, Harper, and Kunze (1979), and Wolff (1981a). In theory, both sets of studies investigate equally important questions. In practice, only the latter can produce unambiguous results; the former suffer from what might be called the *fallacy of levels comparisons*.

Comparing levels of output per unit of input between two sectors presumes that sectoral inputs and outputs are measured in comparable units. If not, the familiar saw about comparing apples and oranges would apply. Unfortunately, although the theoretical requirement is clear, empirical applications have, for understandable reasons, universally adopted two severely limiting conventions: (1) Because inputs must be measured in common units across sectors, and because labor, capital, and material inputs are not denominated in common units even within a sector, nonlabor inputs are ignored. Labor input, typically measured as the number of either employees or hours worked, becomes the denominator in each productivity ratio. (2) Because sectoral outputs are not measured in comparable units, all outputs (regardless of sector origin) are assumed to have a price equal to one dollar in some base year. Price differences in other years depend on movements in product-specific price indexes. In short, current-dollar sales in some base year become the measure of output. That is, one dollar of legal services is assumed to be equivalent to one dollar of barley.

The case against focusing solely on labor input is straightforward. Sector A may be labor-intensive; sector B may be capital-intensive. Which sector has the higher level of productivity? Given the information, the correct answer is indeterminate. Conventional level comparisons, by ignoring technological differences, would always select sector B.

Similar difficulties plague the output convention. Suppose that each sector employs 10 laborers in both 1958 and 1972. Each has current-dollar sales of $100 in 1958 and $200 in 1972. Assume further that output prices between 1958 and 1972 have remained constant at $1 in sector A but have doubled from $25 to $50 in sector B. Conventional levels comparisons using 1958 as the base year would conclude that in 1972, sector A has twice the productivity level of sector B. In contrast, if 1972 were selected as the base year, the same study would conclude that the two sectors had identical productivity levels in 1972. In short, the conclusion is sensitive to the selected base year.[9]

Past levels comparisons, then, are at best inconclusive, and their results must be interpreted carefully. Nordhaus (1972), for example, calculates both level and rate effects. His work is best known for the following conclusion:

> The slowdown in productivity growth can be traced almost exclusively to the level factor, or the effect on aggregate productivity of shifts in employment shares among industries with different levels of productivity. In the early postwar period of 1948–1955, the level terms added 0.75 percentage point to aggregate productivity growth, signifying a marked shift of employment toward industries of especially high productivity; in the most recent period, 1965–1971, the level effects dragged down productivity growth by 0.18 percentage point. Comparing the two periods, the change in the level terms accounts for almost 1 full percentage point slowdown in the growth of aggregate productivity.[10]

The level effects account for over 80 percent of the aggregate slowdown recorded by Nordhaus.

In the same study, Nordhaus (1972) also concluded that "it is striking that the rate effect seems to be negligible, recording a very small shift in the shares of output toward industries with high rates of productivity growth."[11] He contended that although aggregate productivity growth declined by 1.17 percentage points between 1948–1955 and 1965–1971, sectoral shifts contributed a positive 0.04 percentage point.[12] Given the inconclusive nature of levels comparisons, Nordhaus's most important conclusion may well be that shift effects explained none of the slowdown and that, if anything, sectoral shifts served as a partial offset.

The fact that levels comparisons offer no unambiguous evidence regarding the economic issues underlying the industrial strategy debate is not troubling. What is cause for concern is the slowdown in the *rate* of aggregate productivity growth, not a decline in the *level* of aggregate productivity. Studies focusing on shifts among sectors with differing *rates* of productivity growth are the proper medium to identify the sources of the slowdown.

A single important conclusion follows from this discussion: The modeling of sectoral productivity and shift effects cannot be arbitrary. Results of empirical research can be affected greatly if all inputs are not treated symmetrically, if intersectoral linkages are ignored, or if shift effects are characterized in terms of levels rather than rates of growth.

## THE STORY OF POSTWAR ECONOMIC GROWTH

Measures of postwar growth in total-factor productivity have been developed by Fraumeni, Gollop, and Jorgenson for the private domestic business economy and for each of the forty-five sectors that make up that aggregate.[13] A detailed discussion of the methodology, data sources, and early results is presented in Gollop and Jorgenson (1980); estimates for the 1948–1976 period are reported in Fraumeni and Jorgenson (1980). This body of research relies on methods consistent with the economic principles of productivity accounting outlined in this chapter. As such, its estimates of aggregate and sectoral productivity provide an opportunity to break down postwar economic growth into the source components identified in Equation 7-6.

### The Aggregate Economy

The U.S. economy experienced rapid growth in the early postwar period, but its recent performance has been less impressive. The rate of economic growth peaked during the period from 1960 to 1966, slowed substantially between 1966 and 1973, and has declined to disappointingly low levels since then. Concurrent with the decline in economic growth has been the precipitous deterioration of productivity growth.

Analysis of the slowdown must begin with the decomposition of the growth of aggregate output during the postwar period into its basic source components. Using Equation 7-2, the rate of growth of the economy's aggregate output can be expressed as the sum of the contributions of labor and capital inputs and the rate of productivity growth. The contribution of each input is the product of the input growth rate and the average share of the input in the value of output. The results are reported in Table 7-1 for the 1948–1976 period and seven subperiods. With the exception of 1973–1976, each subperiod covers economic activity from one cyclical peak to the next. The last subperiod ends in 1976, a year of recovery from the sharp downturn in economic activity in 1974 and 1975.

Over the full postwar period, output grew at an average annual rate of 3.5 percent. It reached its maximum, 4.83 percent, during the 1960–1966 period but increased at only 0.89 percent during the recession and partial recovery of 1973–1976. Among the source contributions, capital is the most important, with an average of 1.61 percent, or nearly half of the

**Table 7-1. Growth of Output and Source Contributions for the U.S. Economy, 1948 to 1976**

|                           | 1948–1976 | 1948–1953 | 1953–1957 | 1957–1960 | 1960–1966 | 1966–1969 | 1969–1973 | 1973–1976 |
|---------------------------|-----------|-----------|-----------|-----------|-----------|-----------|-----------|-----------|
| Output                    | 0.0350    | 0.0457    | 0.0313    | 0.0279    | 0.0483    | 0.0324    | 0.0324    | 0.0089    |
| Contributions to economic growth: |   |           |           |           |           |           |           |           |
| Capital input             | 0.0161    | 0.0194    | 0.0154    | 0.0109    | 0.0156    | 0.0211    | 0.0161    | 0.0126    |
| Labor input               | 0.0075    | 0.0097    | 0.0013    | 0.0057    | 0.0116    | 0.0108    | 0.0068    | 0.0033    |
| Productivity growth       | 0.0114    | 0.0166    | 0.0146    | 0.0113    | 0.0211    | 0.0004    | 0.0095    | −0.0070   |

*Source*: Barbara M. Fraumeni and Dale W. Jorgenson, "The Role of Capital in U.S. Economic Growth, 1948–1976," in *Capital, Efficiency, and Growth*, ed. George M. von Furstenberg (Cambridge, Mass.: Ballinger, 1980), pp. 9–250. Reprinted with permission.

postwar growth in output. Next in importance are productivity growth and labor input, with average annual contributions of 1.14 percent and 0.75 percent, respectively.

The summary description of economic activity during the 1973–1976 period is striking. The economic growth rate of 0.89 percent a year was a full 2.61 percentage points below the postwar average of 3.5 percent. During this period, the contribution of capital input fell to 1.26 percent, a drop of 0.35 percentage points from the postwar average. The contribution of labor input fell to 0.33 percent, a 0.42-percentage-point drop from its postwar average. The rate of productivity growth, at a negative 0.70 percent, was down 1.84 percentage points from its 1948–1976 average. This decline accounts for 70 percent of the 2.61-percentage-point drop in economic activity. The implication is clear: A detailed explanation of the fall in the rate of productivity growth is needed to account for the slowdown in U.S. economic growth.

## Sources of Productivity Growth

The aggregate economy's rate of productivity growth depends on productivity growth within individual sectors, shifts in economic activity among sectors, and the market's ability to reallocate resources to their most productive uses. Equation 7-6 formally describes this source decomposition. The proper design of an industrial strategy depends importantly on the sign and magnitude of each source component.

The model described in this chapter is applied to the 1948–1976 aggregate and sectoral data developed by Fraumeni, Gollop, and Jorgenson. To examine the resource reallocation and sectoral shift components, the 1948–1976 period is divided into two subperiods, 1948–1966 and 1966–1976. The period is divided at 1966 because that year is commonly accepted as marking both the end of the golden age of postwar economic growth and the beginning of the decline in U.S. productivity growth.[14]

A comparison of pre-1966 and post-1966 economic history in the light of Equation 7-5 provides insights into the economic issues underlying the industrial strategy debate. If the recent slowdown is the result of the market's failure to allocate resources efficiently, post-1966 reallocation effects should be small, perhaps even negative, relative to their pre-1966 counterparts. If shifts in economic activity are responsible, the changing distribution of weights from the golden age to the period of decline should account for much of the recent slowdown. If, in contrast, a widespread and substantial decline in sectoral productivity has occurred since 1966, post-1966 aggregate productivity growth should mirror any constant weighted sum of post-1966 sectoral growth rates.

The results of the complete decomposition are reported in Table 7-2. For the 1948–1966 period, the aggregate rate of productivity growth, 1.68 percent a year, is dominated by the contribution of sectoral rates. The average annual contributions of reallocations of value added, labor input, and capital input are −0.35 percent, −0.03 percent, and 0.09 percent, respectively. The combined −0.29 annual effect of these reallocations is negligible relative to the 1.97 percent annual contribution of sectoral productivity growth.

The 1966–1976 period exhibited a fundamentally different character. Resource reallocations made the largest contribution to aggregate productivity growth. Market reallocation terms annually contributed an

**Table 7-2. Sources of Aggregate Productivity Growth, 1948 to 1976**

|  | 1948–1966 | 1966–1976 | Period-to-Period Change |
|---|---|---|---|
| Aggregate rate of productivity growth | 0.0168 | 0.0018 | −0.0150 |
| Source components: |  |  |  |
|   Sectoral rates of productivity growth: | 0.0197 | −0.0007 | −0.0204 |
|     Shifts in economic activity among sectors | — | 0.0004 | 0.0004 |
|     Changes in productivity growth within sectors | 0.0197 | −0.0011 | −0.0208 |
|   Resource reallocations: | −0.0029 | 0.0025 | 0.0054 |
|     Value added | −0.0035 | 0.0018 | 0.0053 |
|     Labor input | −0.0003 | 0.0000 | 0.0003 |
|     Capital input | 0.0009 | 0.0007 | −0.0002 |

average 0.25 percentage points; sectoral productivity growth declined at an annual 0.07 percent rate. The result was a dismal 0.18 percent annual rate of aggregate productivity growth.

Although the aggregate performance was disappointing, resources responded properly to market signals. Market reallocations of capital input to sectors having higher rates of return on capital and a recomposition of aggregate value added to sectors with lower marginal production costs annually contributed, on average, 0.07 percent and 0.18 percent, respectively. In short, market-directed reallocations were sufficient to maintain a positive rate of productivity growth for the overall economy.

The period-to-period changes reported in Table 7-2 indicate the sources of the productivity slowdown. The average annual rate of aggregate productivity growth decreased 1.5 percentage points between 1948–1966 and 1966–1976, and the average annual contribution of sectoral productivity growth declined a full 2.04 percentage points. What prevented the sectoral decline from causing a comparable decline in aggregate performance was a 0.54 percentage-point gain from the market-directed reallocation of resources to more productive uses.

It is important to emphasize that postwar shifts in economic activity had little to do with the observed deterioration of aggregate performance. In fact, relative to the distribution of economic activity during 1948–1966, post-1966 sectoral shifts made a modest 0.04-percentage-point contribution. That is, if the composition of economic activity had not changed between 1948–1966 and 1966–1976, the contribution of sectoral productivity growth would have been −2.08 percentage points instead of −2.04 percentage points. Moreover, this result is insensitive to the choice of base-period weights. If the 1948–1953 period were selected as the base period, the sectoral shift effect during 1966–1976 would be changed insignificantly; instead of the 0.04 effect associated with 1948–1966 weights, the shift effect would be 0.05.[15]

The decline in aggregate productivity performance after 1966 is clearly due neither to the post-1966 shift in economic activity among sectors nor to any failure of the market system to reallocate resources to their most productive uses. Instead, it is the result of the widespread collapse of productivity growth within individual sectors.

The implications for the industrial strategy debate are equally clear: (1) There is no evidence that sector-targeted intervention would have a significant impact on macroeconomic performance. Although sectoral shifts in economic activity have occurred throughout the postwar period, they have been unimportant in explaining the recent slowdown in aggregate productivity growth. (2) Economic policy should stimulate productivity growth across all sectors. The evidence suggests that the decline in sectoral productivity growth has been both widespread and substantial, thereby lending support to a sector-neutral industrial strategy. (3) Because the market system has responded to the productivity slowdown by reallocating resources to more productive uses, the evidence argues against the need for a sector-biased industrial policy. A sector-neutral industrial policy is indicated.

## The Sectoral Slowdown

The evidence discussed in the preceding section suggests that the collapse of sectoral productivity bears sole responsibility for the recent decline in aggregate productivity growth. A detailed examination of postwar sectoral data confirms this conclusion.

Using Equation 7-4, Fraumeni, Gollop, and Jorgenson developed measures of total-factor productivity for each of the forty-five industrial sectors in the private business economy. The results of that research are summarized in Table 7-3 for the full postwar period and for the 1948–1966 and 1966–1976 subperiods.

Although Table 7-3 demonstrates that rates of productivity growth vary considerably across sectors, it reveals a more important fact: A similar pattern describes the postwar productivity performance of most sectors. Among the forty-five sectors, thirty-four experienced declines in their annual rates of productivity growth between the subperiods. Only ten sectors registered increases. (One sector's rate was unchanged.) Moreover, not only did three-fourths of the sectors exhibit decreasing productivity growth rates, but the average annual decline endured by these thirty-four sectors, $-2.02$ percentage points, was twice the average annual increase calculated for the ten sectors enjoying increased rates of productivity

Table 7-3. Productivity Growth by Sector, 1948 to 1976

|  | Average Annual Growth Rate | | |
|  | 1948–1976 | 1948–1966 | 1966–1976 |
|---|---|---|---|
| Agricultural production | 0.0216 | 0.0240 | 0.0169 |
| Agricultural services | −0.0115 | −0.0013 | −0.0311 |
| Metal mining | 0.0029 | 0.0059 | −0.0025 |
| Coal mining | −0.0046 | 0.0160 | −0.0439 |
| Crude petroleum and natural gas | −0.0057 | 0.0117 | −0.0389 |
| Nonmetallic mining | 0.0012 | −0.0066 | 0.0159 |
| Contract construction | 0.0007 | 0.0098 | −0.0166 |
| Food and related products | 0.0129 | 0.0208 | −0.0020 |
| Tobacco | −0.0044 | 0.0028 | −0.0181 |
| Textiles | 0.0138 | 0.0191 | 0.0038 |
| Apparel | 0.0090 | 0.0071 | 0.0127 |

**Table 7–3. (continued)**

|  | Average Annual Growth Rates | | |
|---|---|---|---|
|  | *1948–1976* | *1948–1966* | *1966–1976* |
| Paper | −0.0038 | −0.0046 | −0.0023 |
| Printing and publishing | 0.0082 | 0.0060 | 0.0125 |
| Chemicals | 0.0187 | 0.0233 | 0.0100 |
| Petroleum and coal products | −0.0015 | 0.0177 | −0.0381 |
| Rubber and plastics | 0.0054 | 0.0054 | 0.0054 |
| Leather | 0.0067 | 0.0079 | 0.0043 |
| Lumber and wood products[a] | −0.0087 | 0.0015 | −0.0283 |
| Furniture and fixtures | 0.0104 | 0.0136 | 0.0045 |
| Stone, clay, and glass | −0.0008 | −0.0013 | −0.0049 |
| Primary metals | −0.0068 | −0.0042 | −0.0116 |
| Fabricated metals | 0.0032 | 0.0081 | −0.0061 |
| Machinery[b] | 0.0034 | 0.0065 | −0.0024 |
| Electrical machinery | 0.0118 | 0.0129 | 0.0098 |
| Transportation equipment and ordnance[c] | 0.0070 | 0.0107 | −0.0001 |
| Motor vehicles | 0.0124 | 0.0132 | 0.0109 |
| Intruments | 0.0060 | 0.0106 | −0.0027 |
| Miscellaneous manufacturing | 0.0115 | 0.0098 | 0.0149 |
| Railroads and rail express | 0.0178 | 0.0232 | 0.0076 |
| Street rail, bus lines, and taxis | −0.0135 | −0.0113 | −0.0176 |
| Trucking and warehousing | 0.0150 | 0.0194 | 0.0065 |
| Water transportation | 0.0081 | 0.0002 | 0.0232 |
| Air transportation | 0.0162 | 0.0377 | −0.0245 |
| Pipelines[d] | 0.0506 | 0.0565 | 0.0393 |
| Transportation services | −0.0263 | −0.0312 | −0.0171 |
| Telephone and telegraph | 0.0229 | 0.0264 | 0.0164 |
| Radio and TV broadcasting | −0.0099 | −0.0087 | −0.0122 |
| Electric utilities | 0.0204 | 0.0408 | −0.0184 |
| Gas utilities | 0.0103 | 0.0219 | −0.0017 |
| Water supply and sanitation services | 0.0084 | 0.0191 | −0.0118 |
| Wholesale trade | 0.0107 | 0.0113 | 0.0095 |
| Retail trade | 0.0098 | 0.0158 | −0.0016 |
| Finance, insurance, and real estate | −0.0002 | −0.0041 | 0.0073 |
| Services[e] | 0.0067 | 0.0043 | 0.0113 |
| Nonprofit institutions | 0.0044 | 0.0022 | 0.0086 |
| Weighted average | 0.0124 | 0.0197 | −0.0007 |
| Unweighted average | 0.0060 | 0.0105 | −0.0025 |

*Source*: Fraumeni and Jorgenson, "The Role of Capital in U.S. Economic Growth, 1948–1976," *op. cit.*, pp. 9–250.

[a] Excludes furniture.
[b] Excludes electrical machinery.
[c] Excludes motor vehicles.
[d] Excludes natural gas.
[e] Excludes private households and institutions.

performance, 1.04 percentage points. The productivity slowdown beginning in 1966 has been widespread and substantial.

This conclusion is robust no matter how the data reported in Table 7-3 are evaluated. The median annual rate of sectoral productivity growth in the 1948–1966 period was 1.02 percent; in the 1966–1976 period, it turned negative, dropping to −0.09 percent. The simple unweighted average of annual sectoral rates fell by nearly the same amount, from 1.05 percent in the pre-1966 period to −0.25 percent in the post-1966 span. That the mean and median both declined by similar amounts is consistent with the conclusion that the productivity decline has occurred rather uniformly across the economy.

The widespread nature of the sectoral slowdown is illustrated by the data in Table 7-4. During the 1948–1966 subperiod, only eight sectors exhibited negative productivity growth rates. Only two sectors (transportation services and street rail, bus lines, and taxicabs) had annual rates of less than −1.0 percent. In sharp contrast, twenty-four sectors had negative growth rates during the 1966–1976 period and fifteen of these had productivity declining at rates exceeding −1.0 percent a year.

The full importance of the decline in sectoral performance for the aggregate economy is determined by weighting each sector's growth rate by the ratio of the value of that sector's total output to aggregate value added.[16] As reported in Table 7-2, the weighted average of annual sectoral productivity growth rates decreased between the two subperiods by more than 2 percentage points, from 1.97 percent to −0.07 percent. The seriousness of the sectoral productivity story is further revealed by focusing on those sectors whose productivity growth rates exhibit a large change

**Table 7-4. Distribution of Sectoral Productivity Growth Rates, 1948 to 1976**

| | Number of Sectors | |
| --- | --- | --- |
| *Average Annual Rates* | *1948–1966* | *1966–1976* |
| Less than −4% | 0 | 1 |
| −4% to −3% | 1 | 3 |
| −3% to −2% | 0 | 2 |
| −2% to −1% | 1 | 9 |
| −1% to 0% | 6 | 9 |
| 0% to 1% | 15 | 11 |
| 1% to 2% | 13 | 8 |
| 2% to 3% | 6 | 1 |
| 3% to 4% | 1 | 1 |
| More than 4% | 2 | 0 |

*Source*: Fraumeni and Jorgenson, "The Role of Capital in U.S. Economic Growth, 1948–1976," *op. cit.*, pp. 9–250.

between the two subperiods. A large change is any positive or negative change exceeding 2.5 percentage points. Table 7-5 identifies ten sectors that meet this criterion; in every case, the large change was negative.

It is also informative to compare weighted and unweighted average rates of productivity growth within and between subperiods. The weighted average of sectoral growth rates for 1948–1966 is 1.97 percent, exceeding the 1.05 percent unweighted average. The implication is that sectors with large shares in national output had higher rates of productivity growth than sectors with small shares. The same holds true for 1966–1976; the weighted average, −0.07 percent, exceeds the unweighted average, −0.25 percent. However, the weighted average declined more between the two subperiods (−2.04 percentage points) than the unweighted average (−1.30 percentage points). This suggests that although industries with large output shares continued to have higher rates of productivity growth than smaller sectors, the large sectors suffered greater declines in their own rates of productivity growth.

In summary, these sectoral results confirm the conclusions derived from the discussion of the sources of aggregate productivity growth. As Table 7-2 indicates, the slowdown in aggregate productivity growth is not the result of shifts in economic activity from high- to low-productivity-growth sectors or the market system's failure to reallocate resources, nor is it the result of a decline in sectoral productivity in only a few important sectors. The economy's overall rate of productivity performance has declined to disappointingly low levels because of widespread and substantial deterioration in sectoral productivity growth.

**Table 7-5. Sectors Exhibiting Large Changes in Total-Factor Productivity Growth**[a]

|                                      | Percentage-Point Change |
| ------------------------------------ | ----------------------- |
| Agricultural services                | −2.98                   |
| Coal mining                          | −5.99                   |
| Crude petroleum and natural gas      | −5.06                   |
| Construction                         | −2.64                   |
| Petroleum and coal products          | −5.58                   |
| Lumber and wood products[b]          | −2.98                   |
| Air transportation                   | −6.22                   |
| Electric utilities                   | −5.92                   |
| Gas utilities                        | −3.36                   |
| Water and sanitation services        | −3.09                   |

Source: Fraumeni and Jorgenson, "The Role of Capital in U.S. Economic Growth, 1948–1976," op. cit., pp. 9–250.
[a] A large change between 1948–1966 and 1966–1976 is defined as any positive or negative change exceeding 2.5 percentage points.
[b] Excludes furniture.

## CONCLUSION

Three dominant conclusions can be drawn from this research: (1) There is no evidence that sector-targeted intervention would have a significant impact on macroeconomic performance. Sectoral shifts in economic activity have occurred throughout the postwar period, but they have been unimportant in explaining the recent slowdown in aggregate productivity growth. In fact, relative to the sectoral distribution of economic activity in either the 1948–1953 or the 1948–1966 periods, post-1966 shifts in economic activity made a modest 0.04 percent annual contribution to economic growth. (2) The evidence suggests that the decline in sectoral productivity growth has been both widespread and substantial, thereby lending support to a sector-neutral industrial strategy. On average, productivity growth within sectors declined by 2.08 percentage points between 1948–1966 and 1966–1976. This more than accounts for the 1.50-percentage-point decline in aggregate productivity growth. (3) The market system has responded to the productivity slowdown by reallocating resources to more productive uses. Had it not been for these reallocations, the decline in aggregate productivity growth would have been 30 percent greater. Thus, economic history argues against the need for a sector-biased industrial strategy.

Those advocating a sector-targeted strategy not only must defend their views against economic history but also must argue persuasively that they have a clear vision of future events. A market economy is a dynamic organism. Demand and supply conditions are continually changing, often in unexpected and uncontrolled ways. Unanticipated innovations occur sporadically, spurring some industries and forcing adjustments in others. Unforeseen changes in market prices send clear signals for reallocating labor, capital, and material inputs across sectors. It is not obvious that policy makers can foresee future events more clearly than a dynamic market.

The implications of the conclusions are clear: Productivity stimulants should be applied broadly across the economy. No constraints should be imposed on the ability of the market system to allocate resources to their most productive uses. Policy should be sector-neutral, not sector-biased.

## APPENDIX: LINKING AGGREGATE AND SECTOR MEASURES OF PRODUCTIVITY GROWTH

### Aggregate Economy

An economy's macroeconomic objective for production is to maximize value added, $V$, given supplies of primary inputs labor, $L$, and capital, $K$:

$$V = f(L, K, T) \qquad (7\text{-}7)$$

where $T$ is an index of time. The rate of aggregate productivity growth, $G$, is determined by taking the total logarithmic derivative of Equation 7-7 with respect to time and solving for $G$:

$$G = \frac{d \ln V}{dT} - \frac{\partial \ln V}{\partial \ln L} \cdot \frac{d \ln L}{dT} - \frac{\partial \ln V}{\partial \ln K} \cdot \frac{d \ln K}{dT} \qquad (7\text{-}8)$$

where $G = \partial \ln f / \partial T$.

Under constant returns to scale and competitive factor markets

$$\frac{\partial \ln V}{\partial \ln L} = \frac{p_L L}{q_v V}$$

$$\frac{\partial \ln V}{\partial \ln K} = \frac{p_K K}{q_v V} \qquad (7\text{-}9)$$

and

$$\frac{p_L L}{qvV} + \frac{p_K K}{qvV} = 1 \qquad (7\text{-}10)$$

where $q_V$ is the price associated with aggregate value added and $p_L$ and $p_K$ are economy-wide average prices for labor and capital inputs, respectively.

The expression for the aggregate rate of productivity growth, Equation 7-8, can then be written in its familiar form:

$$G = \frac{d \ln V}{dT} - \frac{p_L L}{q_v V} \cdot \frac{d \ln L}{dT} - \frac{p_K K}{q_v V} \cdot \frac{d \ln K}{dT} \qquad (7\text{-}11)$$

**The Individual Sectors**

The appropriate specification of an industry's technology is a production function incorporating all primary and intermediate inputs:

$$X_j = h^j(L_j, K_j, X_{1j}, X_{2j}, \ldots, X_{nj}) \qquad (7\text{-}12)$$

where $X_j$ is the quantity of the $j$th industry's gross output, $L_j$ and $K_j$ represent the sector's labor and capital inputs, and $X_{ij}$ is the quantity of the $i$th intermediate input used in the $j$th industry.

When Equation 7-12 is differentiated logarithmically with respect to time, the overall rate of growth in output can be broken down into its source components:

$$\frac{d \ln X_j}{dT} = e_j + \frac{\partial \ln X_j}{\partial \ln K_j} \cdot \frac{d \ln K_j}{dT} + \frac{\partial \ln X_j}{\partial \ln L_j} \cdot \frac{d \ln L_j}{dT}$$

$$+ \sum_i \frac{\partial \ln x_j}{\partial \ln x_{ij}} \cdot \frac{d \ln X_{ij}}{dT} \qquad (7\text{-}13)$$

where $e_j \equiv \partial \ln X_j / \partial T$.

Assuming competitive equilibrium in all input and output markets implies that each input is paid the value of its marginal product, we conclude that

$$\frac{\partial \ln X_j}{\partial \ln L_j} = \frac{p_{Lj} L_j}{q_j X_j}$$

$$\frac{\partial \ln X_j}{\partial \ln K_j} = \frac{p_{Kj} K_j}{q_j X_j}$$

$$\frac{\partial \ln X_j}{\partial \ln X_{ij}} = \frac{p_{ij} X_{ij}}{q_j X_j} \qquad (i = 1, 2, \ldots, n) \qquad (7\text{-}14)$$

where $p_{Lj}$ and $p_{Kj}$ are prices paid by the $j$th sector for labor and capital inputs, respectively, $p_{ij}$ is the price paid by the $j$th sector for intermediate input delivered from the $i$th sector, and $q_j$ is the price of output produced by the $j$th sector.

Maintaining constant returns to scale assures consistency with the sectoral accounting identity:

$$\frac{p_{Lj} L_j}{q_j X_j} + \frac{p_{Kj} K_j}{q_j X_j} + \sum_i \frac{p_{ij} X_{ij}}{q_j X_j} = 1 \qquad (7\text{-}15)$$

It is then possible to write Equation 7-13 in equivalent form:

$$e_j = \frac{d \ln X_j}{dT} - \frac{p_{Lj} L_j}{q_j X_j} \cdot \frac{d \ln L_j}{dT} - \frac{p_{Kj} K_j}{q_j X_j} \frac{d \ln K_j}{dT}$$

$$- \sum_i \frac{p_{ij} X_{ij}}{q_j X_j} \cdot \frac{d \ln X_{ij}}{dT} \qquad (7\text{-}16)$$

## Aggregating Over Sectors

A series of substitutions permits the rate of aggregate productivity growth, $G$, in Equation 7-11 to be separated into terms identifying both the transmission of advances in sectoral productivity and the effects of resource reallocations among sectors. The argument begins with the definition of the value of aggregate value added:

$$q_v V = q_v \sum_j V_j \qquad (7\text{-}17)$$

so that

$$q_v \frac{dV}{dT} = q_v \sum_j \frac{dV_j}{dT} \qquad (7\text{-}18)$$

where $V_j$ is value added originating in the $j$th sector. When Equation 7-18 is substituted into Equation 7-11, the aggregate of productivity growth is given implicitly by the expression:

$$(q_V V)G = q_V \sum_j \frac{dV_j}{dT} - p_L \frac{dL}{dT} \tag{7-19}$$

At the sectoral level, the value of sectoral value added is defined as follows:

$$q_j^V V_j = q_j X_j - \sum_i p_{ij} X_{ij} \tag{7-20}$$

so that

$$q_j^V \frac{dV_j}{dT} = q_j \frac{dX_j}{dT} - \sum_i p_{ij} \frac{dX_{ij}}{dT} \tag{7-21}$$

where $q_j^V$ is the price corresponding to $V_j$.

When Equation 7-21 is substituted into Equation 7-19 and the following market definitions are used,

$$L = \sum_j L_j$$

$$K = \sum_j K_j \tag{7-22}$$

the rate of aggregate productivity growth can be expressed as follows:

$$G = \sum_j \frac{q_V - q_j^V}{q_V V} \cdot \frac{dV_j}{dT} + \sum_j \frac{q_j X_j}{q_V V} \cdot \frac{d \ln X_j}{dT} - \sum_i \sum_j \frac{p_{ij} X i_j}{q_V V}$$

$$\cdot \frac{d \ln X_{ij}}{dT} - \sum_j \frac{p_L L_j}{q_V V} \cdot \frac{d \ln L_j}{dT} - \sum_j \frac{p_K K_j}{q_V V} \cdot \frac{d \ln K_j}{dT} \tag{7-23}$$

Finally, when Equation 7-16 is multiplied by $q_j X_j / q_v V$, all sectors are added together, and the resulting expression is substituted into Equation 7-23, the following statement is produced:

$$G = \sum_j \frac{q_j X_j}{q_V V} e_j + \sum_j \frac{q_V - q_j^V}{q_V V} \cdot \frac{dV_j}{dT} + \sum_j \frac{p_{Kj} - p_K}{q_V V} \cdot \frac{dK_j}{dT}$$

$$+ \sum_j \frac{p_{Lj} - p_L}{q_V V} \cdot \frac{dL_j}{dT} \tag{7-24}$$

The rate of aggregate productivity growth can be broken down into four components: a weighted sum of sectoral productivity growth rates and three terms reflecting the importance of sectoral reallocations of value added, capital, and labor.

## NOTES

1. The values of aggregate output and inputs are defined from the point of view of the producer. Consequently, aggregate value added (or deliveries to final demand) includes subsidies paid to producers and excludes indirect business taxes on output and all excise and sales taxes.

2. Aggregate value added and deliveries to final demand are equivalent concepts only for a macro economy importing no material inputs. However, the closed-economy nature of the framework developed for this chapter does not affect the paper's substantive conclusions. For a discussion of measuring aggregate productivity growth in an economy importing material inputs, see Frank M. Gollop. "Growth Accounting in an Open Economy," in *Developments in Econometric Analyses of Productivity*, ed. A. Dogramaci (Boston: Klumer Nijhoff, 1982).

3. Note that an increase in $e_j$ does not necessarily imply that $Q_j$ will be more productive when used as an intermediate input in the $i$th sector. Sector $i$ has an independent rate of productivity growth, $e_i$. An increase in $e_j$ implies only that the economy now has more output $Q_j$ available for delivery to final demand and to vertically higher sectors purchasing $Q_j$ as an intermediate input.

4. Under the assumption of competitive input markets, relative marginal products reflect relative input prices.

5. William J. Baumol, "Macroeconomics of Unbalanced Growth: The Anatomy of Urban Crisis," *American Economic Review* 57 (June 1967): 415–426.

6. The subject of shift effects appeared in many papers but was the primary empirical topic in the following papers: William D. Nordhaus, "The Recent Productivity Slowdown," *Brookings Papers on Economic Activity* 3 (1972): 493–536; Edward F. Denison, "The Shift to Services and the Rate of Productivity Change," *Survey of Current Business* 53 (October 1973): 20–35; John R. Norsworthy and Leo J. Fulco, "Productivity and Costs in the Private Economy, 1973," *Monthly Labor Review* 97 (June 1974): 3–9; Ronald E. Kutscher, Jerome A. Mark, and John R. Norsworthy, "The Productivity Slowdown and the Outlook for 1985," *Monthly Labor Review* 100 (May 1977): 3–8; Jerome A. Mark, "Productivity Trends and Prospects," *Special Study on Economic Change: Hearings before the Joint Economic Committee*, 95th Congr. 2d sess., pt. 2, 485; Edward R. Denison, *Accounting for Slower Economic Growth* (Washington, D.C.: The Brookings Institution, 1979); John R. Norsworthy, Michael J. Harper, and Kent Kunze, "The Slowdown in Productivity Growth: Analysis of Some Contributing Factors," *Brookings Papers on Economic Activity* 2 (1979): 387–422; Lester C. Thurow, "The U.S. Productivity Problem," *Data Resources Review* (August 1979); Edward N. Wolff, "Compositional Effects, Sectoral Technical Change, and the Productivity Slowdown" (1981); William J. Baumol and Edward N. Wolff, "Productivity and the Shift to the Services" (1982).

7. For a survey of the empirical literature addressing the importance of shift effects, see Edward N. Wolff, "The Magnitude and Causes of the Productivity Slowdown in the United States: A Survey of Recent Studies," in this volume.

8. Wolff, "Compositional Effects, Sectoral Technical Change, and the Productivity Slowdown," pp. 26–29.

9. See Baumol and Wolff, "Productivity and the Shift to the Services," pp. 6–11, for a formal critique of levels of comparisons.

10. Nordhaus, "The Recent Productivity Slowdown," pp. 520–521.

11. Nordhaus, "The Recent Productivity Slowdown," p. 521.

12. Nordhaus, "The Recent Productivity Slowdown," p. 521.

13. The forty-five sectors exhaust the private domestic business economy as defined in Fraumeni and Jorgenson (1980) and Gollop and Jorgenson (1980).

Excluded sectors are general government, government enterprises, households, and rest-of-world.

14. This interpretation of recent economic history is supported by the postwar trends observed in Table 7-1.

15. Quite coincidentally, Nordhaus found that shifts in economic activity between 1948–1955 and 1965–1971 among sectors with differing rates of productivity growth contributed 0.04 percentage points to aggregate productivity growth. See Nordhaus, "The Recent Productivity Slowdown."

16. See Equation 7–5.

## REFERENCES

Baumol, William J. "Macroeconomics of Unbalanced Growth: The Anatomy of Urban Crisis." *American Economic Review* 57 (June 1967): 415–426.

———, and Edward N. Wolff. 1982. "Productivity and the Shift to the Services."

Denison, Edward F. "The Shift to Services and the Rate of Productivity Change." *Survey of Current Business* 53 (October 1973): 20–35.

———. 1979. *Accounting for Slower Economic Growth* (Washington, D.C.: The Brookings Institution).

Fraumeni, Barbara M., and Dale W. Jorgenson. 1980. "The Role of Capital in U.S. Economic Growth, 1948–1976." In *Capital, Efficiency, and Growth*, edited by George M. von Furstenberg (Cambridge, Mass.: Ballinger), pp. 9–250.

Gollop, Frank M. 1982. "Growth Accounting in an Open Economy." *Developments in Econometric Analyses of Productivity*, edited by A. Dogramaci. Boston: Klumer Nijhoff.

———, and Dale W. Jorgenson. 1980. "U.S. Productivity Growth by Industry: 1947–1973." In *New Developments in Productivity Measurement and Analysis*. Studies in Income and Wealth, 4, edited by J. W. Kendrick and B. Vaccara, (Chicago: University of Chicago Press), pp. 17–136.

Kendrick, John W. 1973. *Postwar Productivity Trends in the United States, 1948–1969* (New York: National Bureau of Economic Research).

Kutscher, Ronald E., Jerome A. Mark, and John R. Norsworthy. "The Productivity Slowdown and the Outlook to 1985." *Monthly Labor Review* 100 (May 1977): 3–8.

Mark, Jerome A. 1978. "Productivity Trends and Prospects." *Special Study on Economic Change: Hearings before the Joint Economic Committee*. 95th Congr. 2 pt. 2, 485.

Nordhaus, William D. "The Recent Productivity Slowdown." *Brookings Papers on Economic Activity* 3 (1972): 493–536.

Norsworthy, John R., and Leo J. Fulco. "Productivity and Costs in the Private Economy, 1973." *Monthly Labor Review* 97 (June 1974): 3–9.

———, Michael J. Harper, and Kent Kunze. "The Slowdown in Productivity Growth: Analysis of Some Contributing Factors." *Brookings Papers on Economic Activity* 2 (1979): 387–422.

Thurow, Lester C. "The U.S. Productivity Problem." *Data Resources Review* 7, no. 6 (August 1979): 1.14–1.19.

Wolff, Edward N. 1981a. Compositional Effects, Sectoral Technical Change, and the Productivity Slowdown."

———. 1981b. "The Magnitude and Causes of the Productivity Slowdown in the United States: A Survey of Recent Studies."

# 8

# Toward an Effective Productivity Program

## WILLIAM J. BAUMOL and KENNETH MCLENNAN

To effect a sustained reversal of U.S. productivity performance, to get it to match the rate of growth achieved by other major industrial nations, it will not be enough merely to modify a few government policies or to encourage managers and employees to work together more closely. To believe that all that is needed to solve the productivity problem is a new government expenditure program, additional tax incentives for business, some temporary protection from foreign imports, or even a sustained economic recovery is only an exercise in self-delusion.

The lag in U.S. productivity growth is certain in the long run to have profound effects on the composition of the economy's output. So far, however, there is no evidence on the basis of manufacturing output measures that the U.S. economy is being deindustrialized, even though there has been erosion of the relative importance of manufacturing employment in the U.S. labor force, as is true in most industrialized nations. The contribution of manufacturing output to the gross national product (GNP) varies with the business cycle, and the output of most manufacturing industries will rise substantially during an economic recovery. Indeed, the real value of manufacturing output was 23.7 percent of real GNP in 1980, which is almost the same as it was in 1960 (23.3 percent),[1] and manufactured goods continue to constitute a major share of U.S. exports. Although deindustrialization of the economy is largely a myth, this should not obscure the fact that during the past two decades, an enormous amount of economic change has occurred within industrial sectors. There has been a progressive reduction in the share of the U.S. labor force that is needed to produce our manufactured output, but this reflects primarily a surge of employment in service industries. Within the manufacturing sector, output and employment have grown rapidly in industries that have utilized high technology and highly skilled workers, but many industries are in serious trouble because they have failed to invest sufficiently in the research and development and new plant and equipment that would enable them to match the efficiency of foreign competitors. For those firms that have failed to innovate, neither a more favorable exchange rate nor a strong economic recovery is likely to prove sufficient to restore them to their former competitive position in world markets.

An improved environment and some modifications in current policies will obviously encourage productivity improvement. There is a serious risk, however, that some policy makers and business executives will use weaknesses in overall economic performance, inefficient government programs, and claims of unfair foreign competition as excuses for not facing up to the economic and political costs that must be incurred to increase productivity growth and restore the competitiveness of some U.S. industries. The convergence of U.S. and Japanese *levels* of manufacturing productivity confirms that an economic recovery alone will not solve the productivity problem of many U.S. industries. Indeed, the initial phase of an economic recovery may well increase the competitive advantage of foreign rivals who have matched or surpassed the productivity level of U.S. industries.

## MAJOR COMPONENTS OF A PRODUCTIVITY PROGRAM

A productivity program that effectively improves the performance of industries in all sectors of the economy must entail significant changes in a broad range of public policies. Such changes will require political courage and in the short run will impose costs that will be painful to many segments of the population.

Our study of the productivity issue suggests that three primary and interrelated ingredients must be included in the design of any program to achieve a reasonable set of productivity goals: enhanced innovation, an increased rate of investment, and an unleashing of the market mechanism and its powerful incentives for unceasing effort by management to outstrip its own past performance as well as that of its rivals. A sustained and substantial increase in productivity growth cannot be expected if the market mechanism is subverted by routine penalties on business success and routine protection of firms from the consequences of their failures. Productivity growth will be stunted by a continuation of the meager flow of resources into plant and equipment needed to provide better and more powerful tools to the labor force and to replace those that have become obsolete. Above all, substantial gains in the rate of productivity growth will require a sustained increase in innovation by American industry.

In two senses, innovation may be considered the most critical of the requisites for effectiveness in a productivity program. First, if the economy were to settle into doing things as they have always been done, if innovation were to cease, total-factor productivity would, almost by definition, have to approach a stationary level. Second, although investment and effective use of the market mechanism are of prime importance (as much of the evidence in this volume confirms), from the point of view of productivity growth, both may be considered handmaidens of innovation. That is, both are means, making possible the innovation that is itself the means to increase productivity growth. Accordingly, much of our discussion focuses on innovation and its requisites. (This discussion is outlined in Table 8-1.) We begin our recommendations for a productivity growth program with one that relates primarily to the environment necessary for growth rather than growth itself because we consider this to be of critical importance.

## THE ROLE OF THE MARKET SYSTEM

Interference with the market mechanism's allocation of capital resources must be reduced to the extent that is feasible politically. This requires avoidance of protection of industries and firms with poor economic prospects and abstention from the use of the legal processes to handicap more successful enterprises. Of course, transition processes are often painful and difficult, and it may well be appropriate to undertake measures to soften the blow to failing firms and industries and to facilitate the appropriate adjustments. Help for individuals hurt by the process is certainly defensible. But such measures must be distinguished from unacceptable attempts to prevent the process of change.

The market system does not always produce the optimal allocation of resources and, indeed, if firms are unable to capture fully the returns from their investment in some activities, as in the case of basic research, the market will fail to allocate sufficient resources to this type of economic activity. In the production of most goods and services, however, economists have long emphasized the role of the free market in the efficient allocation of society's resources. Whenever an industry becomes more attractive because of new technology, new products, or increased demand, profitability will rise and capital will automatically flow into it. Similarly, an industry that lags or declines will see its capital stock eroded; low profits discourage replacement investment. This capital-allocation process is a

**Table 8-1. Policies for Stimulation of U.S. Productivity Growth**

| Phase of Technological Innovation | Effect on Productivity Growth | Major CED Recommendation Public | Major CED Recommendation Private |
|---|---|---|---|
| *Favorable economic environment* | Essential precondition for R&D and capital investment | Adoption of policies to control inflation: Control of budget deficits to reduce interest rates | Long-run planning by management to help reduce uncertainty |
| | | Elimination of protectionism and other impediments to market mechanism: Mode of enforcement of antitrust laws; avoidance of impediments to free trade; avoidance of support of firms in financial difficulties | Avoidance of demands for protection by private sector; reduced litigiousness |
| *Research and development* Basic | No measurable effect in short run but in long run important to high-technology sector, crucial for elimination of decline in the long run, but less important for lag in U.S. productivity behind other countries | Basic R&D at universities a high priority—even at expense of other federal programs. Universities should recover full cost under government contracts. Expenditures should be apportioned on basis of excellence rather than "equity" among a large number of institutions | Investment in *basic* research not justified for most industries because of uncertainty of outcomes, unpredictability of identity of beneficiaries |

| | | | |
|---|---|---|---|
| Developmental and applied | No measurable effect in short run but important for technological base in most sectors | Tax policy: support current temporary incremental tax credit but consider permitting flexible write-off (including expensing) of R&D structures and equipment | Important to include in long-term strategic plan |
| *Initial innovation at establishment* | Little measurable effect in short run, but can lead to higher productivity in firm fairly quickly | Tax policies that reduce the effective tax rate on income from capital relative to consumption: Support intent of depreciation policy changes adopted in 1981 | Assess rate of return in relation to cost of capital |
| | | Tax real rather than nominal capital gains (i.e., adjust valuation of capital gains for inflation) | Provide incentives to employees to accept and participate in innovation |
| | | If tax regulations for R&D conducted abroad (regulation 1.861–8) are restored, then only R&D expenses *directly* traceable to foreign earnings should be treated as a deduction from foreign-source income | Entrepreneurship should be encouraged by top management throughout organization, and deviations from traditional approaches protected |
| | | Antitrust rules for joint research by companies should be clarified | Compensation systems that reward successful R&D results and innovations by employees should be considered |

**Table 8-1. (Continued)**

| Phase of Technological Innovation | Effect on Productivity Growth | Major CED Recommendation | |
|---|---|---|---|
| | | Public | Private |
| | | Patent policies: several of CED's past recommendations have now been adopted. In addition, write-off of expenditures for purchase of patent rights or externally designed innovations should be considered | |
| | | Regulatory policies:<br>Speed up regulatory approval of innovations, recognizing that zero-risk is inefficient goal impossible to achieve | |
| | | Social-benefit regulations should avoid zero-risk standards and be subject to benefit-cost analysis | |
| | | Regulatory goals should be pursued via market incentives as in "bubble" concept and "offsets" program | |

*Diffusion and distribution of innovation throughout economy*

Effect on U.S. productivity clearly observable during diffusion process with significant effect on U.S. competitive position

Deregulation of pricing, entry, and exit should continue in markets where competition is present (e.g., transportation and many public utility markets)

Tax policies should:
Stimulate saving and investment
Eliminate bias favoring consumption and discouraging saving
Reduce bias favoring investment in particular types of assets
Support removal of impediments to high-interest earnings on small savings

Elimination of consumption bias in public expenditures
Increased expenditures on public capital (harbors, bridges, etc.)

In future, move toward a more "neutral" tax system should be considered, including:

Company-wide compensation systems should reward productivity improvement

Workers should be helped to recognize that failure to meet competition will result in loss of employment and/or wage

193

**Table 8-1.** (Continued)

| Phase of Technological Innovation | Effect on Productivity Growth | Major CED Recommendation | |
|---|---|---|---|
| | | *Public* | *Private* |
| | | Tax simplification through broadening of tax base and reductions in marginal rates | growth |
| | | Increased "expensing" of capital, trading off a reduction of special tax arrangements against a reduction in corporate tax rate | |
| | | Removal of double taxation of dividends | Management should consider new approaches to work organization that encourage entire organization to achieve productivity growth |

Regulatory policies:
  Accelerate approval of "bubble" concept and "offsets" program

  Permit new plant and equipment to be included in "bubble" (change enabling legislation)

  Proceed with deregulation to avoid devotion of excessive business resources to regulatory processes

  Government should avoid protecting inefficient individual firms or industries

Management should avoid seeking protection from market forces

195

critical component of productivity growth; in this way, without recourse to any government planning agency, the market separates the winners from the losers and assures adequate resources to economic activities that offer the most outstanding prospects.

This suggests that government need not provide special inducements to encourage the flow of capital into particular industries that will lead the economy in the future. Nor does it need to cajole or inveigle investors to act accordingly. Indeed, if our conclusion about the power of the market mechanism is valid, there is no need for any agency even to seek to judge which industries offer the best prospects. The market can determine this very effectively by itself. Rather, what is most urgently needed from government is restraint, abstention from measures that impede the flow of capital or actually encourage it to move in the wrong direction.

There are many ways in which governments do, in fact, impede the allocation of capital through the market mechanism. The most obvious is protection of industries or firms that would otherwise be forced to retrench or to close down altogether. Some of these industries have long been recipients of overt or indirect subsidies. Others seek and receive protection from successful foreign competition.[2] There have been several well-publicized instances in which firms or industries have sought to prevent the effective competition of their more successful rivals.[3] Such measures frustrate the workings of the market mechanism and divert the flow of the economy's investments by retaining resources in areas that are second-best or even less promising, denying those resources to activities whose prospects are most outstanding.

Such interferences with the market mechanism inhibit productivity in other ways as well. For example, one of the prices of the litigiousness entailed in obtaining protection through the courts or the regulatory authorities is an expansion of the role of lawyers in business enterprises at the expense of the entrepreneurs and the engineers. Increased dependence on government assistance inevitably means that resources must be used to meet bureaucratic requirements, and this often inhibits decision making and speedy response to changing market conditions.

It should be emphasized that this sort of interference with the market mechanism does not occur only on the initiative of government. Business, too, has often requested protection by the public sector and undertaken litigation of its own in the courts and before the regulatory agencies.

## THE MACROECONOMIC ENVIRONMENT FOR PRODUCTIVITY GROWTH

Creation of an environment conducive to increased productivity also requires effective control of inflation. Particularly when its rate varies in an unpredictable manner, inflation constitutes a major impediment to planning and decision making by business.

The rapid inflation that beset the United States during much of the 1970s disrupted the capital markets, undermined the value of equities, and thereby made it extremely costly to raise funds for investment through the issue of new stocks. At times, it pushed real interest rates to heights that had no precedent in recent history and in this way impeded the funding of investment through debt. Even when real interest rates were low, the high nominal rates seriously discouraged long-term borrowing because, for example, a long-term agreement to pay a 14 percent interest rate, which is not a great burden when the inflation rate is 12 percent, can become a backbreaking commitment if at some future date the inflation rate declines substantially.

Inflation has thus discouraged investment and impeded long-term contractual arrangements and other enduring commitments. It has led to preoccupation with short-run decisions and short-run results, whereas productivity growth obviously requires the long run to be the major focus of attention.

Inflation has also consumed time and effort better devoted to other purposes. The search for means to prevent the erosion of the value of capital, to avoid the burdens of taxes escalated by inflation, and to deal with the other problems generated by rapid and unpredictable price rises has absorbed considerable amounts of the time and attention of valuable personnel.

All in all, inflation has probably been a major detrimental influence on the economic environment and has thereby constituted a substantial handicap for productivity growth. An enduring reduction in the rate of inflation is almost certainly insufficient by itself to eliminate the nation's productivity problems, but without such a reduction, it will be far more difficult to increase productivity growth.

Although a reexamination of such macroeconomic policy issues as the choice of anti-inflation measures is beyond the scope of this discussion, it is clearly appropriate to recommend that the federal government continue its efforts to contain inflation and resist political pressures to reheat the economy. It is true that unemployment incurs a heavy cost in terms of human tragedy, social disruption, and wasted productive capacity, but it is also true that inflation is not an acceptable solution to the problem of joblessness and that it may only exacerbate that problem in the long run. Therefore, the requirement of productivity growth, as well as a variety of other social goals, calls for continuation of determined efforts to keep inflation under control.

The incentive to invest in the development of new products and more productive processes depends on the demand for goods and services.

Policies designed to dampen effective demand may be appropriate to restrain inflation, but sustained productivity growth nevertheless requires macroeconomic policies that sustain the demand for goods and services over the long run. For this reason, it is desirable—except in periods of severe recession—to avoid large budget deficits that threaten to crowd out private-sector investment through upward pressure on real interest rates.

## STRENGTHENING RESEARCH AND DEVELOPMENT

Because innovation is probably the key element in the stimulation of productivity, the most obvious thing to do is to encourage the research that makes innovation possible.

During the 1963–1967 period, the United States devoted a little more than 3.0 percent of its gross domestic product (GDP) to research and development, with government funds supporting 62.0 to 65.0 percent of this research. From 1967 to 1975, the proportion of GDP invested in research and development (R&D) activities declined to about 2.5 percent, reflecting a major cutback in defense and space expenditures. (The government's share of R&D expenditures dropped to about 51.0 percent.)

The United States spends a slightly higher proportion of its output on research and development than other industrial countries do. Since the mid-1960s, however, several other countries, notably the Federal Republic of Germany and Japan, have devoted an increasing share of their output to research and development, and the proportion of their GNP spent on these activities is now only slightly smaller than that of the United States. In absolute expenditures, however, the United States still dominates the industrial world in resources devoted to research and development.[4]

### Support for Basic Research

A hallmark of basic research is the unpredictability of the uses to which its results will be put and, consequently, of the identity of those who will benefit from it. This gives rise to a variety of issues. The first is the nature of the gains that basic research offers to the country that carries it out. It has been argued that basic research expenditures purchase little advantage in the productivity race because the research results are usually made available to everyone and that other economies may be able to appropriate the bulk of the benefits by concentrating their research resources on application and development.

It is suggestive that the United States appears to have been the world leader in basic research, according to indexes such as shares of GNP devoted to this activity and share of Nobel prizes, throughout the period when the country's productivity growth fell behind that of its commercial rivals. There is something to the argument, although matters are not quite so simple as it suggests. For example, basic research activity contributes to the process of scientific and technical training and helps to provide the skilled labor force necessary for success in innovation. Familiarity with the details of current basic research may also suggest applications more quickly.

Whatever the validity of these qualifications, however, they are not the main point. The primary productivity contribution of basic research is *not* the advantage it confers on one economy relative to others. We have emphasized earlier that the United States is beset by two rather different productivity problems: the slowdown in its own productivity growth and its lag behind other countries. Basic research outlays may or may not make a large difference in the degree to which the United States will succeed in its attempt to catch up with other economies, but it is surely vital for a durable reversal of the fall in U.S. productivity growth.[5]

The unpredictability of the beneficiaries of basic research has a second and more familiar implication: Private enterprise cannot be relied on to devote to this activity the quantity of resources called for by the public interest. Basic research is the illustration *par excellence* of the free-rider problem—that is, the opportunity it presents for beneficiaries to avoid payment of any share of the costs. When it is difficult or impossible to collect payments from the users of a product, that product is obviously not one that will prove attractive to firms operated on the profit motive. This implies that if society is to have the basic research activity that its interests call for, government will have to pay most of the bill. This has, of course, long been recognized. In the United States, the bulk of the basic research has been at universities and research institutes, with funding provided by the public sector. There is little prospect that this arrangement will change and no reason that it should.

The complementarity of the research and teaching activities and the availability of scientists and scholars of outstanding ability at universities make it desirable that much of the nation's basic research continue to be carried out at those institutions.

Given these conclusions, it is appropriate to recommend that the government undertake a commitment to a high level of funding of basic research, particularly that which is carried out in the nation's universities. Moreover, it is important for such funding to achieve a degree of consistency and to offer scope for precommitment of support for substantial periods in order to facilitate long-term planning and to encourage projects that cannot be expected to yield rapid results. In its policy statement *Productivity Policy: Key to the Nation's Economic Future* (1983), the Committee for Economic Development (CED) offered several detailed proposals in this connection, recommending that government pay the full cost of research carried out at universities under contract, rather than continuing to require cost sharing by the universities, an arrangement that has been at best a continuing source of friction and at worst a significant drain on university resources.[6]

In addition, CED recommended that government funds for basic research be apportioned entirely on the basis of the quality of the research personnel and the promise of the projects funded, without any attempt to achieve geographic balance or equality in the treatment of a large number of heterogeneous institutions.

## Applied Research

Whereas basic research may contribute primarily to the nation's effort to grapple with the productivity slowdown rather than with its lag behind other countries, applied research and development almost undoubtedly serves both causes. Yet, despite its importance, this activity can, to a far greater degree, be left to the private sector to finance and carry out. Here, in general, there is little reason to question the efficacy of the profit motive as the requisite stimulus.

Table 8-2 shows that while U.S. government R&D expenditures declined during the 1964–1972 period, business-funded research and development grew at a healthy average annual rate of 4.8 percent. The comparative growth rates indicate that several other countries were allocating increased percentages of resources to R&D activities. This was especially true of Japan, whose growth rates for government and business R&D expenditures were two to four times more rapid than those of the United States. The data also show that since the 1960s' decline in U.S. government R&D expenditures, there has been a significant increase in such outlays. This trend has continued into the 1980s. Expenditures for research and development in the United States have continued to increase in real terms even though the government has reduced the rate of growth of nondefense expenditures.

It is, of course, appropriate for government to carry out or finance research and development in defense, air traffic control, and other areas whose results are likely to have direct uses by the public sector and also to do so in such fields as health and environmental protection, which serve the public interest but are unattractive commercial propositions. But aside from these kinds of direct government participation, the public sector can probably encourage applied R&D activity most effectively by removal or modification of measures that impede or discourage private efforts.

**Table 8-2. Average Annual Real Growth of Business- and Government-Funded Research and Development for Six Large Industrial Nations, 1964–1972 and 1972–1980 (percent)**

|  | Business Funded | | Government Funded | |
|---|---|---|---|---|
|  | *1964–1972* | *1972–1980* | *1964–1972* | *1972–1980* |
| France | 7.3 | 4.2 | 4.3 | 0.0 |
| Federal Republic of Germany | 9.0 | 3.0 | 10.0 | 2.1 |
| Japan | 16.1 | 6.9 | 15.5 | 7.8 |
| United Kingdom | 1.5 | −0.4 | −0.3 | 3.3 |
| United States | 4.8 | 4.3 | −0.9 | 3.2 |

*Source*: Rolf Piekarz, Eleanor Thomas, and Donna Jennings, "International Comparisons of Research and Development and Government Policies," in Kendrick's *International Comparisons of Productivity and Causes of the Slowdown*, copyright 1984, American Enterprise Institute for Public Policy Research. Reprinted with permission from Ballinger Publishing Company.

Five recommendations can be offered to encourage private research and development and to give it advantages similar to those provided in some other industrialized nations.

1. Flexible depreciation rules should be permitted in the case of investment in research and development, and it should be made permissible for outlays on R&D structures and equipment to be treated as expenses for tax purposes. This proposed revision of the tax code is consistent with the purpose of the temporary incentives for R&D investment offered by the 1981 Economic Recovery Tax Act. This procedure would be much simpler than the current incremental R&D tax credit and could be substituted for the credit when it expires in 1986. Flexible depreciation of R&D structures and equipment would provide R&D outlays with the same favorable tax treatment they receive in Japan and other industrialized nations.

2. Firms should be allowed to expense expenditures incurred for the purchase of patent rights or for the use of innovative ideas developed by others. Without this change, such purchases will continue to be treated as acquisition of capital that must be depreciated on a straight-line basis over the useful life of the patent. This can constitute a serious impediment to technology transfer and lead to significant delays in the dissemination and use of new productive techniques.

3. The establishment and expansion of small innovative firms should continue to be encouraged by measures in the spirit of the recent tax changes. Evidence suggests that major innovations are often introduced by small new companies formed especially for that purpose, rather than by

large established enterprises. Recent changes in tax law have encouraged the formation and growth of such firms by removing impediments to the use of last in, first out (LIFO) inventory accounting by small firms, facilitating the use of stock options as an incentive to employees, and increasing the number of shareholders permitted a so-called Subchapter S corporation, with its specially flexible tax status. These changes all seem to be desirable, and further moves in the same direction may well be appropriate.

4. Additional modifications in the patent system should be considered to simplify procedures and increase inducements for applied research. For example, adjustment of the life of a patent should be considered for cases where commercial use is held up by regulatory delays. The promptness with which ownership of patent is decided should perhaps be increased by a first-to-file arrangement, under which the first inventor who submits an application automatically receives the patent. Above all, efforts should be made to provide some sort of patent or copyright protection for intangible contributory products such as software and to make it easier for holders of patents and copyrights to derive appropriate earnings from these assets without inappropriate interference by antitrust authorities. Such modifications would supplement recent changes in the patent laws that have, we believe, contributed to the effectiveness of the system.

5. The antitrust laws should be reexamined to clarify further their implications for cooperative R&D activities. Joint research ventures are now evaluated via a rule of reason, under which a venture will not be declared illegal if the participants have a low combined market share and the joint activities are in the basic rather than the development end of the R&D spectrum.

The Administration has introduced legislation that would increase the protection of joint R&D participants from antitrust prosecution. This legislation would codify current practice by prohibiting the courts from declaring illegal per se any joint research venture or any agreement that concerns the licensing of intellectual property (i.e., a patent or trademark). It limits the awarding of damages for conduct by a joint research arrangement that is eventually found illegal by the courts *provided* that the activities of the arrangement have been fully disclosed to the Antitrust Division of the Justice Department. Damages that can be assessed for anticompetitive conduct with respect to the licensing of intellectual property are also limited. Finally, the scope of what may be deemed misuse of an intellectual property right is limited.

These proposed changes represent major steps toward clarification of the antitrust rules governing joint research and development. However, this still allows the agencies responsible for carrying out antitrust actions considerable discretion in applying the rule of reason. The regulations governing joint R&D activities would be improved if the proposed legislation also were to create a formal review and clearance procedure.[7]

## INNOVATION

### Business Initiatives

Research and development are, of course, only steps on the path to productivity growth; by themselves, they are unlikely to yield any substantial and discernible effects on productivity in the short run. Yet, they are clearly vital components of the future technological bases of most sectors of the economy in the industrial sector of the economy. In the United States, almost three-quarters of business R&D expenditures are concentrated in six major sectors: electrical, electronic and equipment components, chemicals and drugs, aircraft, motor vehicles, and machinery. A similar degree of concentration occurs in other industrial countries.[8] Many of the industries within most of these sectors have had high rates of growth and have given the Unites States a strong absolute advantage in the affected activities.

However, before even developmental and applied research can make a significant contribution, the knowledge that emerges from these activities must attract the attention of someone who is interested in applying it and able to do so. The preparation of ideas for application and their actual adoption and utilization constitute the innovation stage of the productivity-enhancement process.

The literature does not always distinguish adequately between innovation and research and development (where the term "innovation" is used by economists it applies to the process of carrying out in practice the new ideas that emerge from research and elsewhere, for example, the inauguration of manufacture of pocket calculators, in distinction from their invention or design). Therefore, it is possible that arrangements conducive to the one are not always most favorable to the other. For example, much of the empirical evidence[9] indicates that, at least up to a point, increased company size increases the *share* of earnings devoted to research and development; that is, of two industries, the one populated with smaller firms can be expected to devote a smaller quantity of resources to such activities. Yet, anecdotal evidence suggests that small enterprises may have a greater propensity to introduce substantially new methods and new products—that is, to actually carry out the innovations suggested by research and development.

Within a large firm, there is always the danger that bureaucratization and adherence to routine and tradition will stifle entrepreneurship. A distinguishing attribute of an entrepreneur is unwillingness to do things in the way they have always been done. The entrepreneur can make life uncomfortable for others in the firm who have more conservative predilections, pointing out inefficiencies and inadequacies in current procedures and introducing new and disturbing methods and ideas. It is all too easy to pledge allegiance to entrepreneurship while consciously or unconsciously doing much to impede it. Therefore, no large firm can leave the exercise of entrepreneurship to chance. If it really intends to encourage innovativeness, top management must take strong measures to make sure entrepreneurship will not be stifled by the bureaucracy. There are at least four specific means that management can use to prevent this.

1. It must encourage lower-level and middle managers to take reasonable risks, offering substantial rewards for success and avoiding disproportionate penalties for occasional failures.
2. It must go out of its way to provide suitable recognition and rewards for the accomplishments of innovators.
3. It must provide organizational arrangements, such as special divisions or small subsidiaries, that facilitate innovation.
4. It must give protection and rewards to individuals who point out inefficiencies and defects in current operations and other varieties of ineffective business practices.

We recognize, of course, that these are measures of which it is easy to speak approvingly but not so easy to institute and sustain.

## Government Policy

The public sector, too, can do a good deal to facilitate innovation. One of the prime requirements of innovation is capital. Investment is entailed in the very act of introducing the innovation, it is required for the plant and equipment that embody the innovative process or turn out the new product, and it is needed to replace the plant and equipment the innovation renders obsolete. Therefore, one of the main ways government can stimulate innovation is to remove impediments to the formation of productive capital. (See the section "Capital Formation" for a detailed discussion.) More immediately to the point are regulatory impediments to innovation. There are two basic types of regulation:

- *Economic* or *public utility regulation* of profits, prices, entry, and investment of industries such as telecommunications, electricity, railroads, and trucking
- *Social regulation* intended to deal with the matters such as the environment, product safety, and safety in the workplace

Economic or public utility regulation has impeded innovation in the regulated industries in a number of ways. It has slowed decision making by subjecting management to lengthy hearings, competitive challenges, and a variety of other procedures that in some cases have delayed the introduction of new services literally for years, even for more than a decade. By preventing entry or subjecting it to enormous impediments, such regulation has prevented new and innovative firms from operating or delayed their launching significantly. By impeding exit, regulation has exacerbated the risks of entry and tied up capital in economic areas that economic logic and the requirements of productivity growth would have had it leave. Resources were thus prevented from being used in innovative ways in the regulated firm's more profitable activities. Rate-of-return ceilings have often kept regulated firms from deriving profits from successful innovation and have therefore all but removed the incentive for the enterprise to undertake it. Finally, regulatory delays in adjusting prices during periods of inflation have caused the erosion of earnings and made it much more difficult to compete on the capital market for the funds that innovation requires.

We do not mean that regulation of the public utility type is always unjustified. But it does always exact heavy economic costs, not the least of which is its discouragement of innovation. We conclude from this that in any industry in which the degree of competition is sufficient to deprive firms of market power, deregulation should be continued and even hastened. Where monopoly power remains a reality, there may be justification for the heavy economic and social costs of regulation. But where competition can do the job, economic regulation is virtually all cost, with little offsetting benefits; the sooner it can be withdrawn from such markets, the sooner the market mechanism can begin to elicit the full quota of innovation that can be expected to emerge in them.

The arena of social regulation calls for a rather different sort of recommendation. Most such regulations clearly *are* designed to yield social benefits; and although in some cases their ability to pass a cost-benefit test may be questionable, a general policy of deregulation is hardly justified. Instead, the objective here should be, wherever possible, to redesign the regulations in ways that involve no weakening of targets but that reduce the cost of their attainment. Traditional methods of social regulation have impeded innovation in several avoidable ways. They have often been based on particularly rigid direct controls rather than on economic incentives. Instead of allowing management to choose the techniques it employs to meet regulatory targets, it has been told precisely what means to use. The use of low-sulphur coal, smokestack scrubbers, or other narrowly defined techniques has been imposed on business management. Such a technique may be well adapted to the circumstances of some particular plants or firms, but it is hardly likely that it will be the most efficient method for all.

Economists have long maintained that the costs of environmental protection can be reduced substantially and that productivity can be increased—without weakening environmental goals—if financial inducements are substituted for direct controls as the main policy instrument. Several years ago the Environmental Protection Agency undertook some moves in this direction, using the so-called bubble and offsets programs. Under these arrangements, a company is permitted to use any technique to achieve assigned emissions targets, so long as it can demonstrate that it has complied. Moreover, if it is more expensive for company A to eliminate a given quantity of emissions than it is for neighboring company B to do so, the two are permitted and encouraged to enter a voluntary arrangement under which B undertakes to meet *both* A's and its own emissions-reduction requirements and A compensates B for taking over the task.

Unfortunately, the rate of expansion of these flexible programs, with their scope for productivity enhancement, has been disappointingly slow. Moreover, administrative provisions have pointlessly limited their flexibility and in particular have inhibited interfirm trades. Perhaps most important, new plant and equipment have in general been made ineligible for bubble and offsets programs; the government has preferred to issue required standards for engineering designs.

Clearly, such inflexible procedures can constitute major hurdles for productivity growth in general and for innovation in particular. Consequently, it is appropriate to recommend that use of more flexible instruments for environmental protection be simplified, facilitated, and speeded up. New plant and equipment as well as old should be made eligible for inclusion in such programs. This greater flexibility should be designed to reduce costs and encourage innovation and productivity growth without any weakening of defensible environmental goals.

## CAPITAL FORMATION

As we have already noted, expansion of the nation's capital stock is essential both for productivity growth in general and for innovation in particular. However, before discussing the means by which investment can be encouraged, it is desirable to say a bit about the evidence on the role of capital formation in the nation's productivity problems. As we have already noted, there is considerable variation in statistical estimates of the responsibility borne by the behavior of capital formation in the slowdown in the nation's productivity growth. Estimates range from as little as 1 percent to as much as 70 percent; the preponderance of evidence places the figure between 20 and 40 percent. Probably the reason this figure is not higher is that although there was a slight fall in the capital-labor ratio in the early 1970s, the ratio of gross domestic investment to gross domestic output actually increased during a substantial portion of the productivity slowdown period, and it is still above its early postwar level. The rapid increase in labor force participation of women and youths during the 1970s, the effect of the post-1973 oil "shocks" on the rate of obsolescence of some plant and equipment, and the increased capital requirements emanating from regulatory policies are all possible explanations of why the maintenance of or even moderate increases in the rate of capital formation was insufficient to prevent the productivity slowdown. It should be clear from the figures that although the behavior of investment is not the overriding cause of the slowdown, it can be judged with some confidence to be one of the most important contributory influences.

In the case of the lag of the United States behind its leading industrial rivals, the role of investment is even more clear-cut. In Chapter 1, it was reported that both saving out of personal disposable income and investment in manufacturing relative to manufacturing output are nearly twice as high in leading European economies as in the United States and that the disparity between this country and Japan is even greater. Because these differences cumulate and compound, they can over the course of several decades constitute an enormous handicap for the U.S. economy. It is not surprising, therefore, that Chapter 3, which seeks to explain the difference between U.S. and Japanese labor productivity, ascribes 75 percent of the difference to the higher Japanese investment rate during the period 1965–1973.

Since the mid-1970s the rate of growth in capital investment in manufacturing has declined substantially in most European countries. At the same time the rate of growth has been increasing in the United States to the point where we are now devoting to capital investment the same proportion of manufacturing output as are our European competitors. The rate of manufacturing investment has also been declining in Japan and is now probably not much different from the rate for the United States.[10] Since Japanese growth in capital investment was, however, about four times higher than U.S. investment rates for over a decade, on average the stock of Japanese manufacturing capital continues to embody a higher level of technology than U.S. plant and equipment. For the United States to match the average level of technology in Japanese manufacturing plant and equipment, it probably will be necessary for our rate of investment to surpass the Japanese rate of investment for some period of time.

In sum, although the behavior of investment is surely significant for innovation and productivity growth in the United States, it is clearly of overwhelming importance in this country's battle to regain its position of world leadership in productivity expansion. This issue, then, is what can be done about it.

Two major approaches immediately suggest themselves, both involving tax and other institutional arrangements. The first relates to the biases that encourage consumption at the expense of investment; the second concerns the biases that favor investment in consumer durables rather than in industrial plant and equipment.

Both lower- and upper-income groups have encountered significant disincentives to saving, although the nature of these disincentives differed considerably. For a long period, interest ceilings on bank deposits and other usury laws meant that small savers were offered rates of return far below the rate of inflation. They were, in effect, condemned by law to negative real interest rates and to steady erosion of the purchasing power of their savings. Such institutional impediments could, to a considerable degree, be escaped by upper-income groups, whose larger investments could earn market-determined interest rates that compensated for inflation. Because the poor had no such option open to them, it is hardly surprising that saving by the lower-income group was low. Recently, however, matters have been improved. Deregulation of banking, the authorization of postponement of taxes on Individual Retirement Accounts, and increases in the interest rates on U.S. government savings bonds have all served to ameliorate the problem. We recommend the retention of these reforms and elimination of all remaining restraints on the earning by small savers of the full interest rates as determined by the free market.

Large savers have also been subjected to a variety of impediments to saving and investment. Among the more substantial is the fact that capital gains are taxed on the basis of their nominal value rather than their real magnitude. Of course, the entire tax system, like those of most other countries, has been based on nominal values; and in an inflationary period, this has automatically introduced a variety of distortions and disincentives. Yet, there are good reasons for particular concern over the effects of failure to index tax rates in the case of capital gains. It is clear that capital gains are a major component of the return on investment. Therefore, excessive taxation of this type of earning will certainly be a disincentive to capital formation. Most important, because a capital gains tax is a tax on a *differential* in values (the value of the asset when it is sold minus its value when acquired), whereas most taxes (e.g., sales and income taxes) are based on an absolute economic magnitude (the price of the taxed item or the taxpayer's income), the capital gains tax is particularly vulnerable to severe distortion by inflation. An individual whose real income has fallen because of inflation will nevertheless be subject to income taxation only if that real income is positive, but the sale of a capital asset is subject to taxation on the nominal capital gain even when there is a real capital loss. If over the course of two decades when the general price level has risen 150 percent, an asset's price has risen only 100 percent, the holder will have suffered a loss of one-third of the funds invested. Yet, that holder will be taxed as if the asset's value had actually risen 100 percent. Surely, it is difficult to doubt that this significantly discourages investment, particularly by individuals in higher tax brackets.

Recent changes in tax laws that liberalize opportunities for deferral of tax payments on retirement savings, reduce taxes on inheritances, and decrease maximum tax rates on unearned income (including, of course, returns on investment) have served as increased incentives for saving. The modifications may perhaps all be viewed as steps toward a system of taxation based on expenditure rather than income, that, because it would completely exempt from taxation any earnings on saving and investment until they are actually spent, may perhaps be considered the most savings-stimulative of tax arrangements. A number of observers have concluded that a shift to some form of expenditure tax is socially desirable. One possible move in this direction would be a simplification of the individual income tax code through elimination of many of the current individual deductions. This would significantly reduce average and marginal tax rates and at the same time remove some of the consumption bias in the system. We are not prepared to endorse any specific tax reform proposal, but tax reform to remove impediments to saving and investment certainly merits serious consideration as a part of the nation's productivity program.

## TAX BIASES AND MISALLOCATION OF INVESTMENT

The goal of enhanced innovation and productivity growth calls for measures that encourage industrial use of the resources made available by saving and that do not bias their allocation among economic activities. Observers have concluded that U.S. tax laws bias the allocation of capital resources in at least two major ways.

First, they favor investment in housing rather than industrial capital, diverting capital that might otherwise have been used in the innovation process or to enhance productivity in other ways.

In the case of investment in real estate for business purposes, the deduction of mortgage interest and real estate taxes from profits is justified as a normal cost of business. Earnings from real estate investment are subject to real estate taxes, which raise taxes on business investment in housing and other real estate above the tax on profits from other forms of business investment. The deductibility provisions in the tax code partially offset this disadvantage.

There are five provisions in the federal income tax code that favor investment in the housing sector: (1) exclusion of net imputed rent for owned-occupied homes, (2) deductibility of mortgage interest, (3) deferral of capital gains on home sales, (4) one-time exclusion of up to $125,000 in capital gains from home sales for those fifty-five years old and older, and (5) exclusion of interest from tax-exempt mortgage bonds.

The main source of the bias in favor of investment in homes arises because the flow of housing service (the imputed rent) of owner-occupied housing is excluded from taxable income. If taxable income were adjusted for imputed rent, deductibility of mortgage interest and real estate taxes would be appropriate because they constitute a reduction in the net real incomes of homeowners.

Research suggests that the current tax deductibility provisions together with the simultaneous failure to adjust for imputed rent for owner-occupied housing have produced a sectoral bias in the tax code that accounts for about one-fourth of the increase in housing consumption between 1945 and 1974. It is also concluded that government housing assistance expenditure programs, including the provision of public housing, have significantly increased the consumption of housing above what it otherwise would have been. The pertinent implication is that this increase in consumption diverted resources from other economic activities, reduced the rate of long-term growth in overall economic activity, and on balance probably led to a less equitable distribution of income.[11]

Second, the investment tax credit favors investment in equipment over investment in plant, and this bias seems to have been increased recently. Such tax provisions not only influence the usage patterns of capital resources within an industry but may also affect significantly the allocation of capital among industries. By favoring economic activities whose technology calls for relatively large expenditures on equipment rather than plant, they distort capital flows toward such industries and away from industries needing heavy outlays on plant. Obviously, this pattern of modification of capital uses bears little relation to that called for by the most promising opportunities for innovation and enhancement of productivity growth.

Increased neutrality of the tax system, especially in marginal tax rates among industries, is a matter of great importance for stimulating innovation. Perhaps one very effective way to move in this direction would be to permit all outlays for plant and equipment to be treated as expenses, thereby making them deductible at the time of purchase. This expensing approach would make continuation of the investment tax credit inappropriate, and that, too, would remove a source of bias in the treatment of different types of investment. The reduction or elimination of the various types of business tax preferences in exchange for a decrease in the tax on corporate profits also merits serious consideration.

## ALLOCATION OF CAPITAL RESOURCES:
## INDUSTRIAL STRATEGY PROPOSALS

Some observers, both here and abroad, have concluded, usually on the basis of little evidence, that the distribution of the nation's capital among industries through the workings of the market mechanism is not generally the distribution that maximizes production growth in the nation as a whole. Accordingly, the poor U.S. productivity performance has given rise to numerous proposals for particular brands of "industrial policy." Most of these proposals attempt to use government intervention to affect the rate of structural change in the economy through particular designated adjustment mechanisms. Each would attempt to affect significantly the ways in which markets allocate resources in general and capital resources in particular.[12]

Table 8-3 illustrates the central features of several leading proposals for industrial policies to improve the productivity performance and increase the international competitiveness of U.S. industries. Several of the proposals are designed to rationalize U.S. industry through direct government intervention in markets. The first (Table 8-3, alternative I.A.) recognizes the importance of rapid adaptation to structural change as a way of increasing productivity. The advocates of this approach include Ira Magaziner and Robert Reich, who suggest that public policies can preserve this country's absolute advantage by providing incentives to "sunrise" industries and assisting workers to move out of "sunset" industries.[13] To reduce the pressures for protection from imports by the sunset industries, this version of industrial policy recommends a substantial increase in the resources devoted to adjustment. Proponents would also increase tax and loan incentives for the sunrise industries so that capital and labor will be reallocated to "the industries of the future."

The second approach to rationalization is virtually the opposite of the first and involves an attempt to reduce competitive forces by protecting industries in trouble so that the pace of structural change will be moderated. In addition to protection against imports, government grants and loans would be made available for revitalization of industries, and extensive new employment-protection laws would be enacted. The major proponents of these policies, Barry Bluestone and Bennett Harrison, believe that the key to productivity improvement is prevention of the erosion of the

Table 8-3. Alternative Approaches to Industrial Policy: Implications for Productivity Policy

| Alternative Approaches | Intended Effect on Structural Change | Implications for Expenditure Policy | Possible Adjustment Techniques | Institutional Implications |
|---|---|---|---|---|
| I. More intervention with rationalization of domestic and international policies | | | | |
| A. Target specific sectors and industries: Incentives for sunrise industries, adjustment for sunset industries | Increase rate of change through tax and loan incentives and increased expenditures | Increase rationality of current microeconomic intervention; Increase micro interventions to assist winners and help losers adjust so protection is avoided | U.S. development fund for high-risk investment; Joint government-business-university research and development; More tax and loan incentives for winners; Legislation for retraining, adjustment assistance, plant closing, severance, and rehiring | Board of MITI type for development fund; Less labor-management conflict (favors tripartitism) |
| B. Protect sunset industries and compensate workers | Reduce rate of growth through buy-out of worker resistance and constraints on movement of resources | Increase expenditure of assistance to losers; Trade-off—no plant closing, no offshore production | Tax and loan incentives and protection for losers; Use of pension fund assets for assistance | More government planning; National Economic Development Board |

| | | | | |
|---|---|---|---|---|
| C. Partial targeting designed to reindustrialize industrial base | Increase rate of change in basic industries through capital investment in public and private sectors | Reduce cost of capital; more expenditure on public infrastructure<br><br>Temporary protection for industrial base | Target tax incentives to industrial base<br><br>Worker participation in management | No planning board<br><br>Change political system with stronger party system<br><br>More broad-based interest groups |
| II. More intervention to improve local and regional economic development and redistribute resources | Slowdown and a reverse direction of structural change in local economies through revitalization of industry | Use private and public funds to subsidize local development throughout country | Subsidies and direct allocation of capital to industries in declining local areas<br><br>Financed through pension fund assets | Redevelopment Finance Corporation<br><br>Favors tripartitism |

**Table 8-3. (Continued)**

| Alternative Approaches | Intended Effect on Structural Change | Implications for Expenditure Policy | Possible Adjustment Techniques | Institutional Implications |
|---|---|---|---|---|
| III. Reduced and more neutral intervention in all markets | | | | |
| Improve operation of markets, plus justifiable government programs to facilitate adaptation to change without targeting | Increase rate of change by adapting the movement of resources in response to domestic and international market forces (i.e., improve microeconomic-level efficiency in resource use) | Macroeconomic effects: Substantial reduction in budget deficit by 1985–1986 period; remove restrictions on saving and capital investment; reduce consumption bias in federal expenditure<br><br>Microeconomic effects: Reduce regulations; general rather than targeted adjustment assistance; expenditure for basic research and development; reduce/eliminate current subsidies that do not meet market failure, government failure test | Tax and regulatory reform<br><br>Nontargeting of expenditures<br><br>Cost-benefit screening of interventions to correct market failure<br><br>Compensation flexibility and UI-based adjustment assistance and retraining<br><br>Maintain liberal trading system<br><br>Carry out current "unfair" trade remedies | No new bureaucracy |

214

IV. General Economic
    Recovery

| | Increase competitiveness of markets and adapt to change | Macroeconomic effects: Reduce inflation through tighter fiscal policy; raise taxes | Cut expenditures and raise taxes | No new bureaucracy |

Help workers to relocate and retrain

215

U.S. industrial base; otherwise, they claim, a large number of relatively high-paid jobs will be lost to the economy as displaced workers move to a rapidly growing number of low-paid jobs.[14]

The government intervention inherent in both these approaches calls for new political institutions to direct the required public-sector activity. Magaziner and Reich favor the Japanese approach and its use of a special board, similar to the Ministry of International Trade and Industry (MITI), to select and provide incentives for the sunrise industries. In contrast, Bluestone and Harrison recommend a national economic development board that would utilize the assets of pension funds and government incentives to revitalize the U.S. industrial base. This is similar to the industrial policy approach proposed by the AFL-CIO, which is a strong advocate of union, business, and government representation on a national board that would be responsible for the allocation of capital through grants and tax and loan preferences to specific industries and companies. In addition, it is proposed that the policy be carried out with the aid of a complex network of industry and regional boards with authority to reallocate capital among industries. This model of industrial policy is almost identical with the system of some sixty industrial and regional boards used in the United Kingdom in an attempt to revitalize declining industries and regions during the 1970s.

A third variation recognizes the need to stimulate capital investment in both the public and the private sectors. Under this plan, targeting, in the form of temporary import protection and special tax incentives, is to be restricted to basic industries within the manufacturing sector.[15] No planning board would be necessary because the executive branch and Congress would decide which industries are to receive import protection and additional tax incentives. It is also proposed that the party system be strengthened, presumably in the belief that increased discipline in political parties will make it easier to provide special preferences to specific industries.

Although the decline in U.S. productivity growth has been pervasive, the *comparative* productivity problem is most severe in some industries, preponderantly those that have been hardest hit by imports. Since the early 1970s, for example, the Japanese levels of productivity in the steel and automobile industries have been higher than those of the United States. Because basic industries tend to be concentrated geographically, this was a source of particularly severe problems for some regions and a number of localities.

The structural change resulting from poor productivity performance and import penetration has always varied geographically in its effects. This fact has led to proposals for an industrial policy designed to improve local and regional economic conditions. One of the leading proponents of this approach is a prominent investment banker, Felix Rohatyn, and his views have acquired some support within the business community. Particular components of this approach owe much to experience gained under the New York Seasonal Financing Act (1975), under which the federal government provided $2.3 billion in short-term loans to New York City in order to encourage private financing to save the city from bankruptcy. Advocates of this form of industrial policy generally believe that it is useful for government to provide firms in particular areas with similar types of assistance. Revitalization plans assume that the local companies can be restructured to attract private investment into the depressed areas. This approach calls for an institutional structure that will permit government, business, and labor representatives to determine the kind of programs and solutions needed by any sector. These include an industrial development board, to identify the industries that are crucial to economic growth, and a national investment bank (somewhat like the Japan Development Bank or a reconstituted Reconstruction Finance Corporation) with sufficient authority and resources to provide assistance to particular regions and sectors of the economy.

In sharp contrast with these targeted industrial policies, there is the view that a strong economic recovery will solve all, or most of, the problems of U.S. industries. Those who hold this position believe that the proper macroeconomic policies will make any microeconomic measures unnecessary (see Table 8-3, alternative IV).[16] However, the evidence on the nature of the U.S. productivity problem provided in this book indicates that it will take much more than economic recovery to raise productivity growth in most industries to near the rates now achieved by the United States' international competitors. Appropriate macroeconomic policies are an essential foundation for any successful productivity program, but additional public and private measures are also necessary if such a program is to be effective.

The empirical evidence on the ability of markets to allocate resources to their most productive uses suggests that less rather than more government intervention in particular markets is called for. Chapter 7, "Evidence for a Sector-Biased or Sector-Neutral Industrial Strategy," shows that by reallocating resources among industries, the market mechanism made a significant contribution to productivity growth during the late 1960s and early 1970s. On the basis of his analysis of the productivity slowdown between 1946–1966 and 1966–1976, Gollop concludes that the market system responded by reallocating resources to more productive uses. Without this contribution from the market system, the decline in the overall productivity growth in the private sector might well have been 30 percent greater.

The advocates of an industrial strategy that is selective in its treatment of different economic sectors present no evidence indicating that their proposals would in fact reallocate resources from relatively stagnant to more promising industries more effectively than the market system can. Indeed, because the productivity problem is so pervasive, encompassing the entire spectrum of industries, there is no easy way to select the winners and the losers. Under these circumstances, the allocation decisions by any national board would inevitably rely heavily on political judgments.

The case provided by the proponents of a targeted strategy rests largely on the observation that other countries have adopted such programs. However, it is noteworthy that in most countries that use planning agencies in this way, the economic plans are rarely binding and their effects on the allocation of resources in the private sector may well be quite limited. Even in Japan, the role of industrial policy has diminished substantially since the mid-1960s; and most evaluations of Japanese economic progress, including the Norsworthy and Malmquist research reported in Chapter 3, attribute most of the differential Japanese productivity growth to influences other than industrial policy.[17]

Experience under programs such as the Area Redevelopment Act shows that unless they employ strong criteria for the allocation of assistance, most industries inevitably qualify as candidates for aid.[18] In the United Kingdom, the elaborate network of some sixty regional and industry tripartite boards also resulted in the eligibility of almost two-thirds of the country for economic development assistance during the mid-1970s.

The premise that a tripartite board made up of representatives of government, industry, and labor can successfully direct resources toward the most promising industries and improve the overall rate of productivity growth is highly questionable. Whenever interested parties participate directly and collectively in decisions affecting economic change, there is a strong tendency for any consensus to yield policies that resist the economic forces causing the structural change. Under such a program, the movement of resources toward their most productive use will actually be impeded, and society will continue to be denied the benefits of economic change.

This has certainly been the pattern that emerged from tripartite participation in the negotiation of orderly marketing arrangements. Even where a good case was made for providing time for firms and workers to adjust to economic change, many of the temporary arrangements that emerged became remarkably permanent and simply delayed the movement of resources to their most productive uses.[19] If the lesson of the limited number of *ad hoc* programs applies, any national industrial strategy for case-by-case treatment of industries will have exactly the opposite result from that which is called for by retaining resources in those activities in which productivity growth is lowest.[20]

## PRODUCTIVITY GROWTH AND STRUCTURAL UNEMPLOYMENT

The market mechanism reallocates resources among industries that differ in their rates of productivity growth, shifting capital and labor out of industries whose productivity growth is most rapid as innovation reduces the quantity of input required per unit of output. This changes the industrial structure and distribution of employment in the economy. Such structural changes give rise to the concern that if an industry innovates rapidly, it will displace workers from their current jobs and initiate a downward trend in employment in the industry.

Over time, the introduction of technological change rarely has an adverse effect on employment growth in the economy as a whole. In a particular company or industry, innovation frequently results in the substitution of equipment for workers, but this is usually offset in part by the increased output associated with the innovation. The introduction of new technology results in a downward shift in the firm's or industry's cost curves, reducing the price of the output, attracting a larger volume of purchases, and thus at least offsetting partly the reduced demand for labor.

A recent study of innovation in several industries over the 1957–1977 period indicates that in most cases, the employment-generating effect of the increase in output more than offsets the employment loss resulting from the substitution of equipment for labor. In all the industries (steel, automobiles, aluminum, coal, and iron ore), some workers were displaced as new techniques were introduced because the techniques were labor-saving. The average annual rate of worker displacement ranged from 1 to 5 percent, depending on the industry. However, by reducing costs of production, innovation created sufficient employment growth to offset this employment loss in all the industries except steel.

During the 1959–1977 period, the employment loss in the steel industry from the substitution of capital for labor was small, mainly because few innovations were introduced. The output effect of real cost changes was also adverse to employment because increases in input prices such as wages prevented the industry cost curves from shifting downward. In contrast, in the other industries, the employment-generating output effect was sufficient to produce net growth in employment ranging from an average annual increase of about 0.1 percent in autos to 7.5 percent in aluminum. [21] Of course, this does not mean that employment actually grew at these average annual rates; factors other than the introduction of new technology influence employment growth in these industries. For example changes in other input costs, economies of scale, and the comparative performance of foreign producers occur simultaneously with the introduction of new technology. These changes can either increase or reduce the beneficial employment effect of innovation.

If the production process in an industry largely involves low skills, is labor-intensive, or is based on routine technology, innovation is unlikely to prevent a decline in employment because the United States does not have a comparative advantage in this type of economic activity. In order to offset erosion of employment in such an industry, resources must continuously move to its high-skill, high-technology segment. This has occurred in the textile industry as output from high-technology processes has expanded while products requiring labor-intensive production have declined.

Structural change brought about by productivity growth raises the nation's standard of living; it does not reduce overall employment in the long run. But for some workers, innovation will mean the loss of their present jobs. Because only a small proportion of the jobs in an industry (1 to 5 percent annually) is likely to be displaced by innovations, much of the adjustment can be made through normal attrition. However, in some firms, abrupt introduction of productivity-enhancing innovations can lead to the elimination of a significant number of jobs even if the innovations induce long-run growth in the output of the industry. Similarly, as the market reallocates resources, some companies in industries that have lost their regional or international advantage will experience a loss of some or all jobs. In such cases, it is certainly appropriate for the government to facilitate the readjustment of the workers who have been adversely affected.

Over the past two decades, the government has introduced twenty adjustment programs to assist workers suffering from structural unemployment, but these targeted programs have had little success in facilitating labor market readjustment. Indeed, since the beneficiaries of many of the programs were often also eligible for benefits from the unemployment insurance program, as well as severance benefits from their employers, the reemployment of workers was frequently delayed.

Unemployment insurance (UI) is the nation's largest labor market program, accounting for $15 to $30 billion in annual expenditures, depending on the unemployment rate. UI benefits are usually not payable to a worker who enrolls in a retraining program. The present UI program is exclusively an income-maintenance program and does little to encourage the readjustment of structurally unemployed workers. Clearly, the use of these resources should be made much more flexible so that assistance can be provided to help those affected by structural change readjust in the labor market.[22]

In Chapter 6, McKersie and Klein discuss the roles of management and labor in facilitating innovation in the firm. Although there is widespread acceptance by employees as well as employers of the need for companies to innovate, resistance occurs when particular innovations are being instituted. McKersie and Klein have found that there is a trend toward joint efforts by labor and management to increase productivity. Some of the industrial relations arrangements—for example, those referred to as *job-investment bargaining*—also promise to assist those adversely affected by the introduction of new technology, thereby reducing worker resistance to change. By trading off some of the more onerous plant work rules in return for a management commitment to increase capital investment in its facilities, it may be possible to reduce any adverse employment effect of innovation at the plant and to provide management more flexibility in redeploying the work force to other jobs within the firm.

Many of the current attempts to link a company's industrial relations and personnel management system to the goal of productivity improvement are still in the experimental stages in the United States. But there is considerable reason for optimism; renewed interest in various forms of worker participation at various levels of decision making and the trend toward a variety of gain-sharing schemes are evidence that workers and managers recognize their mutual interests in productivity improvement. In the long run, this may be worker's best guarantee of employment security.

## THE OVERALL PROGRAM

This chapter has sought to use the analyses and findings of the previous chapters to provide added support for the major recommendations of the CED policy statement *Productivity Policy: Key to the Nation's Economic Future.*[23] It is clear that for a program to encourage research and innovation, this list of productivity recommendations is far from exhaustive, even within the constraints imposed by our expository approach. Moreover, there are a number of areas that we have discussed only briefly. These include the variety of steps management should consider and undertake to improve labor-management relations and elicit increased contributions to productivity growth from the company's labor force. As Chapters 5 and 6 make clear, there is no one best way for business to improve the contribution of the labor-management climate to productivity growth. Yet, unless this is done, much of any gain from an improved overall public policy can be easily dissipated at the plant. Thus, as Norsworthy and Zabala demonstrate in Chapter 5, increased participation by workers can contribute materially to productivity growth within a given establishment.

The items omitted from our discussion also include the design of reward systems that will elicit innovative suggestions and cooperation in their adoption. In short, we have not analyzed here the much-publicized Japanese practices such as quality circles, gain sharing, and lifetime job tenure.

We have also omitted detailed discussion of the various proposals for simplifying the tax code and for increasing the allocation of public-sector resources to maintenance and improvement of the nation's transportation network, port facilities, and other production-facilitating investments.

These lacunae in our discussion indicate that our recommendations focus only on those elements of productivity policy to which we assign the highest priority. We are convinced that stimulation of research and innovation, encouragement of saving and investment, and removal of impediments to freedom of resource allocation by the market mechanism are the primary components necessary for any really promising productivity program.

Yet, in a sense, this conclusion is misleading. If the target of a productivity program is sustained rates of growth commensurate with those of America's leading industrialized competitors or a sustained rate of growth in the standard of living similar to that achieved before the slowdown began, it will be necessary to undertake perhaps a trebling of the long-term productivity growth rate. That, obviously, will be no easy task. We believe it is not an impossible task. But it cannot be carried out by settling on a few high-priority elements of a full productivity program and discarding those that seem secondary, onerous, or likely to be unpopular. Even the recommendations offered here, when taken together, may prove to be insufficient to achieve the difficult goal that faces the United States. If that turns out to be true, still more demanding measures will have to be considered. Certainly, there is no ground for believing that the goal is beyond us, but its achievement requires the adoption of means commensurate with the task.

## NOTES

1. *Economic Report of the President* (Washington, D.C.: U.S. Government Printing Office, February 1982), p. 245.
2. By using targeting techniques, some governments attempt to allocate resources directly to specific industries in order to improve the competitive position of their industries in world markets. The instruments of targeting include *protection of the home market* through import quotas, tariffs, government procurement, control over the availability of foreign exchange, and prohibition

against foreign investment; *tax benefits* to encourage mergers, joint ventures, and exports; *antitrust exemptions* to permit the formation of cartels, import and export consortia, joint research and development associations; *innovation policies* such as control over licensing of foreign technology, tax write-offs for specific research and development, and government purchasing and leasing of specific technology; *direct financial assistance* such as grants, preferential loans, and easier access to foreign exchange. As part of its strategy to increase its economic growth, Japan has made more use of these techniques than other countries. Until the mid-1960s, it employed protection of the home market more than most countries. Although Japan still uses some targeting to improve the competitiveness of selected industries, the evidence indicates that the most important source of its economic growth in the 1970s was its high rate of saving and capital investment.

The success of these techniques in increasing competitiveness is questionable, even in the case of Japan, which is frequently cited as the model for other countries to emulate. At the same time, if *protection of the home market* is employed as its instrument, targeting may well reduce the ability of all countries to improve productivity and increase real income. Japanese recourse to this instrument has declined substantially since 1965 but is still used for some industries in which the United States has a comparative advantage. If this leads to more protection throughout the industrialized world, the incentive to innovate will be reduced and output growth retarded. Each country will be striving to preserve or increase its share of particular markets, but all will be worse off because the market will not be expanding.

3. See Research and Policy Committee, *Strategy for U.S. Industrial Competitiveness* (New York: Committee for Economic Development, 1984), Chapter 4.
4. See Rolf Piekarz, Eleanor Thomas, and Donna Jennings, "International Comparison of Research and Development and Government Policies" (Paper presented at American Enterprise Institute Conference on International Comparisons of Productivity and Causes of the Slowdown, Washington, D.C., October 1982).
5. On this, see, for example, Edwin Mansfield, "Basic Research and Productivity Increase in Manufacturing," *American Economic Review* 70 (December 1980): 363–373.
6. When such conclusions are offered by academics, there is some reason to suspect that they are at least unconsciously self-serving. That is why it must be emphasized that these recommendations are those of the group of business leaders who are the trustees of the Committee for Economic Development.
7. See Research and Policy Committee, *Strategy for U.S. Industrial Competitiveness*, Chapter 5.
8. See Piekarz, Thomas, and Jennings, "International Comparisons of Research and Development and Government Policies," *op. cit.*
9. For review of the available evidence, see F. M. Scherer, *Industrial Market Structure and Economic Performance*, 2d ed. (Chicago: Rand McNally, 1980), Chapter 15; and M. I. Kamien and N. I. Schwartz, "Market Structure and Innovation: A Survey," *Journal of Economic Literature* 13 (March 1973).
10. See Robert Z. Lawrence, *Can America Compete?* (Washington, D.C.: The Brookings Institution, 1984), p. 31, Table 2-8.
11. See Harvey S. Rosen, *Housing Subsidies: Effects on Housing Decisions, Efficiency and Equity* (Cambridge, Mass.: National Bureau of Economic Research, NBER Working Paper No. 1161).
12. The argument for an increase in the overall U.S. productivity growth rate to match those of our major industrial competitors does not justify an attempt to make *all* U.S. industries outperform their foreign competitors. Such a goal

makes no economic sense. If productivity growth improves the comparative advantage of one sector of the U.S. economy in an open economy with a system of flexible exchange rates, this must automatically lead to a decline in comparative advantage in another sector of the U.S. economy. An increase in the overall competitiveness of the U.S. economy requires that productivity growth be facilitated by movement of resources to their most productive use so that U.S. production is concentrated in those industries whose comparative advantage is growing.

13. Ira Magaziner and Robert Reich, *Minding America's Business* (New York: Harcourt Brace Jovanovich, 1982).
14. Barry Bluestone and Bennett Harrison, *The Deindustrialization of America* (New York: Basic Books, 1982).
15. See Amitai Etzioni, *An Immodest Agenda: Rebuilding America for the Twenty-First Century* (New York: McGraw-Hill Book Company, 1982).
16. The critique of targeted industrial policies by Charles L. Schultze, "Industrial Policy: A Dissent," *The Brookings Review* 2 (Fall 1983): 3–12, seems to come close to relying exclusively on macroeconomic policies as the solution to U.S. productivity and competitiveness. However, Schultze does point out that a more neutral tax code would yield microeconomic advantages, as would training policies to facilitate the movement of labor resources toward their most productive use.
17. See also Philip H. Trezise, "Industrial Policy in Japan" (Paper presented at the Southern Economic Association Meetings, Washington, D.C., November 1983).
18. Schultze, "Industrial Policy: A Dissent," *op. cit.*, pp. 3–12.
19. See "Textiles and Clothing: Economic Forces Stronger than Government Policies," *OECD Observer*, no. 120 (January 1983): 24–29.
20. Robert Z. Lawrence, "The Questionable Case for Selective Industrial Policies" (Paper presented at the Southern Economic Association Meetings, Washington, D.C., November 1983); and Paul Krugman, "Targeted Industrial Policies: Theory and Evidence" (Paper presented at St. Louis Federal Reserve Board, Wyoming, August 1983).
21. Robert A. Levy, Marianne Bowers, James M. Jondrow, "Technical Change and Employment in Five Industries: Steel, Autos, Aluminum, Coal and Iron Ore," in Eileen L. Collins and Lucretia Dewey Tanner, eds., *American Jobs in the Changing Industrial Base* (Cambridge, Mass.: Ballinger Publishing Co., 1984).
22. For a review of the policies to assist workers laid off because of economic change, see Kenneth McLennan, "Policy Options to Facilitate the Reemployment of Displaced Workers," in Kevin Hollenbeck, Frank Pratzner, and Howard Rosen, eds., *The Displaced Worker Problem: Implications for Training and Education Institutions* (Columbus, Ohio: National Center for Research and Vocational Education, Ohio State University, 1984).
23. While this chapter summarizes the recommendations of the CED trustees, it should be emphasized that the authors of the chapter support CED's proposals and believe that the empirical and analytical evidence in this volume is entirely consistent with them. Nevertheless, the authors recognize that if in the next few years the productivity growth problems prove to be too intractable for these steps alone, it may be necessary to turn to more heterodox approaches. For example, more forceful tax reforms may be required to bring saving and investment rates closer to those of other industrialized countries. Stronger incentives (not aimed toward any preselected sectors) may have to be built into the tax mechanism to speed the market's transfer of capital into industries with promising, long-run prospects.

# Contributors

William J. Baumol holds a joint appointment as Professor of Economics at Princeton University and New York University. Dr Baumol is a member of many professional societies, including the Editorial Advisory Board of the Supreme Court Economic Review, the Research Advisory Board of the Committee for Economic Development, and the Board of Trustees of the Joint Council on Economic Education. He is also a founding member of World Resources Institute and a past president of the American Economic Association. Among the many works Dr. Baumol has written are *Economics, Environmental Policy and the Quality of Life*, (with W. E. Oates and S. A. B. Backmun), *Economics: Principles and Policy* (with A. S. Blinder), and *Contestable Markets and the Theory of Industry Structure* (with R. D. Willig and J. S. Panzer). Dr. Baumol, a past Guggenheim Fellow and distinguished fellow of the American Economic Association, was educated at the College of the City of New York and holds a Ph.D. from the University of London. He has also received four honorary degrees.

Kenneth McLennan is Vice President and Director of Industrial Studies at the Committee for Economic Development, and was staff counselor to the CED subcommittee that prepared *Productivity Policy: Key to the Nation's Economic Future*, and he was co-project director for CED's study, *Strategy for U.S. Industrial Competitiveness*. Dr. McLennan served as Deputy Assistant Secretary of Labor for Policy Development from 1972 to 1974. He is a former Division Chief of Social Affairs and Industrial Relations for the Organization for Economic Cooperation and

Development (OECD) in Paris, France. Dr. McLennan is a former chairman of the economics department at Temple University, where he taught for eight years. He is a member of several professional organizations, including the Industrial Relations Research Association and the Western Economic Association, and is the author of many articles on collective bargaining, unemployment, and industrial relations. Most recently he wrote "Unemployment Insurance: To Help Dislocated Workers," in the *Journal of the Institute of Socioeconomic Studies*, and "Policy Options to Facilitate the Reemployment of Displaced Workers," in *Displaced Workers: Implications for Educational and Training Institutions*. Dr. McLennan earned a B.Sc. from the University of London, and M.B.A. from the University of Toronto, and a Ph.D. from the University of Wisconsin.

Martin Bronfenbrenner has been Kenan Professor of Economics at Duke University since 1971. He is also a lecturer in Japanese history and acting director of Duke's Asian/Pacific Studies Institute. He previously taught at the University of Wisconsin, University of Minnesota—Minneapolis, and Carnegie Mellon University, and he is a member of the American Economic Association, the Association of Asian Studies, and Phi Betta Kappa. Dr. Bronfenbrenner has had appointments in the U.S. Treasury, the Federal Reserve System, the Occupation of Japan, and the United Nations Economic Commission for Asia and the Far East, Bangkok, Thailand. His Japanese expertise began during World War II as a Japanese-language officer. Since then he has traveled back and forth eighteen times, lecturing at a number of Japanese universities in addition to working for the Occupation. A frequent contributor to professional journals, Dr. Bronfenbrenner is the author of *Academic Encounter*, *Income Distribution Theory*, and *Tomioka Stories*. Dr. Bronfenbrenner earned his undergraduate degree from Washington University and his Ph.D. from University of Chicago. He is fluent in the Japanese language.

Frank M. Gollop is Associate Professor of Economics at Boston College. Dr. Gollop received many honors and awards, including those from the U.S. Bureau of the Census, the Department of Commerce, U.S. Department of Labor, and the Federal Regulatory Commission. He is a member of the American Economic Association, the Conference on Research in Income and Wealth, the Transportation and Public Utilities Group of the American Economic Association, Western Economic Association, the Antitrust Committee, Boston Bar Association, and since 1976 has been editorial consultant for the *American Economic Review*. Dr. Gollop is the author of articles on the economy, including "Scale Effects and Technological Change as Sources of Productivity Growth," "Growth Accounting in an Open Economy," and "Environmental Regulations and Productivity Growth: The Case of Fossil-Fueled Electric Power Generation." Dr. Gollop has made presentations before the U.S. Senate. the U.S. House of Representatives, the U.S. State Department, and the Committee for Economic Development. He holds an undergraduate degree from the University of Santa Clara and graduate degrees from Harvard University.

Janice A. Klein is an Assistant Professor at the Harvard Business School, where she teaches production and operations management in the MBA program. Dr. Klein has worked for General Electric Company in various manufacturing and human resource management positions. She received her B.S. from Iowa State University, her M.B.A. from Boston University, and her Ph.D. from MIT's Sloan School of Management.

David H. Malmquist holds the office of Chief Economist at the U.S. Securities and Exchange Commission, where he conducts research on financial markets, corporate mergers, and acquisitions. Dr. Malmquist has previously worked as an economist with the U.S. Department of Labor and as a lecturer in the Department of Economics at Hunter College. He is co-author of "Input Measurement and Productivity Growth in Japanese and U.S. Manufacturing" and author of "Inflation and the Growth of Productivity and Factor Costs." Dr. Malmquist received his degrees from Hunter College and the Graduate School of the City University of New York.

Robert B. McKersie is Professor of Industrial Relations at the Sloan School of Management, Massachusetts Institute of Technology. From 1971 to 1979, Dr. McKersie was Dean of the New York State School of Industrial and Labor Relations at Cornell University. He is a consultant for the U.S. Department of Labor and OECD and has served as an advisor on various aspects of industrial relations to government agencies and to private industry. He is a member of the American Arbitration Association and an advisor to the subcommittee on productivity of the Committee for Economic Development. Previously, he was a member of the President's Advisory Committee on Federal Pay and Chairman of the New York State Continuity of Employment Committee. He is the author of many publications and the co-author of *Pay, Productivity and Collective Bargaining* and *A Behavioral Theory of Labor Negotiations*. Professor McKersie earned his undergraduate degree from the University of Pennsylvania and master's and doctoral degrees from Harvard University Graduate School of Business Administration.

John R. Norsworthy is Chief of the Center for Economic Studies in the U.S. Bureau of the Census, where he directs a program of econometric and statistical research and analysis. Prior to joining the Bureau in 1982, Dr. Norsworthy was Chief of the Productivity Research Division in the U.S. Bureau of Labor Statistics. He has participated in a wide range of national and international professional conferences and in 1980 received the Department of Labor Distinguished Achievement Award for Research. Dr. Norsworthy is author or co-author of numerous articles on productivity, capital, energy, input-output analysis, and aggregation theory in domestic and foreign professional journals and books. He received his undergraduate degree and graduate degrees from the University of Virginia and held a post doctoral fellowship in economics at the University of Chicago.

Edward N. Wolff is Professor of Economics at the New York University. Prior to his appointment at New York University in 1974, Dr. Wolff held research positions at the National Bureau of Economic Research and the Yale Economic Growth Center and was a programmer for the Harvard Economic Research Project. He is a member of the American Economic Association and the International Association for Research in Income and Wealth. Dr. Wolff is the author of numerous papers, articles, and manuscripts on the U.S. economy and is currently writing two books, *Economics of the Labor Force* and *Growth, Accumulation, and Unproductive Activity: An Analysis of the Post-War American Economy*. Dr. Wolff received his undergraduate degree from Harvard University and his graduate degrees from Yale University.

Craig A. Zabala is an Economist at the Center for Economic Studies in the U.S. Bureau of the Census. Before joining the Bureau in 1982, Dr. Zabala was a doctoral fellow and an economist at the Productivity Research Division in the U.S. Bureau of Labor Statistics. He conducted four years of participant observation as an assembly-line worker for General Motors in preparation for his doctoral dissertation on collective bargaining. Dr. Zabala is the author or co-author of a number of articles on collective bargaining, industrial relations, and productivity analysis. His current research includes the study of the relationship among worker attitudes, productivity growth, and the structure of production at the firm and industry level. He is a member of Pi Gamma Mu, Phi Beta Kappa, and several other professional societies. Dr. Zabala was a Chancellor Fellow at the University of California from 1974–1980, where he received his A.B., M.A., and Ph.D. in sociology.